THEORY OF INFORMATION TECHNOLOGY

THEORY OF INFORMATION TECHNOLOGY

By

P. K. YADAV

Deptt. of Computer Science & Engineering
Krishna Institute of Engineering & Technology
Ghaziabad (U.P.)

UNIVERSITY SCIENCE PRESS

(An Imprint of Laxmi Publications Pvt. Ltd.)

An ISO 9001:2015 Company

BENGALURU • CHENNAI • GUWAHATI • HYDERABAD
KOCHI • KOLKATA • LUCKNOW • RANCHI
NEW DELHI

Printed and bound in India

First Edition : 2009; *Edition* : 2026

***ISBN* :** 978-81-31807-72-9

UTI-9379-449-THEORY OF INFO TECHNOLOGY

Price: ₹ 449.00

Branches

Bengaluru	080-26 75 69 30
Chennai	044-24 34 47 26
Guwahati	0361-254 36 69
Hyderabad	040-27 55 53 83
Kochi	0484-405 13 03
Kolkata	033-40 04 77 79
Lucknow	0522-430 36 13
Ranchi	0651-224 24 64

PUBLISHED IN INDIA BY

UNIVERSITY SCIENCE PRESS

(An Imprint of Laxmi Publications Pvt. Ltd.)

An ISO 9001:2015 Company

113, GOLDEN HOUSE, GURUDWARA ROAD, DARYAGANJ,
NEW DELHI - 110002, INDIA

Corporate Office : B-33, Sector-5, Noida,
Gautambuddha Nagar (U.P.) - 201 301, INDIA

Telephone : +91-120-44 46 900

www.laxmipublications.com

info@laxmipublications.com

Dedicated
to
My Parents

CONTENTS

PREFACE TO THE FIRST EDITION

The present book "Theory of Information Technology" is meant for the students of B.Tech., MBA and BCA. It has been my personal experience that the first year students find it difficult to prepare for this subject and there are no good books covering the basics of Information Technology. It covers all the basic concept of IT including 'C' Language. 'C' language has been described in detail along with number of solved programs of 'C' and a large number of exercises based on 'C' language.

This book is an outcome of continuous persuasion from my friends and colleagues from different engineering colleges/institutions to develop basic course material for this subject. I have tried to incorporate the suggestions of my colleagues and teachers. I have tried my best to organise the contents of this book with sufficient examples and diagrams.

AUTHOR

Acknowledgement

I would like to acknowledge my deep sense of gratitude to Dr. Ajay Sharma, Director General, KIET, a man of spiritual personality, for his continuous encouragement, effort towards achieving academic excellence in the U.P.

I would also like to thank Dr. P.K. Chakravorty, Director KIET, who has always motivated to achieve high academic values and has always been my source of inspirations. I would like to thank Prof. A.K. Sinha, (HOD CS Deptt.) for acknowledging the work on the subject, his encouragement and critical suggestions.

I would like to express my special gratitude to Dr. V.K. Srivastava, Prof. N.C. Sharma (HOD IT Deptt.), Asst. Prof. A.K. Pandey, Asst. Prof. Snajeev Yadav, Asstt. Prof. Saurabh Chandra, Asst. Prof. A.P. Shukla, Asst. Prof. Pankaj Agarwal, Astt. Prof. Vineet Sharma, Mr. Mohd. Islam, Mr. Piyush Bhushan Singh, Mr. Ankur Bhardwaj, Mr. Vikas Goel, Mr. Sachin Ahuja, Mr. Prabhat Yadav, Mr. Narendera Kumar of KIET for their constructive suggestions.

I am also extremely indebted to Dr. Yashpal Singh (HOD CS Deptt. BIET, Jhansi), Dr. Raghav Yadav (MNNIT, Allahabad), Asst. Prof. B.S. Roohani (HOD CS + IT) Deptt. BBIET and RC (BSR), Asst. Prof. Abhay Bansal (ITS, Gzb.) Asst. Prof. Vijay Shukla (IIMT, G.N.) who have been the driving force behind this effort.

I am very thankful to my colleagues Mr. Arun Yadav (IMSEC, Gzb.), Mr. Lokesh Jain (Ideal Institute, Gzb.), Mr. Dharmendra Tripathi (RKGIT, Gzb.), Mr. Nitin Goel (MIET, Meerut), Mr. Ankit Vishniki (IFTM, Moradabad), Mr. Ajeet Kr. Yadav (RDEC, Gzb.) Mr. Raj Kumar Goel (NIET, G.N.), Mr. C.L.P. Gupta (Sagar Institute, Lucknow), Mr. Sunit Vishwarkarma, (Azad University), Lucknow, Mr. Kulwant Patel (BBDIT, Gzb.) Mr. Tripathi (KEC, Gzb.) for continuous encouragement and necessary help whenever required.

I would like to express my special gratitude to my parents Shri Shankar Prasad Yadav and Smt. Bella Devi for their perpetual love and concern. Their contribution to this book cannot be summed up in words.

I would like to express my heartiest thanks to my wife Suman Yadav, daughter Akansha Yadav, Son Yuvraj Yadav and younger brother Vinod Yadav for their patience and continuing support to make this task complete with pleasure.

—AUTHOR

1

FUNDAMENTAL CONCEPT OF INFORMATION

1.1 DEFINITION OF INFORMATION

Information is the processed data, on which decisions are taken and the subsequent actions are performed thereafter. Information can be defined as data acquired by informing or by being informed. It is knowledge defined from data, study, experience and research.

For decisions to be meaningful and useful, the information must possess the following attributes :

(*i*) **Accurate.** To be useful, information must be accurate at all levels because all further developments are based on the available information.

(*ii*) **Timely.** Information is appreciated only if it is available on time. If the information is available ahead of time, its value may be diminished because the information might get archaic or the user may simply forget it.

(*iii*) **Complete.** Complete information tends to be comprehensive in covering the issue or topic of interest. Without complete information, a decision-maker may get a distorted view of reality.

(*iv*) **Precise.** Apart from being complete, information must also be precise, containing all the essential elements of the relevant subject areas. In order to provide complete information, usually large amount of data is gathered.

(*v*) **Relevant.** Information is relevant if it can be applied to a specific situation, problem or issue of interest.

1.1.1 Information Technology

Information is the collection of facts gathered through various means of communication and plays a vital role in drawing a conclusion. At the same time, technology makes information gathering fast and easy. Information along with technology has created a new branch called Information Technology (IT).

Information technology can be define as the combination of telecommunications and computing to obtain, process, store, transmit and output information in the form of voice, pictures or text. This includes are following below:

- Software application and operating systems.
- Web-based information and application such as distance learning.
- Telephones and means of telecommunications.
- Video equipment and multimedia products.
- World wide web.
- Electronic devices such as photocopiers.

1.1.2 Components of Information Technology

The components of information technology include hardware, software, data and people. These components are essential in the proper functioning of a system in IT.

(*i*) **Hardware.** Hardware consists of physical components that form a computer system or any other electronic gadget. To run computer, both hardware and software are required. Hardware is the physical unit that stores and transmits information.

(*ii*) **Software.** Software is a set of instructions in the form of programs, which control the sequence of operation (tasks). Software runs along with the hardware on the computer system.

(*iii*) **Data.** Data is an unprocessed collection or representation of raw facts, concepts, or instructions in a manner suitable for communication, interpretation, and processing by humans or by automatic means.

(*iv*) **People.** People play an important role in information technology. They perform various functions with the help of hardware and software to produce the desired output using IT.

1.1.3 Applications of Information Technology

Information technology has been applied in almost easy sphere of human use :

- Information technology in Business.
- Information technology in Manufacturing.
- Information technology in Mobile computing.
- IT in Public sector.
- IT in Defence services.
- IT in Media.
- IT in Eduction.

1.2 DATA VERSUS INFORMATION

Data is the collection of unprocessed facts, which when processed, grouped, organized, sequenced and presented in an easy-to-understand manner becomes information. Data are raw facts and when it processed, it becomes an information.

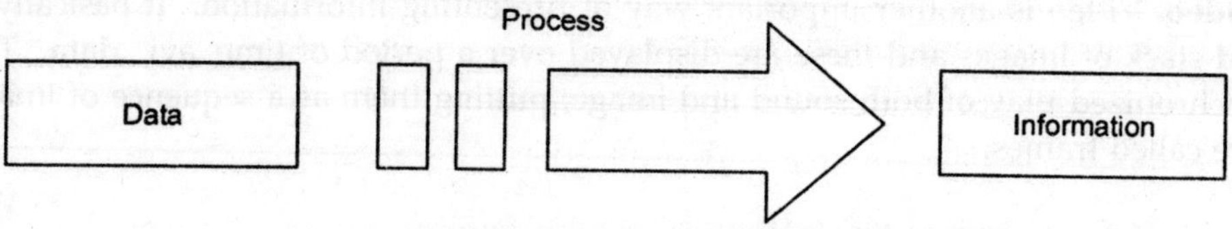

Fig.

Data	*Information*
1. Data is the raw form of information.	It is processed Data.
2. Data is more difficult to understand.	It is easy to understand.
3. It is complex and unclear.	It is simpler and more clear.
4. Examples : 10, pay slip of employee.	*e.g.*, 10 students, payroll repeat of a month.

1.3 REPRESENTATION OF INFORMATION IN DIGITAL MEDIA

Information can be represented in various forms in the digital media, but the most popular way of representing information is in the textual form. In this form, a combinations of letters, numerals, and some special characters are used. However, today these are several other ways in which data can be represented. These are text, Images, Graphics and Animation, Audio and video forms.

1. **Text.** The most common form of data representation is in textual form. It is a collection of alphabets (both upper and lower case), numeral (0–9) and special characters (*, ?, :, #) etc. Data presented in textual form may be written and read. When these text are organized in some order then only it gives some informative values.

2. **Image.** Information may be represented in the form of images. Images refer to data in the form of pictures, photographs, hand drawings etc. These images may be processed and several software programs have been developed to process images.

3. **Graphics and Animation.** Graphics and animation are another way of presenting the information. For instance, to present the information about an organisation systematically. It combines together the text, images, and sound pertaining to the organization in order to prepare a good presentation, *e.g.*, powerpoint tools.

The popular graphics file extension used by microsoft :

- Enhanced metafile (.emf)
- Joint photographic Experts Group (.jpg)
- Portable Network Graphics (.Png)
- Windows Bitmap (.bmp, .rle, .dib)

4. **Audio.** The meaning or value of information contained in audio can be interpreted by hearing. It is the data in the form of sounds. The audio may be stored in a database in the form of files. Different types of sounds produce different information.

5. **Video.** Video is another important way of presenting information. It basically combines sound and stack of images and these are displayed over a period of time, avi, .data. This format stores synchronized play of both sound and image, putting them as a sequence of images. These images are called frames.

1.4 VALUE OF INFORMATION

The value of information plays an important role in decision making process. It is possible to quantity the amount of the information but it is difficult to compute the absolute value of the information. The value of information is different to the different groups of persons value of information is related to the parameters like, who uses the information under what circumstances the information is used and most importantly how it is used, *e.g.*, for the value of information regarding the rain is of high value rather than other person.

There are different types of value of information :

- Normative value.
- Realistic value.
- Subjective value.

1. **Normative Value:** The difference of estimated cost with prior knowledge of order and without the knowledge of order would be normative value of information.
2. **Realistic Value:** The major drawback of normative value of information is that it is based on the theoretical and standard procedures and ignores the human factor, environment and other risk factors. The value of information obtained after taking the behavioural aspects into consideration is known as realistic value of information.
3. **Subjective Value:** The value obtained by using the intuitive guess is known as subjective value of information. In real life, mostly we use the subjective value of information.

1.5 QUALITY OF INFORMATION

Quality of Information refers to the extent to which it enables decision making. It is always desirable that the information be presented in such a way that it enables one to take decisions. In order to make decisions at various levels, the different managers in an organization need different kinds of information. The types of quality of information are :

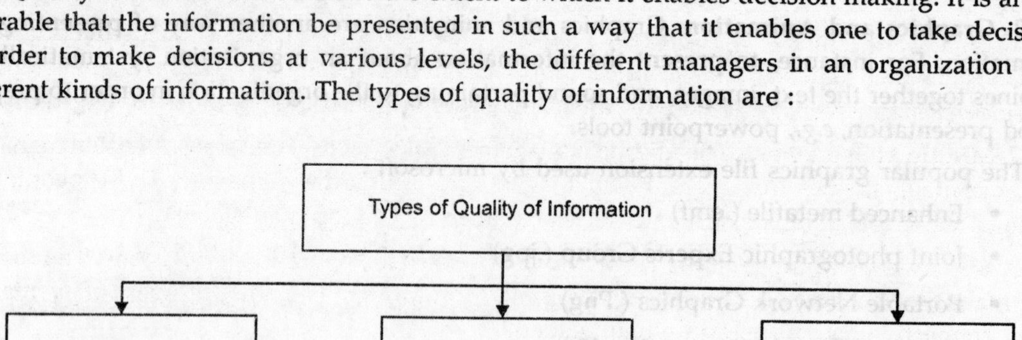

Fig.

1. **Unstructured Information.** This type of information is summarized, may be outdated, subjective in nature, related to the future events, deals with a number of areas and covers the activities inside and outside an organization.

2. **Semistructured Information.** This type of information is a combination of the other two types of information.

3. **Structured Information.** This type of information is up-to-data, detailed not subjective, concerned with past events, deals with a small range of facts and deals with the internal details of an organization.

1.6 CATEGORY AND LEVELS OF INFORMATION IN BUSINESS ORGANIZATION

The secret of any successful organisation lies in the quantity of information it has, and the way it uses that information to achieve its objectives. Any organization aims at delivering a product, or providing a service. Organizations are usually made up of groups, such as Administration, Finance, Payroll, Projects, Human Resources, etc., within each group, there is usually a hierachy of people, such as the managers, then the leaders, and then the people on job. An organization chart depicts these levels and their functions. If also tells us about the reporting hierarchy, and thus, indicates who holds power to make various decisions.

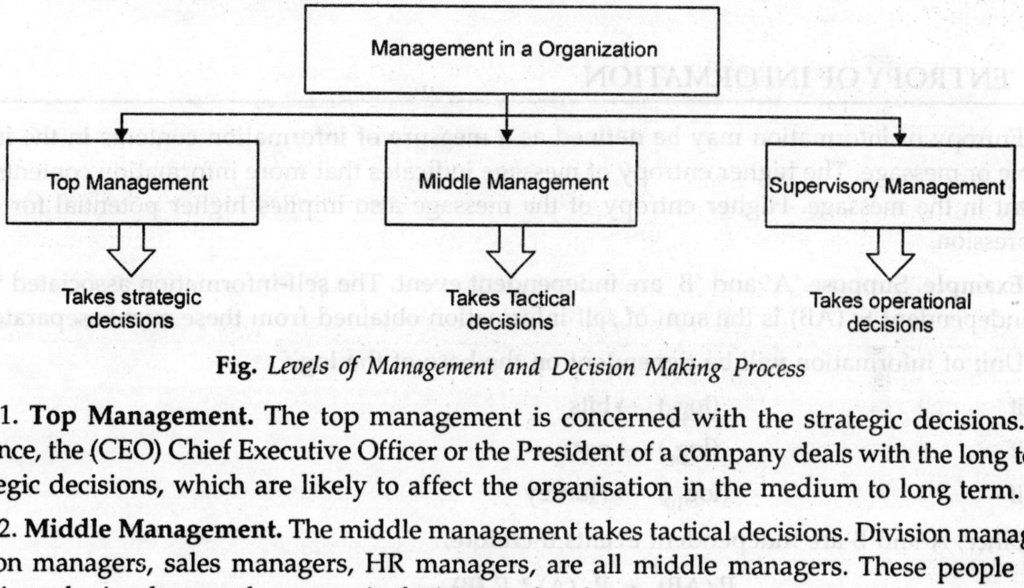

Fig. *Levels of Management and Decision Making Process*

1. **Top Management.** The top management is concerned with the strategic decisions. For instance, the (CEO) Chief Executive Officer or the President of a company deals with the long term, strategic decisions, which are likely to affect the organisation in the medium to long term.

2. **Middle Management.** The middle management takes tactical decisions. Division managers, section managers, sales managers, HR managers, are all middle managers. These people take decisions the implement the strategic decisions taken by the top management.

3. **Supervisory Management.** The supervisory takes the operational devisions. The focus of these managers is mainly the Supervision of staff. Monitoring day-to-day progress of events, and taking connective actions as and when needed.

Another way of representing the management structure is with the help of the management triangle which shows the hierarchy of people in an organisation.

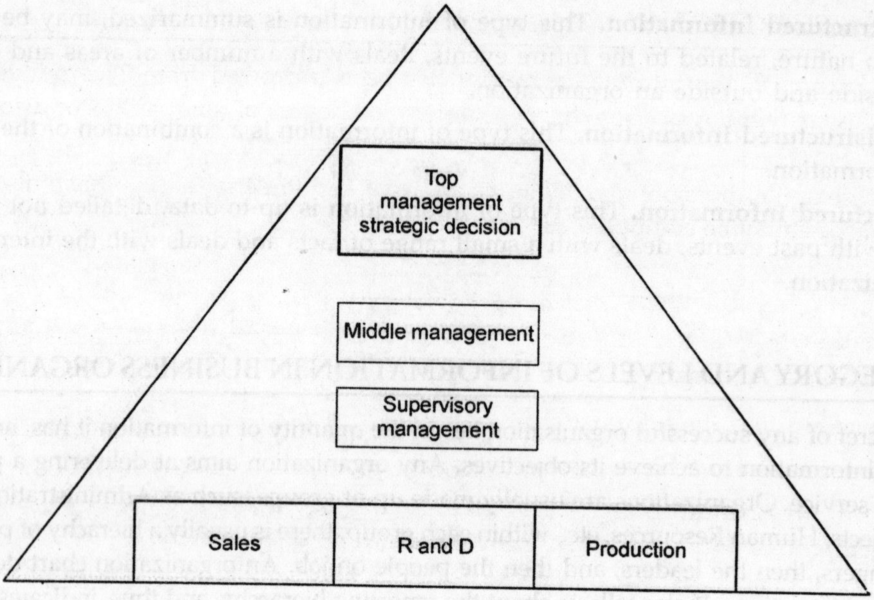

Fig. *Management Triangle*

1.7 ENTROPY OF INFORMATION

Entropy of information may be defined as a measure of information contents in the input sample or message. The higher entropy of message indicates that more information contents are present in the message. Higher entropy of the message also implies higher potential for data compression.

Example. Suppose 'A' and 'B' are independent event. The self-information associated with two independent *Si* (AB) is the sum of self-information obtained from these events separately.

Unit of information will be dependent on the base of the log.

if $(\log_2) \rightarrow$ bits

if $(\log_e) \rightarrow$ nats

if $(\log_{10}) \rightarrow$ Hartley

Since, A and B are independent events therefore,

$$P(AB) = P(A) * P(B)$$

Self-information of event 'A' and 'B' are:

$$Si(A) = -\log_2 [P(A)]$$

$$Si(B) = -\log_2 [P(B)]$$

$$Si(AB) = -\log_2 [P(AB)]$$

$$= -(\log_2 [P(A)] + \log_2 [P(B)]$$

$$\boxed{Si(AB) = Si(A) + Si(B)}$$

1.8 ENTROPY FUNCTION

The term entropy in the information theory has been borrowed from Thermodynamics. Shonnon used this term in information theory to determine degree of randomness or disorder in the data.

Suppose there are *'n'* possible of outcome of an event and Pi denotes the probability of *'i'*th outcome, the entropy may be computed as.

$$\text{Entropy} = -\sum_{i=1}^{i=N} p_i * \log_2 (p_i)$$

1.8.1 Application of Entropy

- It is used to find the information content of a symbol.
- It is used to evaluate Redundancy.

The entropy of whole message can be defined as average self-information of all (N) characters. The self-information of a character is also known as entropy of characters.

$$\text{Entropy of Message} = \frac{1}{N} * \sum_{i=1}^{i=N} \text{entropy of character.}$$

Entropy of a character is related with the probability of occurrence of character. It is defined as follows :

Entropy (self-information) of character = $-\log_2$ (Prob. of character).

The entropy of whole message is therefore, the sum of entropy of individual characters. Entropy is also used to determine that how many bits of information are actually present in the message stream.

Example 1. *Compute the self-information and entropy of the following message stream. "AABACDACDBABCAB"*

Solution. Total number of characters in message (N) = 15

Character	*Probability*	*Self-information* $= -\log_2$ *(Prob of characters)*
'A'	6/15	$= \log_2\left(\frac{1}{p_i}\right) = \log_2\left(\frac{15}{6}\right) = 1.32$
'B'	4/15	= 1.90
'C'	3/15	= 2.32
'D'	2/15	= 2.90

A	A	B	A	C	D	A	C	D	B	A	B	C	A	B
1.32	1.32	1.90	1.32	2.32	2.90	1.32	2.32	2.90	1.90	1.32	1.90	2.32	1.32	1.90

$$\text{Entropy of message} = \frac{1}{N} * \sum_{i=1}^{i=N} \text{entropy of character.}$$

$$= \frac{1}{15} * [1.32 + 1.32 + 1.90 + 1.32 + 2.32 + 2.90.......]$$

$$= 1.88 \text{ bits/message}$$

$$\text{Entropy} = -\sum_{i=1}^{i=N} p_i * \log_2 (p_i)$$

$$= \frac{6}{15} * 1.32 + \frac{4}{15} * 1.90 + \frac{3}{15} * 2.32 + \frac{2}{15} * 2.90$$

$$= .528 + .506 + .464 + .386$$

$$= 1.88 \text{ bits/message.}$$

1.9 STATIC CODING

In this scheme, fixed length codes are generated uniquely to identify each symbol. The whole message or text is converted into coded form by replacing each symbol with its code. This method has a disadvantage that it does not consider the frequency or probability of occurence of a particular symbol in a message.

Suppose there are M symbols, which are used to constitute a message.

and Let N = minimum number of digits required to represent indistinct symbol. Let I = base of number system.

$N = [\log_I (M)]$ since, in digital computer system, we represent data is binary form *i.e.*, I = 2.

$N = [\log_2 (M)]$

Example 2. *A message is composed of 5 symbols, 'a', 'b', 'c', 'd', 'e'.*

(i) Find the minimum number of bits required to represent/code each symbol uniquely.

(ii) Generate the code for all symbols.

(iii) Find the coded form of message string "bddac'.

Solution. Total number of distinct symbol

i.e., $M = 5$

Total number of bits required

$$N = [\log_2 (m)] = [\log_2 (5)] = 3$$

Thus, 3 bit code will be required to represent each symbol or the minimum number of bits required to represent a symbol uniqually is 3.

Static code	***Symbol***
000	'a'
001	'b'
010	'c'
011	'd'
100	'e'
101	—
110	—
111	—

Total number of unique code generated

$= 2^3 = 8.$

Coded string of 'bddac' is

"001001011000010" **Ans.**

Ans. String 'bddac' would require

$5 \times 3 = 15$ digits to code.

1.10 DYNAMIC CODING : (VARIABLE SIZE CODES)

This method is based on the principle of identifying the symbols which appear frequently. Suppose a symbol '*a*' appears in the text most frequently. This property may exploited by assigning a minimum number of digits to represent '*a*'. Since, '*a*', appears most frequently, then we may assign one bit code to same space. The symbols which appears in the text less frequently are assigned higher bit code. For example, Shannon Fano & Huffman coding.

Example 3. * → 1/8 *Probability (Given). How many bits required to represent this character in compression, if a message string '*****' has to be " then determine number of bits saved in comparison to ASCII code?*

Solution. Probability of characters '*' = 1/8

Entropy of characters = $-\log_2$ (Probability of characters)

$$= -\log_2 (1/8) = \log_2^8 = \log_2^{2^3} = 3$$

Thus, entropy of character '*' = 3, It means character will be represented by 3 bit code in compressed form.

Total number of character in string '*****' = 5

∴ Total number of bits required to represent a message string '*****' = $5 \times 3 = 15$ bits.

Characters or symbol require 8 bit code to represent in ASCII code.

∴ Total number of bit required to encode the text '*****' in ASCII code = $5 \times 8 = 40$ bits.

∴ Total number of bits saved = $40 - 15 = 25$ bits.

Static code:

Example 4. *Consider the above example and show how many bits will be saved by using static coding over ASCII code for string 'bddac'.*

Solution. Using static code 'bddac', required = $5 \times 3 = 15$ bits.

Using ASCII $= 8 \times 5 = 40$

$40 - 15 = 25$ bits saved.

Dynamic Coding :

Symbol	*From*	*Prob.*
a	15	.15
b	10	.10
c	75	.75
d	5	.05

"This method is based on the principle of identifying the symbols which appear frequently, suppose a symbol *'a'* appears in the text most frequently. Then assign minimum number of digits to represent *'a'*.

Symbol	*Frex.*	*No. of Bits*	*Code*
c	75	1	1
a	15	2	01
b	10	3	001
d	5	4	0001

EXERCISES

1. What do you understand by Information Technology? What are its applications? Explain in brief.
2. Define information. Describe various attributes of information.
3. What is the information content of the statement? "The sun rises in the east."?
4. What do you mean by information? What are levels of information in business organization?
5. Explain the terms audio, video and animation.
6. Define entropy. Explain its significance.
7. Let X represent the out come of a single roll of a fair die. What is entropy of X?
8. Differentiate between static and Dynamic coding.
9. Discuss entropy of information. What is its significance?
10. Differentiate between data and information giving suitable examples. Explain the various data formats.

2

INFORMATION REPRESENTATION

2.1 INFORMATION CONTENT

Information content of a symbol is entropy of a symbol. The information content of a symbol represents the minimum number of bits required to code the symbol.

> Information Content of a Symbol (IC)
> (Entropy) = $-\log_2$ (Probability of Symbol)

> Information Bits (IB) = Frequency of Symbol × Information Content

Example:

S. No	***Symbol***	***Frequency***	***Probability***
1.	A	40	0.40
2.	B	20	0.20
3.	C	15	0.15
4.	D	10	0.10
5.	E	10	0.10
6.	F	5	0.05

$I_C(A) = -\log_2 (P_A)$

$= -\log_2(.40)$

$= 1.32$

$I_C(B) = -\log_2 (P_B)$

$= 2.32$

$I_B(A) = 40 \times 1.32$

$= 52.8$

$I_B(B) = 20 \times 2.32$

$= 46.4$

$I_C(C) = -\log_2(P_C)$

$= -\log_2(.15)$

$= 2.73$

$I_C(D) = -\log_2 (P_D)$

$= -\log_2(.10)$

$= 3.32$

$$I_B(C) = 15 \times 2.73 = 40.95$$

$$I_B(D) = \text{Freq} \times I_C = 10 \times 3.32 = 33.2$$

$$I_C(E) = -\log_2(P_E) = -\log_2(.10) = 3.32$$

$$I_C(F) = -\log_2(P_F) = -\log_2(.05) = 4.32$$

$$I_B(E) = \text{Freq} \times I_C = 10 \times 3.32 = 33.2$$

$$I_B(F) = \text{Freq} \times I_C = 5 \times 4.32 = 21.6.$$

2.2 DATA COMPRESSION

Data compression is one of the applications of Information memory. The objective of compression is to convert the input data into a format which requires less space for storage. Basic principle behind compression is to code the input data using coding techniques in such a way that the coded data takes less amount of storage space. Therefore, it's basic aim is to minimize the storage requirement.

It is two types of compression:

1. Lossless Compression.
2. Lossy Compression.

2.2.1 Lossless Compression

In loss-less compression, no information is lost. It refers to the compression where the exact input data value will be produced after decompression, *i.e.,* No data will be lossed. At the decompression end we get the original data. This type of compression is used when we must not lose or misplace even a single bit in the original message.

For e.g., : Textual data, S/w programs.

2.2.2 Lossy Compression

In lossy compression, redundant information is discarded. In lossy compression, data may loose some of contents and the exact information will not be reproduced after decompression. Clearly, this type of compression must not be used in text/message compression. It is more appropriate for the compression of graphics, images etc.

For e.g., : Images, audio, videos etc. JPEG.

2.2.3 Compression Ratio

Compression Ratio can be define as :

$$\text{C.R.} = \frac{\text{Size of original data} - \text{Size of compressed data}}{\text{Size of original data}} \times 100$$

Example 1. *A text containing 38 KB is compressed using Shannon–Fano coding. The size of 11 code is 20 KB. Find the C.R.?*

Solution.

$$\text{C.R.} = \frac{(38 - 20)}{38} \times 100\%$$

$$= \frac{18}{38} \times 100$$

$$= 47.36\% \ \textbf{Ans.}$$

2.3 ENCODING VS COMPRESSION

There is a fine difference b/w encoding and compression. The objective of compression is to convert the I/P data into a format which requires less space for storage. The graphics, audio, video, data usually take very high amount of storage ranging from sensal megabyte to gigabytes. Storage, retrieval processing and communication of such huge data is a very costly affair. Basic principle behind compression is to code the I/P data using coding techniques in such a way that the coded data takes less amount of storage. For this purpose many coding techniques are used and this process is called encoding. Encoding is therefore a part of compression. The objective of compression is to minimize the storage requirement and produce the same input data at the decompression phase. The objective of encoding is to generate the code for I/P data which after decoding produces the same information.

2.4 SHANNON-FANO ALGO

It was developed by Claude Shannon at Bell Laboratories and RM fano at M/T. The algorithm deals with text compression. It takes a stream of characters in the form of text or message and produces the code which when decompressed, produces the input text. The coded form of I/P text require lesser number of bytes, and thus, it will require less disk space to store.

Steps:

1. Find the total number of distinct symbols which may appear in the text. Develop a list of frequency count for each symbol.
2. Arrange the symbols in the decreasing order of frequency.
3. Divide the list horizontally in such a way that the sum of frequencies in the upper half and the sum of frequencies in the lower half is approximately same. This process is applied recursively to all of the halves untill each half contains only one symbol.
4. Construct the Shannon Fano free in such a way that the upper half represents the left subtree and the lower the right subtree. Keep doing untill all of the symbols appear at leaves of tree 1.3.
5. Assign Shannon Fano code to each symbol. It is done by representing the left branch of SF Binary tree as 'O' and righ as '1'.

   Traversing from root to that symbol will give the code for that symbol.

2.4.1 Examples of SF Algorithm

Example 2.

Symbol	*Frequency*
A	*50*
B	*25*
C	*10*
D	*?*

Solution.

Step 1 : Find out the frequency of symbol D by subtracting from 100.

i.e., 100 – (50 + 25 + 10)

= 100 – 85 = 15

Step 2 :

Symbols	*Frequency*
A	50
B	25
C	10
D	15

Step 3 : Arrange in decreasing order of frequency.

Symbols	*Frequency*
A	50
B	25
D	15
C	10

Step 4 : Now divide the table into two half.

Symbols	*Frequency*	
A	50	1st Division
B	25	
D	15	
C	10	

Step 5 :

Symbol	*Frequency*	
A	50	1st Division
B	25	2nd Division
D	15	3rd Division
C	10	

Step 6 : Constructing SF Tree.

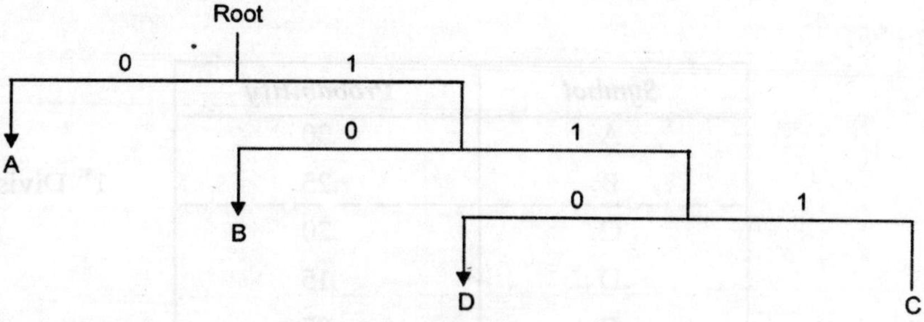

Fig. *SF-Tree*

SF Code:

S. No.	*Symbol*	*SF CODE*	*No. of Bits*	*Frequency*
1.	A	0	1	50
2.	B	10	2	25
3.	C	111	3	15
4.	D	110	3	10

The total number of bits required to represent the text

$$= (50 \times 1) + (25 \times 2) + (15 \times 3) + (10 \times 3)$$

$$= 50 + 50 + 45 + 30 = 175 \text{ bits/symbols.}$$

Since, the sum of all frequencies is 100.

$\therefore$ Average number of bits per symbols by using Shannon-Fano Algorithm.

$$= \frac{175}{100} = 1.75 \text{ bits/symbols.}$$

But in ASCII we need, 8 bits/symbol.

$\therefore$ Total $= 100 \times 8$

$= 800$ bits/symbol

$\therefore$ Total number of bits saved $= 800 - 175$

$= 625.$

Example 3.

Symbol	*Probability*
A	*.30*
B	*.25*
C	*.20*
D	*.15*
E	*.05*
F	*.05*

Solution. Since the given probability is already in decreasing order, so we apply step 1.

Step 1:

Symbol	*Probability*	
A	.30	
B	.25	1st Division
C	.20	
D	.15	
E	.05	
F	.05	

Step 2:

Symbol	*Probability*	
A	.30	2nd Division
B	.25	1st Division
C	.20	
D	.15	
E	.05	
F	.05	

Step 3:

Symbol	*Probability*	
A	.30	2nd Division
B	.25	1st Division
C	.20	
D	.15	3rd Division
E	.05	
F	.05	

Step 4:

Symbol	*Probability*	
A	.30	2nd Division
B	.25	1st Division
C	.20	4th Division
D	.15	3rd Division
E	.05	5th Division
F	.05	

Step 5:

Symbol	*Probability*	
A	.30	2nd Division
B	.25	1st Division
C	.20	4th Division
D	.15	3rd Division
E	.05	5th Division
F	.05	

Construct SF-Tree:

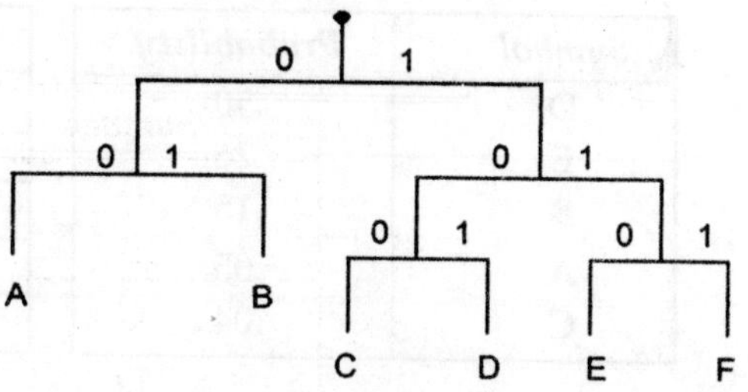

Fig. *SF Tree*

SF Code Table:

S.No.	*Symbol*	*SF Code*	*No. of Bits*	*Probability*
1.	A	00	2	.30
2.	B	01	2	.25
3.	C	100	3	.20
4.	D	101	3	.15
5.	E	110	3	.05
6.	F	111	3	.05

Example 4.

Symbol	*Probability*
A	*.05*
B	*.15*
C	*.04*
D	*.50*
E	*.26*

(i) Calculate the entropy of the source?

(ii) Obtain SF code for the characters?

(iii) Find average length of characters?

(iv) Compute the redundant bits/symbol in SF Code?

Solution (*i*). We know that Entropy Function is given by.

$$E = \sum_{i=1}^{i=N} Pi * \text{Log}_2 (Pi)$$

Putting the values from the table

$= -[(.05) * \log_2(.05) + .15 * \log_2 (.15) + .04 * \log_2 (.04) + .50 * \log_2 (.50) + .26 * \log_2 (.26)]$

$= .21 + .41 + .18 + .50 + .51$

Entropy = 1.81

(*ii*) First arrange the symbols in decreasing order of their probability.

Symbol	*Probability*
D	.50
E	.26
B	.15
A	.05
C	.04

Symbol	*Probability*	
D	.50	1st Division
E	.26	2nd Division
B	.15	3rd Division
A	.05	4th Division
C	.04	

Construct SF Tree:

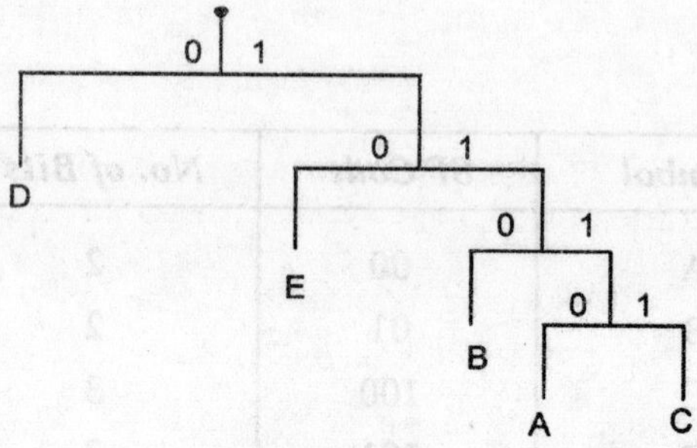

Fig. *SF Tree*

SF Code Table:

Symbol	*Probability*	*SF Code*	*No. of Bits*
A	.05	1110	4
B	.15	110	3
C	.04	1111	4
D	.50	0	1
E	.26	10	2

(*iii*) Average length of character

$= .05 \times 4 + .15 \times 3 + .04 \times 4 + .50 \times 1 + .26 \times 2$

$= 1.83$ bits/character.

(*iv*) Redundancy = Average length—Entropy

$= 1.83 - 1.81$

$= 0.02$ bits/character.

2.5 HUFFMAN CODING ALGORITHM

The Huffman coding Algorithm is an improvement over the Shannon-Fano algorithm. The Huffman algorithm is also a dynamic coding mechanism, in the sense that it assigns variable-length codes to the symbols, based on their frequencies.

The Huffman Algorithm assigns short codes to symbols occuring more frequently, and longer codes to symbols occuring less frequently.

The major technical difference between the Shannon-Fano algorithm and the Huffman algorithm is that the former techniques builds a binary tree from the top to bottom, whereas the later builds it from the bottom to the top.

Steps:

1. Calculate the symbols frequency if not given.
2. Arrange the symbols in decreasing order of frequencies.
3. Now consider the two symbols from the bottom of the sorted list of symbols and find their sum.
4. Now again arrange the sorted list.
5. Repeat step (3) and (4) till there is only one symbol left with a frequency = 100.
6. Now Generate HF Tree.
7. Now Develop HF codes with the help of HF Tree.

2.5.1 Example of HF Algo

Example 5.

Symbol	*Frequency*
A	*30*
B	*10*
C	*20*
D	*05*
E	*15*
F	*10*
G	*?*

Solution.

Step 1: Frequency of G = 100 – (30 + 10 + 20 + 05 + 15 + 10)

= 100 – 90 = 10.

Symbol	*Frequency*
A	30
B	10
C	20
D	05
E	15
F	10
G	10

Step 2 : Arrange the symbols in decreasing order.

Symbol	*Frequency*	*Symbol*	*Frequency*
A	30	A	30
C	20	C	20
E	15	E	15
B	10	H	15
F	10	B	10] I
G	10] H	F	10]
D	05]		

Symbol	*Frequency*	*Symbol*	*Frequency*
A	30	A	30
C	20	J	30
I	20	C	20] K
E	15] J	I	20]
H	15]		

Symbol	*Frequency*	*Symbol*	*Frequency*	*Symbol*	*Frequency*
K	40	L	60] M	M	100
A	30] L	K	40]		
J	30]				

HF Tree:

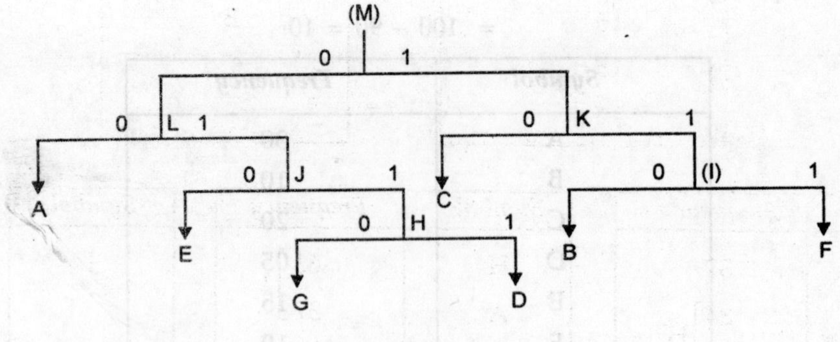

Fig. *HF Tree*

HF Code:

S. No.	Symbol	HF Code	No. of Bit	Frequency
1.	A	00	2	30
2.	B	110	3	10
3.	C	10	2	20
4.	D	0111	4	05
5.	E	010	3	15
6.	F	111	3	10
7.	G	0110	4	10

Example 6.

Symbol	*Frequency*
A	*37*
B	*18*
C	*16*
D	*15*
E	*14*

(i) Construct Huffman Tree and Generate Huffman codes?

(ii) Compute the entry bits and calculate redundancy in the code?

Solution (*i*).

Symbol	*Frequency*
A	37
B	18
C	16
D	15] F
E	14] F

Symbol	*Frequency*
A	37
F	29
B	18] G
C	16] G

Symbol	*Frequency*
A	37
G	34] H
F	29] H

Symbol	*Frequency*
H	63] I
A	37] I

Symbol	*Frequency*
I	100

HF Tree:

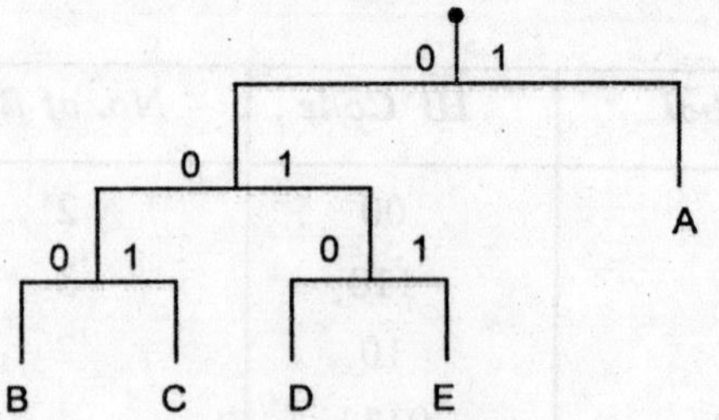

Fig. *HF Tree*

HF Code Table:

Symbol	*Frequency*	*HF Code*	*No. of Bits*
A	37	1	1
B	18	000	3
C	16	001	3
D	15	010	3
E	14	011	3

Total number of bits required to represent a text of 100 *i.e.*,

$= 37 \times 1 + 18 \times 3 + 16 \times 3 + 15 \times 3 + 14 \times 3$

$= 226$

Average number of bits per symbol = 226/100

= 2.26

(*ii*) Entropy $= -\sum_{i=1}^{i=n} Pi * \log_2 (Pi)$

$= -[.37 * \log_2(.37) + .18 * \log_2(.18) + .16 \times \log_2 (.16) + .15 * \log_2 (.15) + .14 * \log_2 (.14)]$

$= .530 + .445 + .423 + .410 + .397$

= 2.205 bits.

∴ Redundancy in the code

= 2.26 – 2.205

= .055 bits/symbol

2.6 DIFFERENCE B/W SHANNON-FANO AND HUFFMAN

Major difference in Shannon-Fano and Huffman algorithm is that in SF algo, the tree is built on the Top-down approach while Huffman Tree is built using the Bottom-up Approach.

Huffman performance is similar to that of Shannon-Fano, but Huffman algo has an edge over SF Algo. Huffman codes even in the worst case, will at least perform equal to SF codes.

2.6.1 Redundancy

Redundancy can be define as the difference between Entropy and Average size of code.

Redundancy = Entropy – Avg. size of code
Shannon-Fano > Huffman > Extended Huffman

2.7 EXTENDED HUFFMAN ALGORITHM

The primary objective of designing Huffman code is that it gives minimum redundancy. But it does not yield good performance when probabilities are skewed.

A drawback to Huffman coding is that they transmit a copy of the probability table with the compressed data. The solution to this problem lies in using Extended Huffman code.

The Extended Huffman codes are obtained by grouping more than one symbol in on group and Huffman code is obtained for whole group. Major advantages for using Extended Huffman code is that it reduces the redundancy considerably.

2.7.1 Example of Extended Huffman Coding

Symbol	*Probability*
A	.40
B	.50
C	.10

A = .40, B = .50, C = .10

Group	*Probability*
AA	.40 × .40 = .1600
AB	.40 × .50 = .2000
AC	.40 × .10 = .0400
BA	.50 × .40 = .2000
BB	.50 × .50 = .2500
BC	.50 × .10 = .0500
CA	.10 × .40 = .0400
CB	.10 × .50 = .0500
CC	.10 × .10 = .0100

Extended HF Tree:

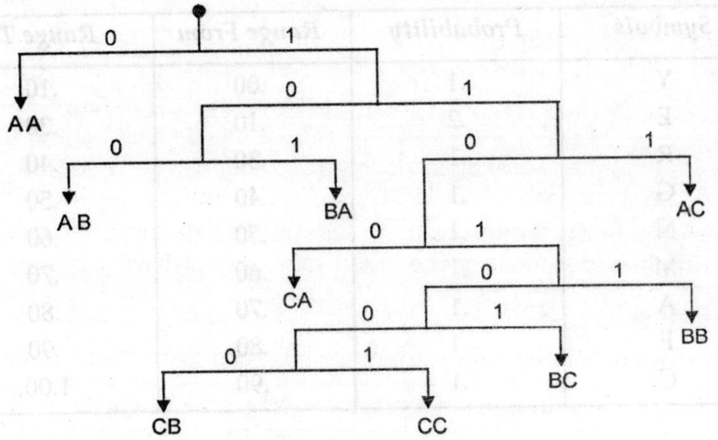

Fig. *Extended HF Tree*

S. No.	Symbol	Extended HF Code	No. of bits	Probability
1.	AA	0	1	.16
2.	AB	100	3	.20
3.	AC	111	3	.04
4.	BA	101	3	.20
5.	BB	11011	5	.25
6.	BC	110101	6	.05
7.	CA	1110	4	.04
8.	CB	1101000	7	.05
9.	CC	1101001	7	.10

2.8 ARITHMETIC CODING

In A.C, it is not required to represent a symbol with a fixed integral length code. The arithmetic compressor takes the stream of symbols and produces of floating point number. This number is less than one and it represent the coded form of input text. The arithmetic coding technique also exploits the probability of occurence of a symbol similar to Shannon-Fano and Huffman coding. Arithmetic coding has proved to be efficient coding techniques for compression and communication of binary numbers.

The only problem is that if produces a large size floating point number and it is difficult to deal by digital computers.

Example 7. *Arithmetic Coding.*

Y	*E*	*R*	*G*	*N*	*M*	*A*	*F*	*C*
.1	*.2*	*.1*	*.1*	*.1*	*.1*	*.1*	*.1*	*.1*

Code the letter "GERMAN" using Arithmetic coding.

Solution. Probability Table

Symbols	Probability	Range From	Range To
Y	.1	.00	.10
E	.2	.10	.30
R	.1	.30	.40
G	.1	.40	.50
N	.1	.50	.60
M	.1	.60	.70
A	.1	.70	.80
F	.1	.80	.90
C	.1	.90	1.00.

2.8.1 Algorithm for Arithmetic Coding

Initialize

Low-value = 0.0 ;

High-value = 1.0 ;

Difference = 1.0 ;

For every symbol in Input Repeat

Low-value = Low-value + Difference × Range-From (symbol) ;

High-value = Low-value + Difference × Range-To (symbol) ;

Difference = High-value – Low-value

Table. Coding

Symbol	*Low-value*	*High-value*	*Difference*
Initial	0.0	1.00	1.01
G	0.0 + 1 × .40 = .40	.00 + 1 × .50 = .50	.1
E	.40 + .1 × .10 = 0.41	.40 + .1 × .30 = .43	.02
R	.41 + .02 × .30 = .416	.41 + 0.02 × .4 = .418	.002
M	.416 + .002 × .6 = .4172	.416 + .002 × .7 = .4174	.0002
A	.4172 + .0002 × .7 = .41734	.4172 + .0002 × .8 = .41736	.00002
N	.41734 + .00002 × .5	.41735 + .00002 × .6	.000002
	= .41735 Answer.	= .417352	

2.8.2 Algorithm for Decoding

$$\text{Code} = \frac{\text{Code} - \text{Range From (Symbol)}}{(\text{Range\_To(Symbol)} - \text{Range\_From(Symbol)})}$$

Table. Decoding

Coded Fractional Number	*Output*	*Range From*	*Range To*	*Difference*
.41735	G	.4	.5	.1
(.41735 – .4)/.1 = .1735	E	.1	.3	.2
(.1735 – .1)/.2 = .3675	R	.3	.4	.1
(.3675 – .3)/.1 = .675	M	.6	.7	.1
(.675 – .6)/.1 = .75	A	.7	.8	.1
(.75 – .7)/.1 = .5	N	.5	.6	.1
(.5 – .5)/.1 = .0	–	–	–	–

O/P of this procedure is fractional No. .41735, which lies in the range .4 – .5. Thus, the first character of the code is 'G'.

Example 8. *The following is the probability distribution of symbols:*

A	*B*	*E*	*G*	*I*	*L*	*S*	*T*	*
.1	*.1*	*.1*	*.1*	*.1*	*.2*	*.1*	*.1*	*.1*

Code the word "BILL GATES" using Arithmetic Coding?*

Solution. Probability Table:

Symbols	*Probability*	*Range From*	*Range To*
A	0.1	0.0	0.1
B	0.1	0.1	0.2
E	0.1	0.2	0.3
G	0.1	0.3	0.4
I	0.1	0.4	0.5
L	0.2	0.5	0.7
S	0.1	0.7	0.8
T	0.1	0.8	0.9
*	0.1	0.9	1.0

Coding Table:

Action	*Low-value*	*High-value*	*Difference*
Initial	0.0	1.0	1.0
Input B	0.0 + 1.0 × 0.1 = 0.1	0.0 + 1.0 × 0.2 = 0.2	0.1
Input I	0.1 + 0.1 × 0.4 = 0.14	0.1 + 0.1 × 0.5 = 0.15	0.01
Input L	0.14 + 0.01 × 0.5 = 0.145	0.14 + 0.01 × 0.7 = 0.147	0.002
Input L	0.145 + 0.002 × 0.5 = 0.146	0.145 + 0.002 × 0.7 = 0.1464	0.0004
Input G	0.146 + 0.0004 × 0.3 = 0.14612	0.146 + 0.00004 × 0.1 = 0.14616	0.00004
Input A	0.14612 + 0.00004 × 0.0 = 0.14612	0.14612 + 0.00004 × 0.1 = 0.146124	0.000004
Input T	0.14612 + 0.000004 × 0.8 = 0.1461232	0.14612 + 0.000004 × 0.9 = 0.1461236	0.0000004
Input E	0.1461232 + 0.0000004 × 0.2 = 0.14612328	0.14632 + 0.0000004 × 0.3 = 0.14612332	0.00000004
Input S	0.14612328 + 0.00000004 × 0.7 = 0.146123308	0.14612328 + 0.00000004 × 0.8 = 0.146123312	0.000000004
Input *	0.146123308 + 0.000000004 × 0.9 = 0.1461233116	0.146123308 + 0.000000004 × 1.0 = 0.146123312	0.0000000004

Arithmetic Code for "BILL GATES*" = 0.1461233116

2.9 DICTIONARY BASED COMPRESSION TECHNIQUES

Dictionary Based coding depends on the concept of maintaining the indexes. In all dictionary Based Coding Technique, the word, phrases or sentences are represented by tokens. Suppose a text has to be transmitted over a communication channel, then an equivalent token of that is transmitted. These tokens are generated corresponding to the index where they have been stored in the dictionary. The dictionary may be generated according to the nature of the text to be compressed.

The first algo proposed using D.B.C.T. was LZ77 developed by Ziv and Lampel. This algo with certain improvement was proposed by Ziv and Lampel in 1978 and it become known as LZ78. The next variant of LZ78 was introduced in 1984 called LZW Compression Technique developed by Teery welch.

2.9.1 LZ77

In this scheme, when a input text is taken for compression, it starts building the dictionary. Thus the symbols/words/phrases which have been scanned previously, appear again in the same text then a token corresponding to the entry of that phrase in the dictionary is generated. LZ77 schemes uses a text window, which is divided into two parts.

2.9.2 Drawbacks

1. Bottleneck in the LZ77 compression scheme is to decide the size of text window performance of LZ77 depends on the size of the text window, *i.e.*, if it is higher than a better performance will be achieved. This is one of the major drawbacks of LZ77.
2. Another drawback is that a limited size of phrase can be matched because of small size of look-ahead-buffer.

2.9.3 LZ78

LZ78 compression begins with a new dictionary. It seems the input characters and an entry to the newly created directory is made. Whenever, a new phrase is found which has a match with the phrase already stored in the dictionary, a new phrase which contains the phrase is stored in dictionary. If next time same phrase appears along with a new symbol/phrase, a new phrase is created. This strategy helps in building and entering new phrases into the directory which may appear in the future.

Example 9. *Code the following using LZ78 "WYS * WYGWYS * WYWWYSG".*

Solution.

Step	*I/p phrase*	*O/P phrase*
1.	'W'	<0, 'W'>
2.	'Y'	<0, 'Y'>
3.	'S'	<0, 'S'>
4.	'*'	<0, '*'>

5.	'WY'	<1, 'Y'>
6.	'G'	<0, 'G'>
7.	'WYS'	<5, 'S'>
8.	'*W'	<4, 'W'>
9.	'YW'	<2, 'W'>
10.	'WYSG'	<7, 'G'>

Dictionary Tree:

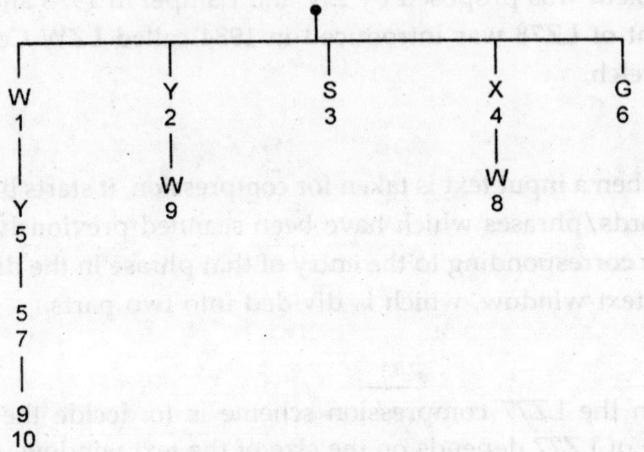

Fig. *Dictionary Tree*

Decode Table:

O/P phrase	*Text Generated*
1. <0, 'W'>	W
2. <0, 'Y'>	Y
3. <0, S>	S
4. <0, '*'>	*
5. <1, 'Y'>	WY
6. <0, 'G'>	G
7. <5, 'S'>	WYS
8. <4, W>	*W
9. <2, W>	YW
10. <7, 'G'>	WYSG.

2.9.4 Drawback of LZ78

In this there is a problem of handling the dictionary tree. However, the dictionary tree is quiet efficient infinding the phrase matches. It is also not suitable for compressing a small amount of data, as in certain cases, the compressed code and the size of dictionary tree groms faster and the resultant code generated is larger than the I/P text.

Example 10. *Encode the message "MAHAN*MAHABHARATH" using LZ78 Algo?*

Solution.

Step	*Input phrase*	*O/P phrase*
1.	'M'	<0, 'M'>
2.	'A'	<0, 'A'>
3.	'H'	<0, 'H'>
4.	'AN'	<2, 'N'>
5.	'*'	<0, '*'>
6.	'MA'	<1, 'A'>
7.	'HA'	<3, 'A'>
8.	'B'	<0, 'B'>
9.	'HAR'	<7, 'R'>
10.	'ATH'	<2, 'T'>
11.	'H'	<0, 'H'>

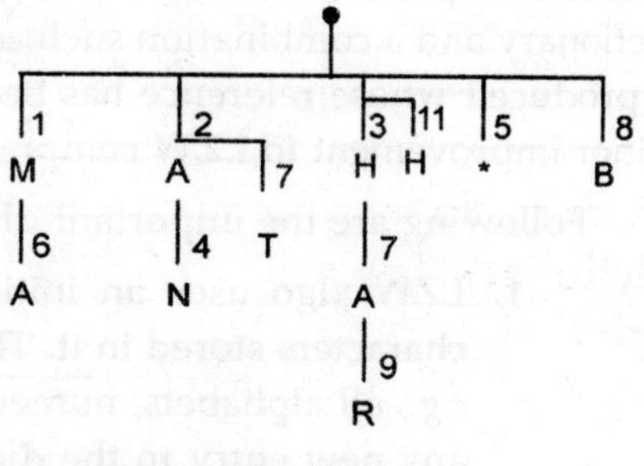

Fig. *Dictionary Tree*

Example 11. *Encode the message "BABABBABUBABABAP" using LZ78 Algo?*

Solution.

Step	*Input phrase*	*O/P phrase*
1.	'B'	<0, 'B'>
2.	'A'	<0, 'A'>
3.	'$'	<0, '$'>
4.	'BA'	<1, 'A'>
5.	'B$'	<1, '$'>
6.	'BAB'	<4, 'B'>
7.	'U'	<0, 'U'>
8.	'BABA'	<6, 'A'>
9.	'BAP'	<4, 'P'>

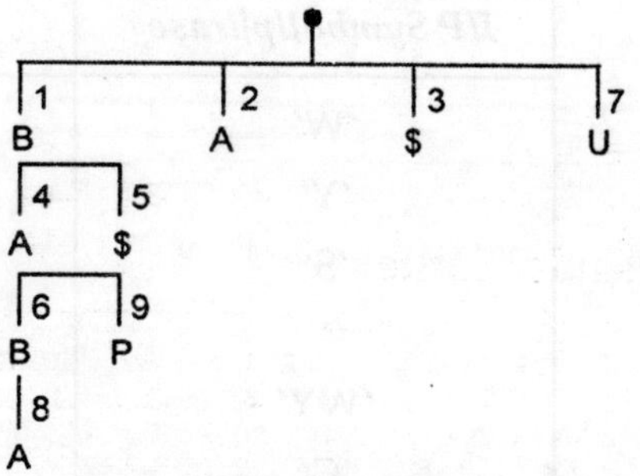

Fig. *Dictionary Tree*

Example 12. *Encode the message "ABACACBDACBDBDACBDAACD" using LZ78 Algo?*

Solution.

Step	*Input phrase*	*O/P phrase*
1.	'A'	<0, 'A'>
2.	'B'	<0, 'B'>
3.	'AC'	<1, 'C'>
4.	'ACB'	<3, 'B'>
5.	'D'	<0, 'D'>
6.	'ACBD'	<4, 'D'>
7.	'BD'	<2, 'D'>
8.	'ACBDA'	<6, 'A'>
9.	'ACD'	<3, 'D'>

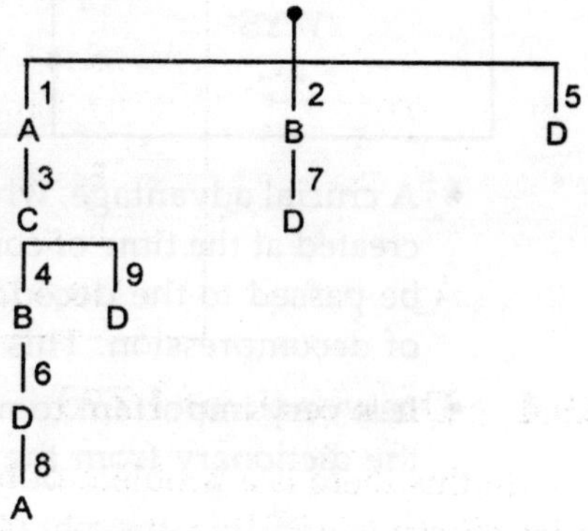

Fig. *Dictionary Tree*

2.9.5 LZW (Lampel, Ziv and Welch)

Terry welch proposed LZW compression algorithm in 1984. It is an improved version of LZ78 compression algorithm. It is different from LZ78 in such a way that LZW, does not produce the character along with the output phrase. In LZ78, a combination of phrase and a character is produced when a string or phrase of input text is matched with the phrase in the dictionary and a combination such as <4, 'W'> is produced. In LZW, only a code such as <201> is produced whose reference has been made to dictionary at the time of decompression. This minor improvement in LZW compression algorithm makes it more effective.

Following are the important difference between LZW and LZ78 algorithm.

1. LZW algo uses an initialized dictionary. The dictionary is initialized with 255 characters stored in it. These are the characters which may be contained in the text *e.g.*, all alphabets, numerals and special character like '@', 'and', '?' etc. Therefore, any new entry to the dictionary will occupy the place at position 256.
2. While scanning the characters of the text, at every character input, a phrase containing the character and the next character at input line, is entered to the dictionary.

Example 13. *Compress the text using LZW algo. "WYS*WYGWYS*WYSWYSG".*

Solution. Suppose the entries for single character 'W', 'Y', 'S', '*', 'G', occupies the positions at 63, 65, 59, 15, 47.

I/P Symbol/phrase	*O/P code*	*Addition to Dictionary*
'W'	<63>	–
'Y'	<65>	'WY' 256
'S'	<59>	'YS' 257
'*'	<15>	'S*' 258
'WY'	<256>	'*W' 259
'G'	<47>	'WYG' 260
'WY'	<256>	'GW' 261
'S*'	<258>	'WYS' 262
'WYS'	<262>	'S*W' 263
'WYS'	<262>	'WYSW' 264
'G'	<47>	'WYSG' 265

- A crucial advantage, which LZW coding offers is that it does not use the dictionary, created at the time of compression. Thus, after compression, the dictionary need not be passed to the decoder because the code itself creates the dictionary at the side of decompression. This saves a lot of space and processing cost.
- It is very important to note that at every step, a symbol or phrase will be added to the dictionary from the position starting with 256.

Decode:

Steps	*Code*	*Generated Symbol/phrase*	*Dictionary*
1.	<63>	'W'	'WY' 256
2.	<65>	'Y'	'YS' 257
3.	<59>	'S'	'SX' 258
4.	<15>	'*'	'*W' 259
5.	<256>	'WY'	'WYG' 260
6.	<47>	'G'	'GW' 261
7.	<256>	'WY'	'WYS' 262
8.	<262>	'WYS'	'S*W' 263
9.	<262>	'WYS'	'WYSW' 264
10.	<47>	'G'	'WYSG' 265

Output Phrase : "WYS*WYGWYWYSWYSG."

Example 14. *'ABACACBDACBDBDACBDAACD'*.

Solution. Assume. A, B, C, D → 63, 64, 65, 66

Coding:

I/P Symbol/phrase	*O/P code*	*Addition to Dictionary*	
'A'	<63>	–	–
'B'	<64>	'AB'	256
'A'	<63>	'BA'	257
'C'	<65>	'AC'	258
'AC'	<258>	'CA'	259
'B'	<64>	'ACB'	260
'D'	<66>	'BD'	261
'ACB'	<260>	'DA'	262
'D'	<266>	'ACBD'	263
'BD'	<262>	'DB'	264
'ACBD'	<260>	'BDA'	265
'A'	<63>	'ACBDA'	266
'AC'	<258>	'AA'	267
'D'	<66>	'ACD'	268

Example 15. *Encode the message "EJSEJESEJEJSEJEJTEJEJ" using LZW Algo?*

Solution. Initially E = 30, J = 31, S = 32, T = 33

I/P Symbol/phrase	*O/P code*	*Addition to Dictionary*	
'E'	<30>		
'J'	<31>	'EJ'	<256>
'S'	<32>	'JS'	<257>
'EJ'	<256>	'SE'	<258>
'E'	<30>	'EJE'	<259>
'SE'	<258>	'ES'	<260>
'J'	<31>	'SEJ'	<261>
'EJ'	<256>	'JE'	<262>
'SEJ'	<261>	'EJS'	<263>
'EJ'	<256>	'SEJE'	<264>
'T'	<33>	'EJT'	<265>
'EJE'	<259>	'TE'	<266>
'J'	<31>	'EJEJ'	<267>

Example 16. *Encode"/WED/WE/WEE/WEB" using LZW Algo?*

Solution. Initially / = 40, W = 41, E = 42, D = 43, B = 44

I/P Symbol/phrase	*O/P code*	*Addition to Dictionary*	
'/'	<40>		
'W'	<41>	'/W'	<256>
'E'	<42>	'WE'	<257>
'D'	<43>	'ED'	<258>
'/W'	<256>	'D/'	<259>
'E'	<427>	'/WE'	<260>
'/WE'	<260>	'E/'	<261>
'E/'	<261>	'/WEE'	<262>
'WE'	<257>	'E/W'	<263>
'B'	<44>	'WEB'	<264>

Example 17. *Encode "D1$D1D$D1D1$D1D1A$D1D1" using LZW Algo?*

Solution. We have initialize the dictionary D = 60, I = 61, $ = 62, A = 63.

I/P Symbol/phrase	*O/P code*	*Addition to Dictionary*	
'D'	<60>		
'I'	<61>	'DI'	<256>
'$'	<62>	'I$'	<257>
'DI'	<256>	'$D'	<258>
'D'	<60>	'DID'	<259>
'$D'	<258>	'D$'	<260>
'I'	<61>	'$DI'	<261>
'DI'	<256>	'ID'	<262>
'$DI'	<261>	'DI$'	<263>
'DI'	<256>	'$DID'	<264>
'A'	<63>	'DIA'	<265>
'$DID'	<264>	'A$'	<266>
'I'	<61>	'$DIDI'	<267>

2.10. IMAGE COMPRESSION

2.10.1. Joint Photographic Experts Group (JPEG)

JPEG has laid down the guidelines for compression of various real world images. It works well on photographs, naturalistic art-work. JPEG recommendations are used only for static images. JPEG is lossy compression technique, therefore, the image obtained by decompression will not be exactly similar to the original one.

JPEG files are platform-independent. This file format is developed as a compression technique for storing graphic files by the group mentioned in the title. JPEG uses 24-bit color, and hence JPEG files are almost like real-life. The efficiency of JPEG format is based on the spatial frequency or concentration of detail.

The JPEG compression algorithm consists of three steps:

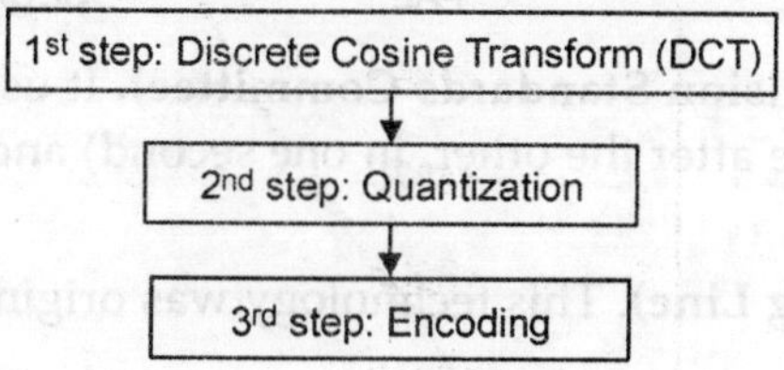

Fig. *JPEG Compression Steps*

1. **Discrete cosine transform.** In this step, the image is divided into a series of blocks. Each blocks contains dots (called as pixels) of 8 rows and 8 columns, *i.e.*, consisting of an 8 × 8 matrix. Here we basically performs a mathematical operation, called as discrete cosine, a detailed study of which is outside of the scope of the current text.

2. **Quantization.** At this steps, the small differences in an image which do not have any significance are ignored *i.e.*, we ignore those portions of an image, which when excluded do not cause any perceptible impact.

3. **Encoding.** The earlier two steps are only transformation steps. There is no compression there. Those steps only transform the image to a format, which can be compressed. The actual compression takes place in encoding. The encoding steps accepts a two dimensional array as input, and produces a linear sequence of bits corresponding to compressed image. Internally, it uses the Huffman algorithm or another compression technique called as Run Length Encoding (RLE).

2.10.2 Moving Picture Expert Group (MPEG)

MPEG is used as ISO standard for digital video compression. It is actually a family of formats supporting video, audio. MPEG does the data stream compression upto 1.2 MBPS which is equal to CD-Rom data transfer rate. MPEG standards always make use of JPEG compression because digital video is represented as a sequence of still colour images.

MPEG has two types of compressions:

1. Asymmetric Compression
2. Symmetric Compression

In Asymmetric Compression, compression is done in a single attempt but the decompression is done in multiple stages, whereas symmetric compression requires the same amount of effort for both compression and decompression.

MPEG has many versions. The MPEG-1 standards was originally developed for VHS quality video transfer. MPEG-2 is a better-quality standards for television broadcasts. MPEG-3 never became popular. The current standard is MPEG-4, which is intended to support video conferencing on communication links of low speed.

There are broadly three types of televsion display formats.

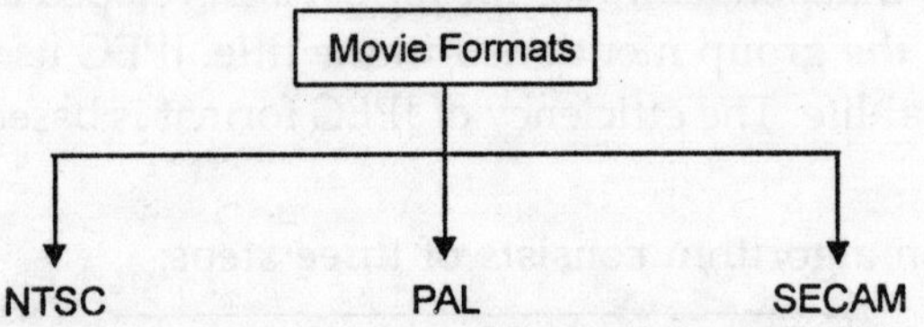

1. **NTSC. (National Television Standards Committee).** It uses 30 frames per second (*i.e.*, it shows 30 pictures quickly one after the other, in one second) and is quite predominant in the US, South America & Japan.

2. **PAL (Phase Alternating Line).** This technology was originated in Germany and it uses 25 frames per second.

3. **SECAM (Sequential Colour Avec Memoire).** This format is quite popular in France, and it also uses 25 frames per second.

2.10.3 Multimedia Hypermedia Expert Group (MHEG)

MHEG is a body setup by ISO for standardizing multimedia presentation and formats. The main objective of this group was to create the standard method of storage, exchange and display of multimedia presentation. This group has many standard formats, the most current being MHEG version 5, which appeared in 1994. The motive of this group are:

- Provide a simple format for multimedia presentations with least number of resources.
- Define a digital format suitable for multimedia presentations, so that these presentations can be exchanged among the users and presented seamlessly.
- Make the formats easily adaptable and extensible as newer and better solutions emerge.

MHEG is based on object oriented (00) technology. The MHEG classes define how video/ audio should be played. There are three main types of classes in MHEG: content classes, behaviour classes and user interface classes.

- *Content classes:* There classes describe the actual content of the video/audio, *i.e.*, the bits corresponding to the pictures, motion or sound.
- *Behaviour classes:* These classes describe how data is presented to the user. This is useful in synchronizing the events with the user interface.
- *User interface classes:* These classes describe the elements of the user interface, such as the buttons, menus, lists, boxes, slider, etc., that appear on the user's screen.

2.10.4 Graphics Interchange Format (GIF)

The GIF uses bitmap images, where 8 bits represent one pixel. It was introduced by compuserve in 1987. Since then, it has been in widespread usage on the world wide web due to its wide support and portability. The format uses upto 256 distinct colours from the 24-bit RGB colour space. It also supports animations and allows a separate 256 colors for each of the frames. But this colour limiations makes the GIF format a bit unsuitable for reproducing color photographs and other images with continuous color. However, it is well-suited for more simple images such as graphs or logos with solid areas of color.

GIF images are compressed using the LZW data compression technique to reduce the file size without reducing the visual quality. In general, we can say that GIFs are suitable for sharp-edged line art (*e.g.*, Logos) with a limited number of colors.

EXERCISES

1. What is data compression? Why is it needed? Differentiate between lossy and lossless data compression techniques with suitable examples.
2. Differentiate between Compression and Encoding.
3. Explain LZW coding Algorithm. What are its advantages and disadvantages?
4. What is dictionary based compression? Differentiate between LZ78 and LZW compression schemes.
5. What are steps of Shannon-Fano Algorithm?
6. Differentiate between SF and HF Algorithm.
7. Explain various file formats used for multimedia data.
8. Write short notes on (1) JPEG (2) MPEG.
9. Construct Huffman Tree and Generate Huffman code for the message "IAMINDIAN".
10. Encode the message "A VABAAVABC$AB" using LZW coding technique.

3

Computer Appreciation

3.1 HISTORY OF COMPUTERS

The effort toward development of computing machines had started long back in the 16th century. An initial attempt in this direction was a mechanical computer developed by Blaise Pascal in 1640. This m/c was based on wheels and it used to add and subtract numbers. Long before, this, the first computing instrument known as ABACUS was developed in 400 B.C.

Gradually, in course of time, Napier's bones (1600), Pascal's first computer (1642), Leibnitz's mechanical calculator (1771), Babbage's difference engine (1822) were developed.

The development of the first computer, named MARK-1, marked the beginning of modern computer technology and generation of computers. The first general purpose digital computer was called ENIAC (Electronic Numerical Integrator and Calculator) developed at University of Pennsylvania. It was very huge m/c and it did not become popular. Vin Neuman, was the one of the chief architects of ENIAC computer.

3.1.1 Definition of Computer

The term computer is derived from the word *'compute'*, which means to *'calculate'*. A computer is an electronic device, designed for performing calculations and controlling operations that can be expressed either in logical or numerical terms. In simple words, a computer is an electronic device that performs diverse operations with the help of instructions to process the information in order to achieve the desired result.

Technically, a computer is a collection of electronic devices used to process data.

3.1.2 Digital Vs Analog Computer

Digital Computers operates an binary digits *i.e.,* 0 and 1. They understand information composed of only 0s and 1s. Whereas Analog Computers are those which can process analog quantities.

Analog and Digital computers differ in many respects but the most important distinction is the way they represent data. Digital systems represent data as having one distinct value or another, with no other possibilities. Whereas Analog systems, however, represent data as variable points along a continuous spectrum of values. This makes analog computers some what more flexible than digital ones, but not necessarily more precise or reliable.

Microcomputer

Microcomputer are general purpose computer which is (Formed) developed by the combination of I/P and O/P devices along with microprocessor and memory.

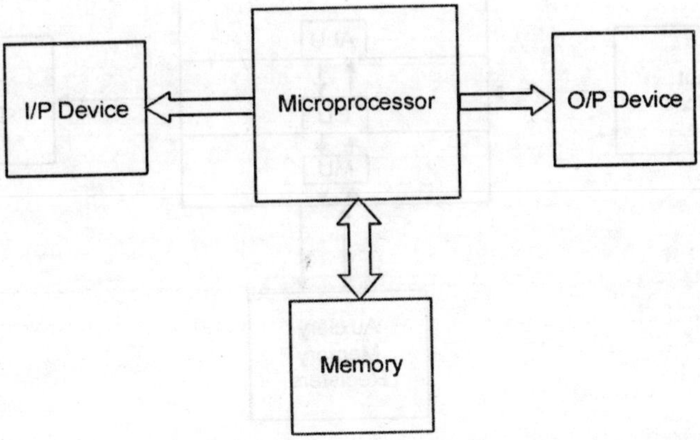

Microprocessor

A CPU built on a single, VLSI or ULSI chip is called a microprocessor. It is the latest development in the field of computer technology as well as semiconductor technology. A digital computer has a microprocessor as its CPU. A microprocessor combined with memory, an input device and an output device form a microcomputer. The CPU of a large computer contains a number of microprocessors. Each microprocessors performs a specified task within the CPU. The microprocessors in the CPU of a large computers operates in parallel. It is basically a part of micro computer.

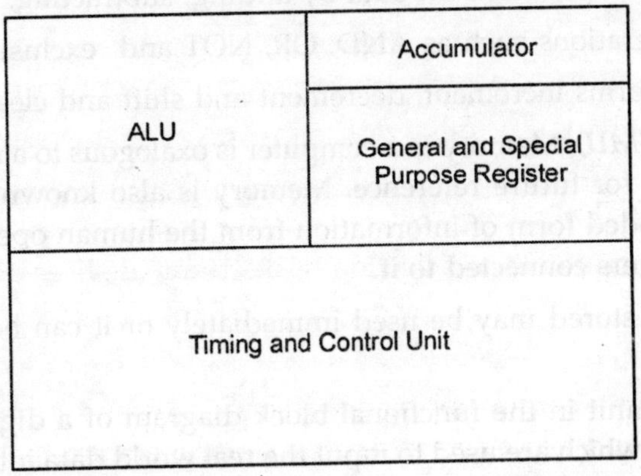

3.1.3 Central Processing Unit (CPU)

The CPU is the brain of a computer where all kinds of processing is done. This unit takes the input data from the I/P devices and processes it according to the set of instructions called program. The O/P of processing of the data are directed to the O/P devices for use in the outside world. The major function of the CPU is to store the data temporarily in the registers and perform arithmetic and logical computations. This unit also controls the operation of all other functional units of the computer such as memory, I/P and O/P devices. CPU has three major parts :

1. CU 2. ALU 3. Memory Unit.

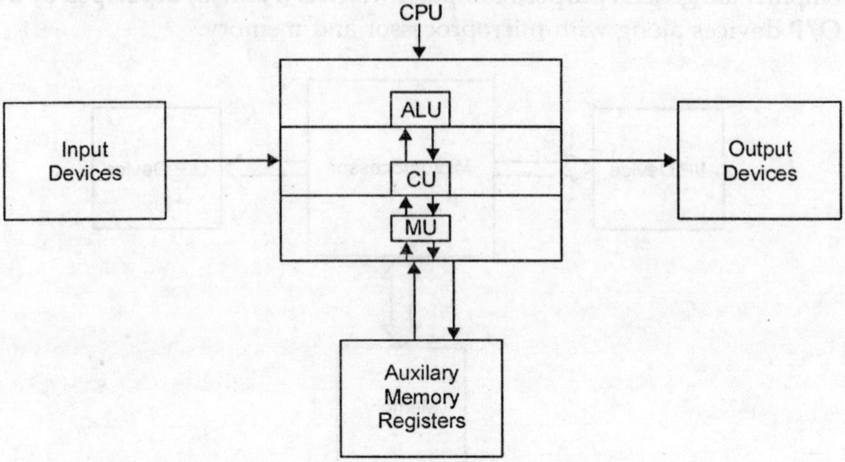

Fig. *Block Diagram of Digital Computer*

1. ***Control Unit (CU).*** This unit is mainly used for generating the electronic control signals, for the synchronization of various operations. All the related functions for program execution such as memory read, memory write, I/O read, I/O write, execution of instruction are synchronized through the control signal generated by the control unit. It controls all the operations of the computer. The computer can copy or more data around to create any kind of report or listing of any order.

2. ***Arithmetic and Logical Unit (ALU).*** This unit is responsible for carrying out:

- Arithmetical operations on data by adding, subtracting, multiplying and dividing.
- Logical operations such as AND, OR, NOT and exclusive OR operation.
- It also performs increment, decrement and shift and clearance operations as well.

3. ***Memory Unit (MU).*** Memory in a computer is oxalogous to a notebook, where we may note down various things for future reference. Memory is also known by the term storage and its function is to store coded form of information from the human operator through the I/P device or from other computers connected to it.

The information stored may be used immediately or it can be kept for later reference for processing by CPU.

4. ***I/P Unit.*** I/P unit in the functional block diagram of a digital computer represents the various input devices which are used to input the real world data into the computer. The function of the input unit is to accept coded information from the human operator or from an electromechanical device or from other computers connected to it through the internet or by any other media, *e.g.,*—keyboard, mouse, scanner, touch screen.

5. ***O/P Unit.*** The O/P unit is used to represent the information processed by the digital computer. The function of the O/P unit is to store the processed information and display it as and when needed by the user, *e.g.*,—Monitor and Printers.

3.2 GENERATIONS OF COMPUTER

There are five Generations of Computers :

1. First Generation (1945–1955)
2. Second Generation (1955–1965)
3. Third Generation (1965–1975)
4. Fourth Generation (1975–1994)
5. Fifth Generation (1994– .....)

1. First Generation (1945-1955)

This Generation of computers is said to have started in 1945. The first computer developed was UNIVAC–1 in 1950, where *Vacuum tubes* were used, and their memory were made of thin tubes of liquid mercury and magnetic drums.

Most of the computer systems developed during this period were IBM 701, IBM 704, IBM 709. During this period, the stored program concept was introduced by Von Neuman. His idea was basically to store the instruction program in a separate memory. The high cost of memory, because of the high cost of vacuum tubes, had discouraged the manufacture from using vacuum tubes for the memory. Instead, electrostatic memories were used to store the data in this generation of computers.

2. Second Generation (1955-1965)

- The second generation of computers lasted from 1955 to 1965.
- A new technology called *Transistor* was introduced in 1959.
- Transistors replaced the vacuum tube technology and it used finite core for memory.
- The size of computers were reduced by using transistors.
- The transistor were made from germanium semiconductor material and hence they were more reliable and faster than vacuum tubes.
- Computer system like IBM 1401, Honey and well-800 and IBM 1620, PDP services were developed.
- Programming language like COBOL, FORTRAN and ALUOL were developed.

3. Third Generation (1965–1975)

- It started in 1965.
- The major development in this period was the introduction of the integrated circuit (IC).
- IC contains number of transistors.
- This generation computers used the small scale integration (SSI) and Medium Scale Integration (MSI).

- In SSI, 10–100 transistors were fabricated on a single wafer, whereas in MSI , more than 100 transistors on a single wafer.
- Semiconductor memories were used.
- The introduction of operating system, DBMS, use of semiconductor memories, use of magnetic tape and disk as storage devices and introduction to each memories were the major milestones of this generation.

4. Fourth Generation (1975–1994)

- Microprocessor were developed.
- The new technology called VLSI (Very Large Scale Integration) was developed due to which it become possible to fabricate more than fifty thousand transistors an a chip.
    - In this generation, the chip replaced the integrated circuits.
    - The personal computers were manufactured.
    - Query languages, Report writers, Graphics, Computer Aided Design were the major software development in this period.
    - Vector processor and Array processors were also used during this period.

5. Fifth Generation (1994 – ...)

- This generation started with major innovations in computer architecture like parallel processing, Intelligent programming, application of A I and knowledge based system.
- The new technology called ULSI (Ultra Large Scale Integration) was developed due to which it has become possible to have the fastest microprocessor with a clock speed ranging from 100 MH_Z to $1GH_Z$.
- This period saw the wide use and popularity of personal computers.

3.3 CHARACTERISTICS OF COMPUTERS

1. Speed

Computers have very fast processing speed. And time measurement is done in terms of

- Milliseconds (10^{-3} seconds)
- Microseconds (10^{-6} seconds)
- Nanoseconds (10^{-9} seconds) and
- Picoseconds (10^{-12} seconds)
- Fermi seconds (10^{-15} seconds).

2. Accuracy

Computers are highly accurate machines and they never make mistakes.

3. Dilligence

Since, the computer lacks the human tendencies such as fatigue, boredom with repeated work, tiredness, lack of concentration, etc., it can perform repeated, mundane tasks with the same level of accuracy and enthusiasm. This is in contrast to the way human beings work, who can make mistake and get board.

4. Reliability

Computers can perform the jobs quite reliably.

5. Memory Capability

Computers have the memory unit as one of their logical blocks.

6. Versatility

Computers are quite versatile machine in many different respects such as in business

- At homes.
- For making movies.
- Creating paintings/music.
- In schools for education purposes.
- In scientific and engineering application.
- For controlling satellites.
- Measuring natural phenomenon.
- For playing games.
- In the medical field.
- For research and management etc., and so on.

7. Networking Capability

Now computers are interconnected through networking technology.

3.4 APPLICATIONS OF COMPUTERS

Computers are used in many areas some of the most prominent ones are :

1. **Science.** Scientists use computers for many purposes like :
    - To develop theories.
    - Gather data and test results.
    - Exchange information with colleagues.
    - For semiulating complicated events such as predicting rainfalls or change in weather patterns.
    - In satellites to explore the outer space.

2. **Education.** Computers can be found everywhere from classrooms to museums and from libraries to labs.
3. **Medicine**
   - Used extensively in area of medicine and healthcare.
   - In diagnosing diseases and
   - Monitoring patients.
   - In controlling the robotic movements of surgical assistants.
   - Medical appliances themselves use computers internally.
4. **Legal Practice.** Computers are used by lawyers, judges, attorneys and all others concerned with the legal profession.
5. **Manufacturing.** Extensively used in factories. Manufacturing with computer and robolie is called computer aided manufacturing (CAM), computers can take over the entire productions process, from design to manufacturing.
6. **Entertainment**
   - In movies
   - Live shows
   - Dramas
   - Creating and recording music
   - Games, etc.

3.5 CLASSIFICATION OF COMPUTERS

The most common classification of computer is as follows:

1. Mainframe
2. Minicomputer
3. Microcomputer or Personal Computer.
4. Super Computer
5. Handlheld Computer

1. Mainframe

- Used in large organisations *e.g.*, by banks, airlines, insurance companies, stock exchanges foreign exchange markets etc.
- Typically, employees work at computer terminal. A terminal is keyboard and screen connection to the mainframe.
- A terminal does not have its own CPU or storage (That is why it is also called as a *dumb terminal*).
- All the terminals are connected by a mainframe computer that handles the input, output and processing needs of the terminals connected to it.

- Mainframe computers are quite huge in size, hence, they used to occupy entire rooms or even a floor of a building.
- Used in governments for maintaining people's demographic data, 100 information etc.
- Many big stores use mainframes to track sales, update inventory positions and manage purchase transactions.
- Mainframes can hold billions of record, and can execute about 1,600,000,000 instructions per second.
- Cheapest mainframe costs about US.$ 30,000. High end mainframes typically cost millions of dollars.

2. Minicomputer

- First minicomputer appeared in the 1960. Manufactured by Digital Equipment Corporation (DEC).
- They were called as *mini*, because they were smaller in size as, compared to the computers of those days (*e.g.*, mainframe). However, now-a-days we can call them giants.
- Minicomputers are considered between mainframes and personal computers.

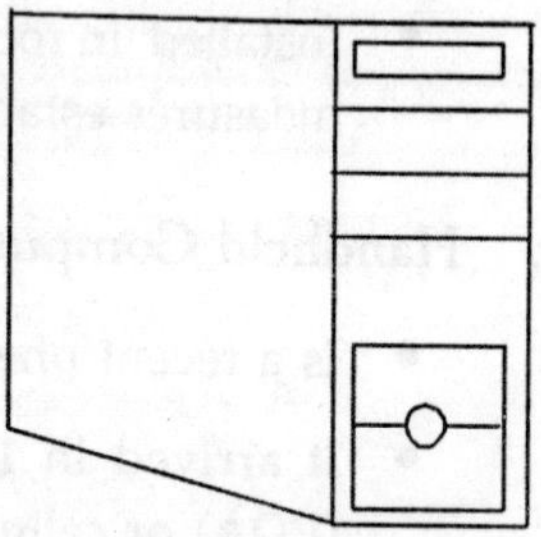

Fig. *Minicomputer*

- Can process large inputs as compared to personal computers.
- Are cheaper than mainframe, but have some features of mainframes.
- Cost between US.$ 18,000 and US.$ 500, 000.

3. Personal Computer

- Is also called as the microcomputer.
- Are found usually at homes, workplaces and classrooms.
- PC appear in many forms, sizes and brands.
- 1BM first brought the PC in 1981.
- The popularity of the PC's is due to:
  - Their economical nature.
  - Ease of use and availability.
  - Rapidly declining costs of hardware devices such as memory I/O etc.
  - Competition between the manufacturing companies.
  - Continuously increasing capability of PC.
- Variations of the PC are the *notebooks.* (also called as laptops), *handheld computers* (also called as palmtops) etc.
- Notebook— It's size is about 8.5 × 11 inch.
  - Can be folded and carried inside a briefcase.
  - It is very lightweight and perform tasks similar to PC.

- Can work using normal power connections or by using batteries.
- Priced between US.$ 500 and US.$ 5,000.

4. Super Computer

- Most powerful type of computers.
- Can process huge amount of data very fast (one trillions calculations/second)
- Used in modelling nuclear fission and fusion, weather pattern modelling and forecasts, managing space shuttles etc.
- Are very expensive. (tens of millions of dollars)
- Consume heavy amount of electricity.
- Installed in rooms having special cooling systems, security features and other protections measures established.

5. Handheld Computer

- Is a recent phenomenon.
- It arrived in 1990s and came in many versions such as Personal Digital Assistance (PDA) or cellular phone with, computing capabilities.
- These computers are very small close to the size of an appointment book.
- Significantly less powerful than a PC or a notebook.
- Not used for normal PC applications.
- But are used for keeping a track of the notes in
  - Meetings
  - Appointments
  - Names
  - Addresses and
  - Phone numbers of people etc.
- Can be connected with PC's for exchanging data periodically.

3.6 MEMORY CLASSIFICATION

Memory is broadly divided into two categories :

1. Main or Primary Memory
2. Auxiliary or Secondary Memory.

1. Primary or Main Memory

Is the fastest memory in a digital computer system. This memory is primarily used to store the data and program temporarily during the execution of a program. It stores program along with data to be processed. It also stores necessary S/W programs which themselves, are required for processing of user's program. CPU directly accesses this memory.

Main memory is further classified into two categories:

(*i*) Random Access Memory (RAM) (Volatile)

(*ii*) Read Only Memory (ROM) (non-volatile)

3.6.1 RAM (Random Access Memory)

It is also called volatile memory. The term volatile is used for RAM because it holds the data temporarily and when the power is switched off, all data stored in this memory is washed. RAM is also referred to as read write memory because it is used by the CPU to temporary load the program instruction and intermediate results. The program instructions and data keep on changing by the process of reading and writing to it therefore, it is also called read/write memory. The accessing of data from the memory takes places randomly and thus, it is referred to as Random Access Memory (RAM). It's access time is in nano seconds.

RAM may be classified into two categories :

(*i*) Static RAM

(*ii*) Dynamic RAM

Static RAM. It is made-up of flip-flops, an, electronic device, which stores a bit as *a* voltage. Static RAMs are fast but the disadvantage is packing of flip-flops. A comparatively lesser number of flip-flops are packed on a memory chip and therefore, the memory density of static RAM is low.

Dynamic RAM. It is based on the technology called MOS transistor gates. The advantage of MOS transistor gates is that a comparative higher number of MOS gates may be packed on the memory chip, and therefore, the memory density of dynamic RAM is high. The drawback of dynamic *memory* is that its flip-flop, based on MOS transistor gates, uses change as a bit. This charge is stored across the capacitor. The property of capacitor is that the charges leak with time. Therefore, a special circuit, called refreshing circuit, is placed with the dynamic RAM to refresh the memory.

3.6.2 ROM (Read Only Memory)

It is also a part of primary memory and it is called non-volatile memory. ROM can be used only for reading or fetching of data from it. The data or program are written into ROM only once and once it has been written, it cannot be modified or altered. ROM is used to store the programs or data which are critical and used frequently. The term non-volatile means that even if the power is switched off, the data or program stored in ROM is not destroyed. Whenever the power comes, the same data appears once again. One of the important usage of ROM is to store the Basic Input Output Software (BIOS). This program is very important because as if used by the operating system at the time of starting up or booting the system.

There are four types of ROM :

1. MROM (Masked ROM)
2. PROM (Programmable ROM)
3. EPROM (Erasable programmable ROM)
4. EEPROM (Electrically Erasable PROM)

MROM. It is manufactured by the masking and metalization process. The pattern or matrix once created is permanent and no change or alteration is permissible afterwards.

PROM. It is programmed by the programmer. PROM is manufactured by placing a fuse at all the positions. A special device called PROM programmer is used to store the desired pattern by selectively buming the fuses. Those fuses are burnt whenever, a bit 0 has to be stored. The presence of a fuse represents the presence of bit 1. The pattern stored through this process is permanent in nature.

EPROM. Are PROM which may be programmed again and again. This so happen because the pattem stored on EPROM is semi-permanent.

EEPROM. Are the same as EPROM, the only difference being that electrical signals are used to program ROM.

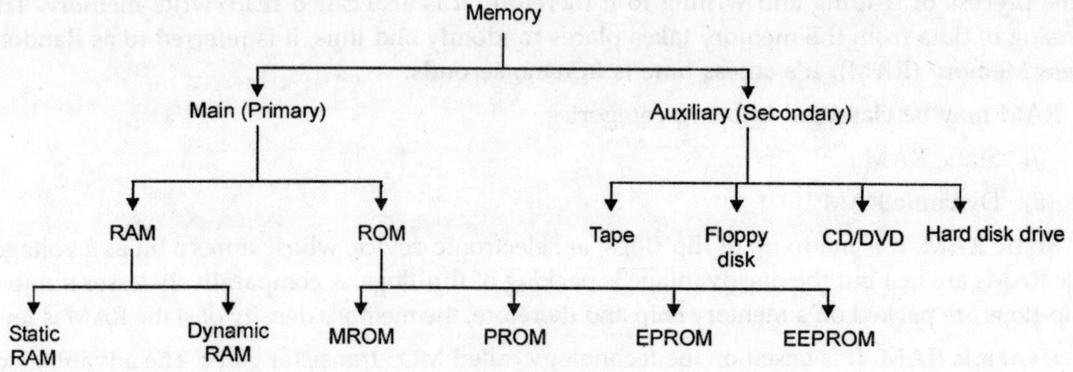

Fig. *Memory Classification*

2. Auxiliary or Secondary Memory

The magnetic memory is used as secondary (Auxiliary) memory. The information which is not being currently processed resides in the secondary memory. The secondary memory is employed for bulk storage (mass storage) of programs, data and other informations. It has much larger capacity than main memory. It stores system software, assemblers, compilers, useful packages, large-data files etc. The secondary memory should not be of volatile nature. It must store information permanently. The magnetic memory has this property. It retains the information once stored in it. The magnetic memories such as hard disks are the most common secondary memories used in computers.

Cache Memory. The cache memory is very high speed memory and it is costlier too. It is placed in between CPU and main memory. The processor is connected to the cache memory through a cache controller. It is a semiconductor memory. It consists of static RAMs. Its access time is about 10 nanoseconds, which is much less than that of the main memory of 50 nanoseconds. (1 nanoseconds = 10^{-9} seconds).

Memory Hierarchy

The processor is the 'brain' of the computer where all the essential computing takes place. Unlike a human brain, which combines memory with processing power a computer processor has very little memory. There are general storage devices which may be categorized on the basis of storage and retrieval time, capacity and technology.

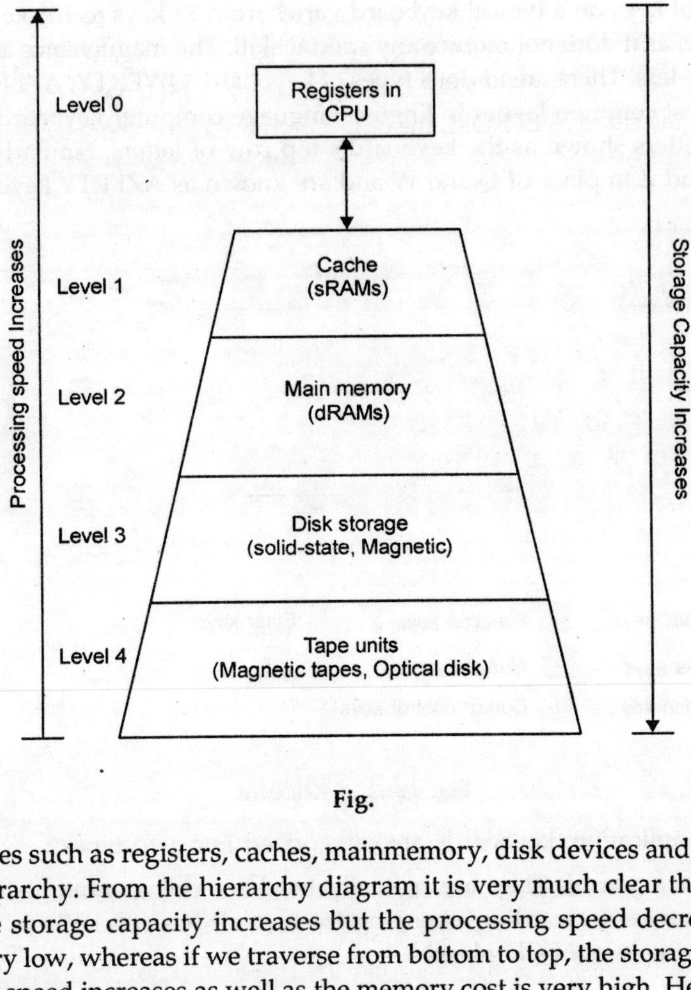

Fig.

Storage devices such as registers, caches, mainmemory, disk devices and tape units are often organized as a hierarchy. From the hierarchy diagram it is very much clear that as we move from top to bottom, the storage capacity increases but the processing speed decreases as well as the memory cost is very low, whereas if we traverse from bottom to top, the storage capacity decreases but the processing speed increases as well as the memory cost is very high. Hence, we can predict that registers are the fastest memory whereas the magnetic tapes drives are the showest. If we talk in terms of storage capacity than registers have very less storage space whereas magnetic tapes has large storage space.

3.7 INPUT DEVICES

An input device is a device through which data is entered into the computer system. They are also used to enter the command, program, images as well as the devices which are used to control various operations related to games and graphics etc.

1. Keyboard

A keyboard is the most popular and common data entry device. It is basically used for entering textual commands, data and programs to the digital computer. Using a keyboard, the user can type text and execute commands. Data is entered into computer by simply pressing keys. The keyboard contains three types of key: One each for each alphabet and numerals; secondly for various special characters; and the third set of keys are the special purpose keys known as functions keys. The number of keys on a typical keyboard varies from 82 keys to 108 keys. Keyboard is the easiest input device, as it does not require any special skill. The maintenance and operational cost of keyboards is also less. There are various types of keyboard: QWERTY, AZERTY and DVORAK. QWERTY is the most common layout in English language computer keyboards. It takes its name from the first six letters shown as the keyboard's top row of letters. Similarly, French language keyboards use A and Z in place of Q and W and are known as AZERTY keyboards.

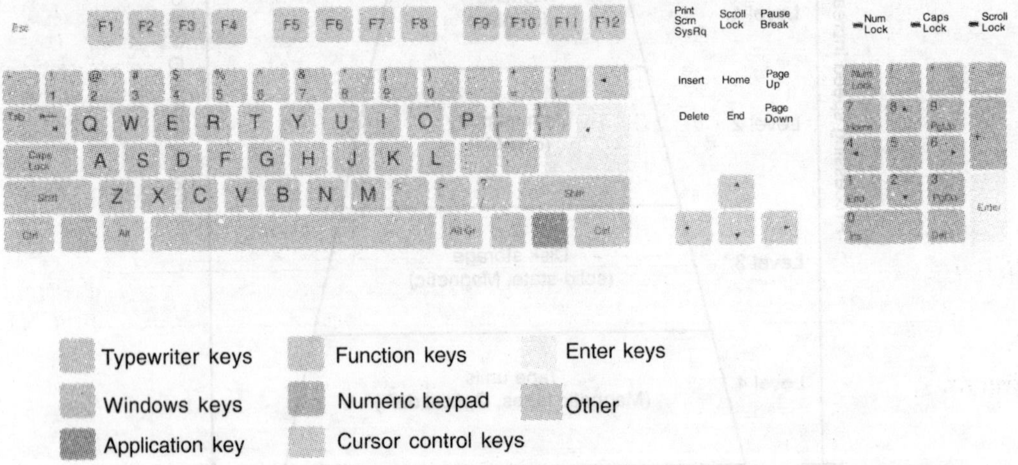

Fig. *Parts of Keyboard*

Based on the application, keyboards are categorized into two types :

(a) *Multimedia Keyboard.* They are basically used for doing multimedia works. Such as playing movies, forwarding, changing track etc. It has special keys which works very similar to the keys of CD players.

(b) *Internet Keyboard.* These are used for accessing internet on the computer.

2. Scanner

A scanner scans an image and transforms the image to ASCII codes and graphics. The coloured images may be scanned by the scanner and may be stored and processed in the graphical format. There are some popular scanners which can also read the text as images that may be converted into text files. Scanners use a light beam to scan the input data. If the data to be scanned is an image, it can be changed by using the image editing software. The two most common types of scanners are :

(*a*) ***Hand-held Scanner.*** The hand-held scanner consists of light emitting diodes, which are placed over the material to be scanned. This scanner performs the scanning of the document very slowly from the top to the bottom, with its light on. In this process, all the documents are converted and then stored as an image. While working, the scanner is dragged very steadily and carefully over the document and it should move at a constant speed without stopping, or jerking in order to obtain best results. Due to this reason, hand-held scanner are widely, used where high accuracy is not of much importance.

(*b*) ***Flat-bed Scanner.*** Flat-bed scanners look similar to a photocopier machine. It consists of a box containing a glass plate on its top and a lid that covers the glass plate. This glass plate is used for placing the document to be scanned. The light beam is placed below the glass plate and when it is activated, it moves from top to bottom. The flat bed scanners are larger in size and more expensive than the hand-held scanner.

Fig. *Flat-bed Scanner*

3. Mouse

Mouse is a small hand-held pointing device, which is rectangular shaped with a rubber ball embedded at its lower side and buttons on the top. It is one of most widely used input devices, after the keyboard. The mouse is used as point and click device with the operating system or programs which have the graphical user interface usually, a mouse contains two or three buttons, and a ball, which can be used to input commands or information. A mouse allows use to create graphic elements on the screen such as lines, curves and freehand shapes. It is of various types:

(*a*) ***2 Buttons with a ball.*** These are the very first developed mouse of earlier days. It has two buttons and at bottom their is a ball. It is kept on a smooth sensitive pad called a touch pad.

(*b*) ***2 Buttons with scroll bar.*** This is very similar to the previous mouse except the scroll bar, which is placed in between the 2 buttons. The scroll bar helps to scroll the page up and down.

(*c*) ***Optical mouse.*** This mouse uses a light beam instead of a rotating ball to detect movement accoss a specially patterned mouse pad. As the user rolls the mouse on a flat surface, the cursor on the screen also moves in the direction of the mouse's movement.

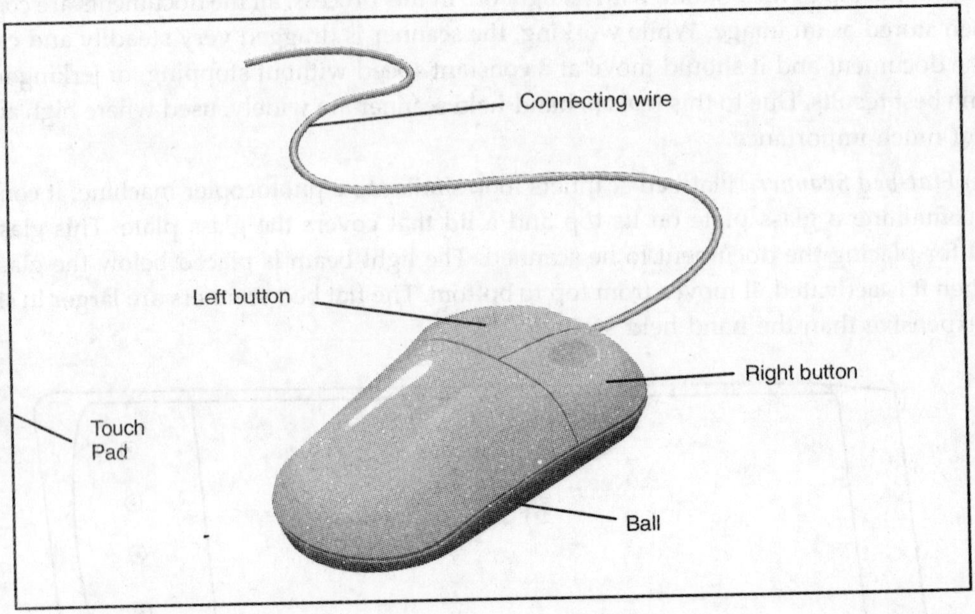

Fig. *Mouse*

(*d*) ***Touch pad mouse.*** Touch pad mouse are also very common and are used with the laptop computers. In the touch pad mouse, the finger is moved on the pad and accordingly, the mouse points moves on the CRT display. A soft press on the mouse pad is treated equivalent to the pressing of a button of the mouse.

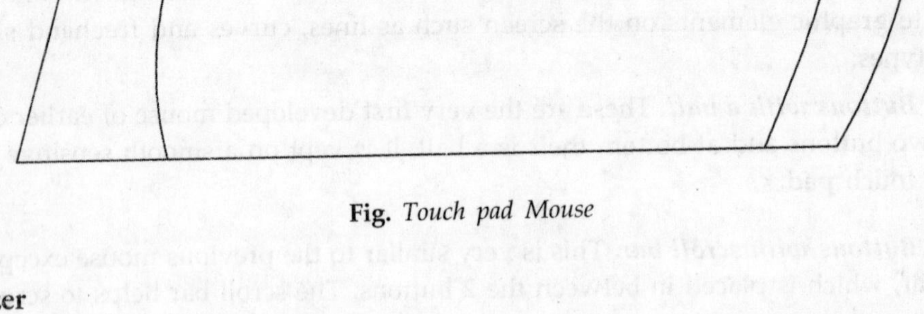

Fig. *Touch pad Mouse*

4. Digitizer

Digitizer is an input device used for drawing free hand images and graphics. This is a pad with a grid of sensor's wire. A pen is moved on to the grid and every movement of the pen on the pad is captured. This pen is also known as stylus.

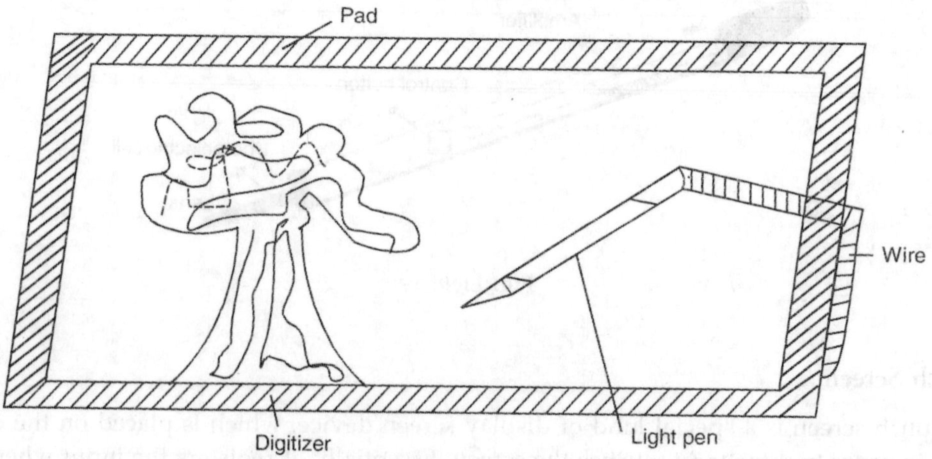

Fig.

5. Track Ball

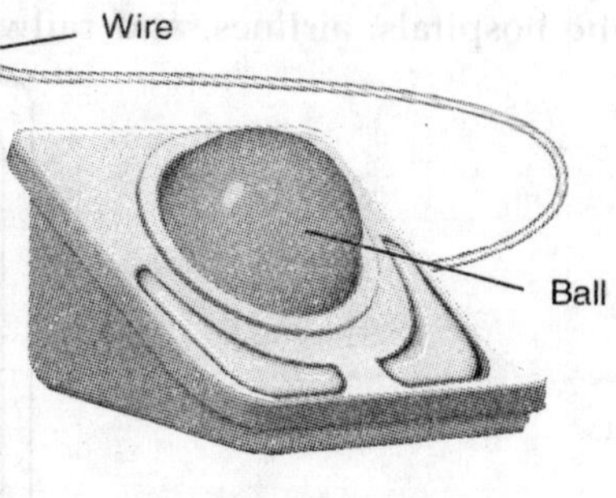

Fig. *Track Ball*

Track ball is another pointing device that resembles a ball nestled in a square cardle and serves as an alternative to a mouse. It has a ball, which can be rotated by fingers in any direction, the cursor moves accordingly. The size of the ball in the trackball vanes from as large as a cue ball, to as small as a marble. Since, it is a static device, instead of rolling the mouse on the top of the table the ball on the top is moved by using thumbs, fingers and palms. Like the mouse, a track ball is also used to control cursor movements and the actions on a computer screen.

6. Joystick

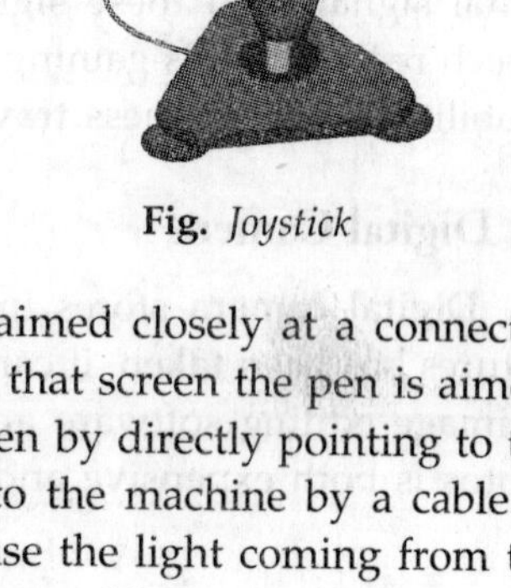

Fig. *Joystick*

A joystick is a device that moves in all directions and controls the movement of the cursor. A joystick is generally used to control the velocity of the screen cursor movement rather than its absolute position. Joysticks are mainly used for computer games, for other applications which includes flight simulators, CAD/CAM systems and for controlling industrial robots.

7. Light Pen

A light pen is a pointing device which when touched to or aimed closely at a connected computer monitor, will allow the computer to determine where on that screen the pen is aimed. It facilitates drawing images and selects objects on the display screen by directly pointing to the objects with the pen. It is a pen like device, which is connected to the machine by a cable. It actually does not emit light but its light sensitive diode would sense the light coming from the screen. The light coming from the screen causes the photocell to respond by generating a pulse.

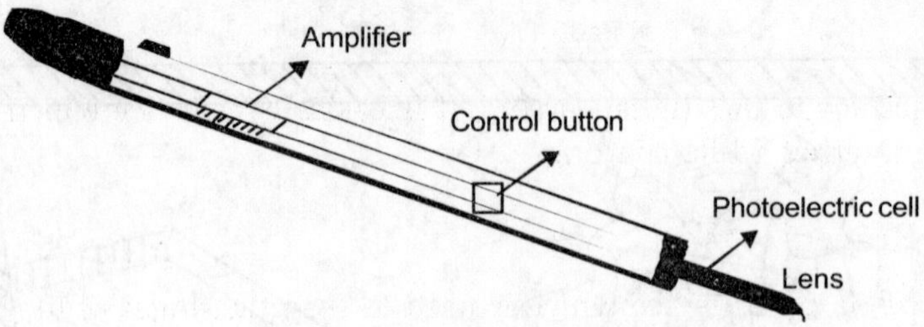

Fig. *Light pen*

8. Touch Screen

A touch screen is a special kind of display screen device, which is placed on the computer monitor in order to somebody touches the screen. Essentially, it registers the input when a finger or other objects is touched to the screen. Touch screen is normally used when information has to be accessed with minimum effort. Typically, they are used in information-providing systems like the hospitals, airlines, and railways and Bank.

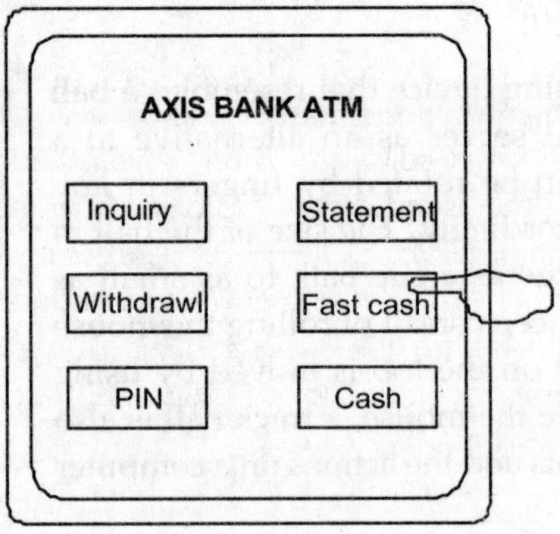

Fig.

9. Speech Recognition

Speech recognition is one of the most interactive systems to communicate with the computer. It is the technology by which sounds, words or phrases spoken by humans are converted into digital signals and these signals are transformed into computer generated text or commands. Speech recognition is gaining popularity in the corporate world among non-typists, people with disabilities, and business travellers who tape-record information for later transcription.

10. Digital Camera

Digital camera stores images digitally rather recording them on a negative film. Once a pictures has been taken, it can be downloaded to a computer system and then manipulated with an image editing software and printed. The big advantage of a digital cameras is that making photos is both expensive and fast because, there is no film processing.

11. Web camera

This is very similar to the digital camera. It is basically a device which is used to transmit the images on the internet while chatting.

12. Finger Print Reader

It is also a type of input device which is used to scan the finger of the person. This device contains scanners in built and scans the mark on the finger.

13. Optical Scanners

Recent technology have developed altemative method to input data instead of entering data through key strokes. Devices such as bar code reader can interpret machine printed marks or codes.

There are four types of optical recognition :

(*i*) Optical Character Recognition (OCR)

(*ii*) Optical Mark Recognition (OMR)

(*iii*) Magnetic Ink Character Recognition (MICR)

(*iv*) Bar Code Reader.

I. *Optical character Recognition.* OCR is a process of scanning printed pages as images on a flat-bed scanner and then using OCR software to recognise the letters as ASCII text. In the OCR system, a book or a magazine article is fed directly into an computer file, and then this file is edited by a word processor. The first major use of OCR was in processing petroleum credit card sales draft. Using an OCR system, one can consolidate data entry and reduce data entry errors. The result of OCR is very human readable and can be used with many printing techniques. However, it is a very expensive input device and if the document is not typed property, it will become difficult for the OCR to recognise the characters.

II. *Optical Mark Recognition.* Optical mark recognition is the process of detecting the presence of intended marked responses. Optical mark reading is done by a special device known as optical mark reader. In order to be detected by the OMR reader, a mark has to be positioned correctly on the paper and should be significantly darker than the surrounding paper. The OMR technology enables a high speed reading of large quantities of data and transfering this data to computer without using a keyboard.

Generally, this technology is used to read answer sheets (objective type tests). In this method, special printed forms/documents are printed with boxes, which can be marked with dark pencil or ink. These forms are then passed under a light source and the presence of dark ink is transformed into electric pulses, which are transmitted to the computer.

III. *Magnetic-Ink Character Recognition.* MICR refers to the special magnetic encoding, printed on the bottom of a negotiable check. This information is machine readable via bank readers/ sorters, which read the visual patterns and magnetic waveforms of the MICR encoding. The characters are printed using special ink, which contains iron particles that can be magnetised. Magnetic ink character readers are used generally in bank to process the cheques. In case of bank cheques, the numbers written at the bottom are recorded in MICR, representing unique cheque numbers, bank, and branch code, and so on. An MICR reads these characters by examining their shapes in a matrix form and the information is then passed on to the computer.

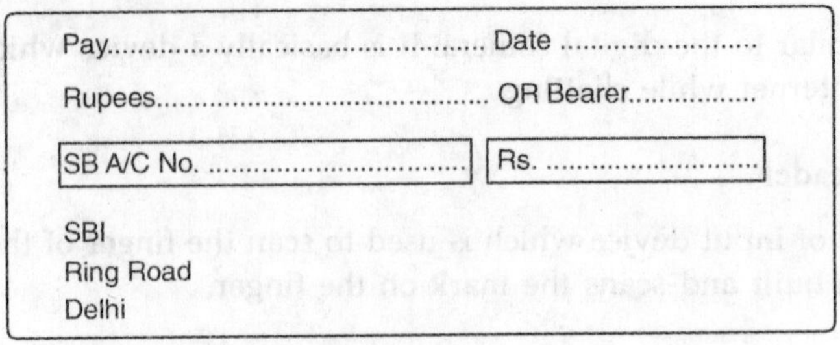

"'000439"' 52" 2106i : 0024065"' 0.2

Cheque number writen in MICR font.

IV. ***Bar Code Reader.*** Bar code is a machine-readable code in the form of a pattern of parallel vertical lines of varying widths. They are commonly used for labelling goods that are available in super market and numbering books in libraries. These codes are sensed and read by a bar code reader using reflective light. The information recorded in bar code reader is then fed into the computer, which recognises the information from the thickness and spacing of bars. Bar code readers are either hand-held or fixed mount.

Bar code

9870654632

3.8 OUTPUT DEVICES

The output devices receives informations from the computer and provide them to users. The computer sends informations to the output devices in binary coded forms. The output devices convert them into a form which can be used by users such as printed form or display on a screen. These devices are used for producing and presenting the data processed by digital computer to the real world, *e.g.*, —printers, monitors, plotters, speakers etc.

1. Monitor (Video Display Unit)

The monitor is the most frequently used soft copy output device. A computer monitor is a TV like display attached to the computer on which the output can be displayed and viewed. Monitors are available in various sizes like 14, 15, 17, 19 and 21 inches. Cathode Ray tube monitors have been used for a number of years with desktop computers. They provide bright and clear picture for a low cost. But the main disadvantages with the CRT monitors are that they are quite big in size, and they need a lot of power supply, whereas flat-panel monitors are quite small in terms of occupying space, and their power requirements are also not that much high.

Liquid Crystal Display (LCD)

A LCD screen is a collection of multiple layers. In LCDs a liquid crystalline material is sandwiched between two glass or plastic plates. The front plate is transparent and the back plate is reflective. There is a coating of thin film on the front plate. The coating is transparent and conductive. Light passes though the first two polarising filters. The polarised light then passes through a layer that contains thousands of liquid crystal blobs aligned in tiny containers called cells. LCDs do not emit their own light. Therefore, a light source is to be used. LCDs simply change the reflection of available light.

Difference between LCD and CRT

1. **Size.** LCD is light weight and compact, which saves desktop space as compared to a CRT.
2. **Resolution.** LCD is designed to work in a single resolution while CRT is designed for many resolution.
3. **Brightness.** The illuminated phosphor of a CRT is not nearly as bright as what the LCD can produce with its fluorescent backlight.
4. **Power consumption.** LCD consumes significantly less power than CRT and has a low emission risk.
5. **Viewing angle.** CRT can be viewed at almost any angle, but LCD is best viewed 'head on'.

2. Printers

A printer is also one of the common output device. A printer prints information and data from the computer on to a paper. Some printers produce only textual information, whereas others can produce graphics as well. Generally, the printer prints 80 or 132 columns of characters in each line, and prints either on single sheet or on a continuous roll of paper, depending upon the printer itself.

Printers are divided into two basic categories: Impact printers and non-impact printers.

The Impact printers. The impact printers print the document character by character. Every character is pressed in a sequential order over a ribbon on to the paper. The drawback of impact printers is that since, these printers print characters by character, they are slow. For example, Dot matrix, Daisy wheel printer, Drum Printer.

The Non-Impact printers. Non-Impact printer print the document on to the piece of paper in a block. *e.g., the line printers print the document line by line.* These printer are usually costly and are used for high speed printing. For example, Ink-jet printer and laser printer.

Dot Matrix Printer. Dot matrix printer is the oldest printing technology and it prints one character at a time. Usually dot matrix printers can print any shape of character, which a user can specify.

This allows the printer to print many special characters, different sizes of print, and enables it to print graphics, such as charts and graphs. The speed of Dot Matrix Printers is measured in characters per second (CPS). Dot matrix printers are inexpensive and have low operating costs. The major drawback of dot matrix printer is that it prints only in black and white.

Daisy Wheel Printers. Daisy wheel printers produce high-resolution output and are most reliable than dot-matrix printers. They can have speed upto 90 cps. These printers are also called as smart printers because of its bidirectional printing and built-in microprocessor control features. However, daisy wheel printers give only alphanumeric output. They cannot print graphics and cannot change fonts unless the print wheel is physically replaced. Daisy wheel printers are slower and more expensive than dot matrix printers.

Drum printers. The dot matrix and daisy wheel printer are character or serial printers, that is, they print one character at a time. However, drum printer is a line printer; it can print a line in a single operation. Generally, line printer is used because of its speed as it uses special tractor fed paper with per-punched holes along each side. This arrangement allows a continuous high-speed printing. Its printing speed varies from 150 lines to 2500 lines per minute.

Ink-Jet Printer. The most common type of printer found in homes today is the ink-jet printer. An ink-jet printer is a printer that places extremely small droplets of ink on to paper to create an image. Being a non-impact printer, it does not touch the paper while creating an image. Instead, it uses a series of nozzles to spray drops of ink directly on to the paper. These printers are costlier than dot matrix printers, but the quality is much better.

Laser Printer. A laser printer provides the highest quality text and images for personal computers today. It is a very fast printer, which operates on the same principle as that of a photocopy machine. Most laser printers can print text and graphics with a very high quality resolution. They are also known as page printers because they process and store the entire page before they actually print it. They produce sharp, crisp images of both text and graphics. Laser printers are often faster than ink-jet printers, but are more expensive to buy and maintain than the other printers.

3. Plotter

A plotter is a pen-based output device that is attached to a computer for making vector graphics, that is, images created by a series of many straight lines. It is used to draw high resolution charts, graphs, blueprints, maps and other line-based diagrams. Plotters are similar to printers, but they draw lines using a pen. As a result, they can produce continuous lines, whereas printer can only simulate lines by printing a closely spaced series of dots.

Plotter is considered a very slow output device because it requires excessive mechanical movement to plot. They are mainly used for Computer Aided Design (CAD) and Computer Aided Manufacturing (CAM).

4. Audio Output (speakers)

Audio output has become common in many places like airlines bus terminals, banks and brokerage houses. It is typically used when an inquiry is followed by a short reply. Automatic telephone voices take sumeys, inform customers that catalog orders are ready to be picked up, and perhaps, remind customers that they have not paid their bills.

3.9 STORAGE DEVICES

Storage Devices are those devices which are used to take the back-up (copy) of important files and data. These are also called as Secondary Storage Devices. The data and the programs are loaded into the main memory prior to the execution of the program. The processed data and the results are kept in the secondary storage device for future reference. Auxiliary storage devices are slower than the main memory and are almost inexpensive in comparison to the main memory. The main purpose of using the secondary or auxiliary storage devices is to provide a large storage at lower lost.

Primarily, there are two methods of accessing data from the secondary storage devices :

(i) **Sequential Access.** Sequential access means the computer system must search the storage device from the beginning unit it finds the desired information. The most common sequential access storage device is magnetic tape where data is stored and processed sequentially. For example, magnetic tapes.

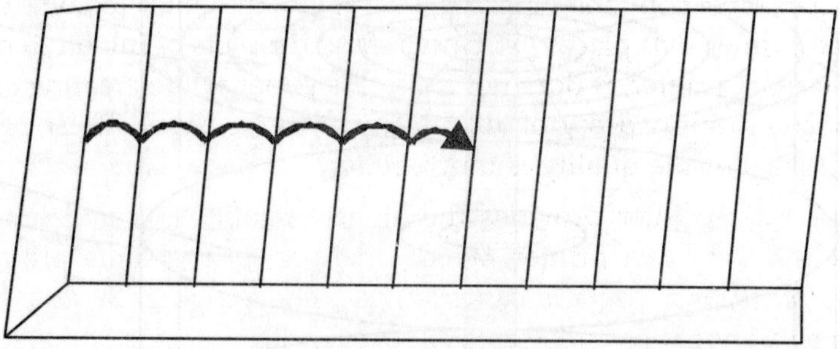

Fig. *Sequential Access*

(ii) **Direct Access.** Direct access, also known as random access, means that the computer can go directly to the information that the user wants. The most common direct access storage are magnetic and optical disks. In this method, information is viewed as a numbered sequence of blocks. It maintains the index or directory of all the data which contains the name of the file and address of the data. Whenever a required data is to be fetched, the head is directly placed to the place where the data exists on the device. For example, Floppy disk, Hard disk.

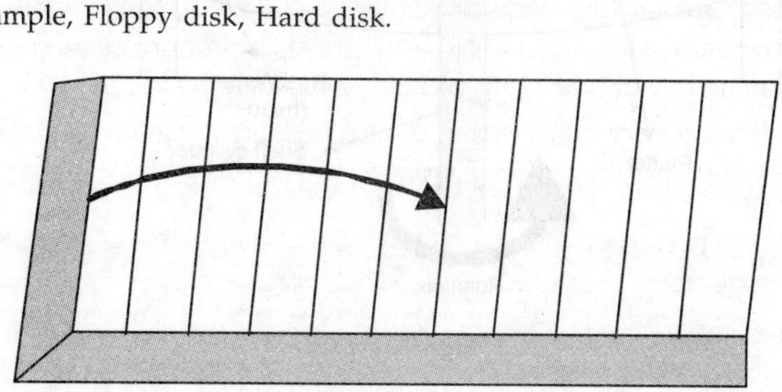

Fig. *Direct Access*

3.9.1 Magnetic Storage Devices

Magnetic disks are the widely used popular storage medium for direct access storage. They offer high storage capacity, reliability, and have capability to access the stored data directly. A magnetic disk consists of plastic/metal circular plate/platter, which is coated with magnetic oxide layer. Data is represented as magnetised spots on a disk. A magnetised spot represents a 1 (bit) and the absence of a magnetised spot represents a 0 (bit). To read the data, the magnetised data on the disk is converted into electrical impulses, which is transfer to the processor. The data in a magnetic disk can be erased and reused virtually infinitely.

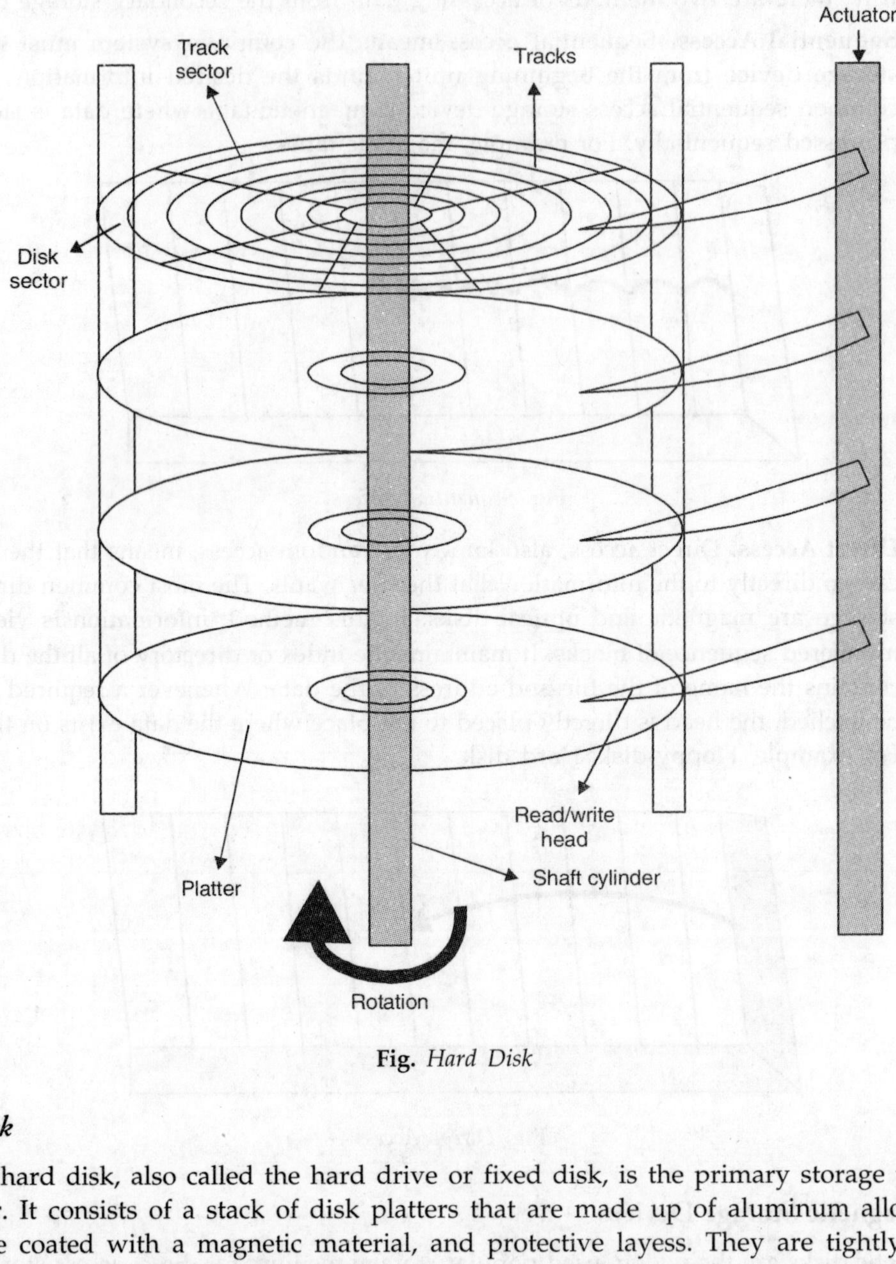

Fig. *Hard Disk*

Hard Disk

The hard disk, also called the hard drive or fixed disk, is the primary storage unit of the computer. It consists of a stack of disk platters that are made up of aluminum alloy or glass substracte coated with a magnetic material, and protective layess. They are tightly sealed to prevent any foreign matter from getting inside which causes head crash. The capacity, or amount of information that a hard drive can store, is measured in bytes. The average computers today comes with a 20-80 GB hard drive. Data is regarded on to the magnetic surface of the disk in exactly, the same way as it in on floppies. In floppy disk, the read/write heads actually touch the surface of the material, whereas the heads in most hard disks float slightly off the surface.

Floppy Disk

A floppy disk is a removable, round, flat piece of mylar plastic, coated with ferric oxide and encased in a protective plastic cover. This kind of disk is read and written by a (FDD) Floppy Disk

Drive, which is a device that performs the basic operation on a disk, including the rotating the disk, reading and writing data on to the disk. Floppy disks were used on personal computer to distribute software, transfer data between computers, and create small backups. Earlier, 5 1/4 inch floppy disk were used but now 3 1/2 inch floppy disk now came into existence. Floppy diskettes are small, inexpensive, readily available, early to store and have a good shelf life it stored properly.

Zip Disk

Zip disk is a removable storage device and it has a capacity to store 100-250 MB of data. Zip disk's drive unit is measured in 18 × 13 × 4 cm and weights about half kilogram. It has rubber feet to stabilise the unit in either vertical or horizontal position. It has an eject button, but no ON/OFF switch. On installation, the zip drive is automatically assigned a logical drive letter, and you can transfer files to and from the zip drive as if you are accessing hard disk or floppy drive. The Zip disk is similar in diameter to that of the 3 1/2 inch floppy diskette.

3.9.2 Optical Storage Device

An optical disk is a flat, circular, plastic disk coated with material on which bits may be stored in the form of highly reflective areas and significantly less reflective areas, from which the stored data may be read when illuminated with a narrow-beam source, such as a casses diode. These disks are capable of storing enormously high amount of data in a limited amount of space. The optical disk storage system consists of a rotating disk coated with a thin layer of metal that acts as a reflective surface and a laser beam, which is used as a read/write head for recording data on to the disk. An optical disk consists of single long track in the form of spiral shapes. This track starts form the outer edge and spirals inward to the centre of the disk. The spiral shape of the track makes the optical disk suitable for reading large blocks. The read/write operations are performed through laser beams, therefore, no access arm movement is required that is used in the case of the magnetic disk.

The laser beam technology used for reading/writing of data on the disk surface of the optical disk uses two laser beam sources of different intensities. The greater intensity laser beams is used to write on the recording surface by turning it ON and OFF at varying rate so that the tiny pits are burnt into the metal coating of the disk.

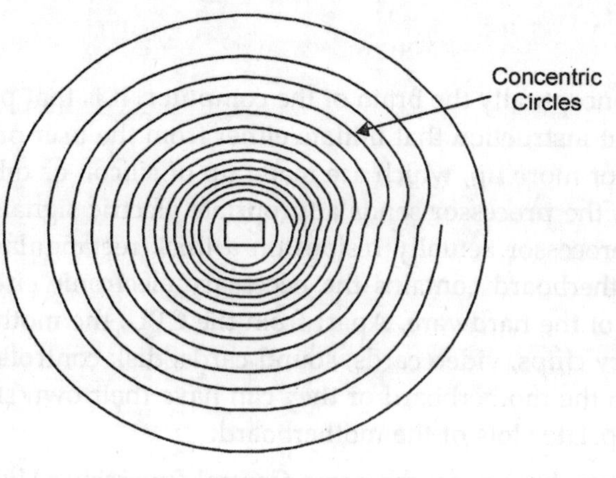

Fig. *Optical Disk*

3.9.3 Compact-Disk-Read only Memory (CD-ROM)

A compact disk is an optical disk that was originally intended only for storing music. A CD-ROM is capable of being used as a data storage device along with storing of digital audio. A CD-ROM disk is a shiny, silver colour metal disk of 12 cm in diameter. It is the most popular and the least expensive type of optical disk and as the name implies, it comes prerecorded with the data, which cannot be altered. A typical optical disk is made up of three layers: A poly carbonate base through which light can pass, a layer of aluminium, and a protective layer of acrylic on top of that. The pits of CD-ROM are typically 0.5 microns wide, 0.83 to 3 microns long and 0.15 microns deep. A CD-ROM has one track that spirals from the centre to the outside edge. If one could remove the track from a standard 12 cm CD, it would stretch for three and a half miles.

3.9.4 Digital Versatile Disk (DVD-ROM)

DVD-ROM is a high-capacity data storage medium. In DVD the tracks are placed closer together, thereby allowing more tracks per disc. The DVD's track pitch is reduced to 0.74 micron, less than half of CD's 1.6 micron. DVD's reduced track pitch and pit size alone give DVD-ROM discs four times the storage capacity of CDs. An interesting feature of DVD is that the disk's second data layer can be read from the inside of the disc out, as well as from the outside in. In standard density. CD's the information is always stored first near the hub of the disc. DVD allows for double-sided discs.

3.10 COMPUTER H/W

The internal components of a computer's H/W can be classified into the following catagories :

- Processor
- Memory
- I/O Devices
- Storage Devices.

3.10.1 Processor

The processor is conceptually the brain of the computer. It is that part of a computer, which organizes and cames out instruction that initiate either from the user or the S/W. The processor usually consists of one or more up, which are made up of silicon or other material. In order to execute an instructions, the processor sends appropriate electric signals via the various circuits of the computer. The processor actually resides on a thick rectangular plastic card (called the motherboard). The motherboard contains the necessary electronic circuits, which connect the processor with the rest of the hardware. Apart from the CPU, the motherboard also hosts other devices, such as memory chips, video cards, sound cards, disk controller etc. These devices can be directly connected to the motherboard or they can have their own small cards, which can be plugged into the appropriate slots of the motherboard.

The processor is often known by the name Central Processing Unit (CPU).

3.11 FIRMWARE

Firmware is defined as software contained in a CD-ROM device. It is the software that is embedded on to a piece of hardware in order to control that hardware. Generally, firmware can be upgraded and is placed on an erasable memory (EEPROM). It allows reading and executing the software, but does not allow its modification. For *e.g.*, BIOS (Basic Input Output System). The BIOS is the piece of software that makes sure that all the hardware devices attached to the computer are working perfectly. It is stored on ROM. Firmware is created and tested like software.

3.11.1 Humanware

Humanware is hardware and software that emphasizes user capability and the design of the user interface. It talks about both H/W and S/W that are designed primarily around the end user experience and user interface rather than focusing on the task that the product is meant to accomplish. The design of humanware often begins with understanding the needs and limitations of the end user and working backwards to design the final product.

For example, technology designed to aid persons with disabilities typically begins with understanding the needs of the end user before designing the product.

3.12 SOFTWARE DEFINITION ROLE AND CATEGORIES

Programs can be define as a specific set of instructions, that perform a specific task. Software is a collection of programs, which are used to do any specific task.

Software can be broadly classified into two categories :

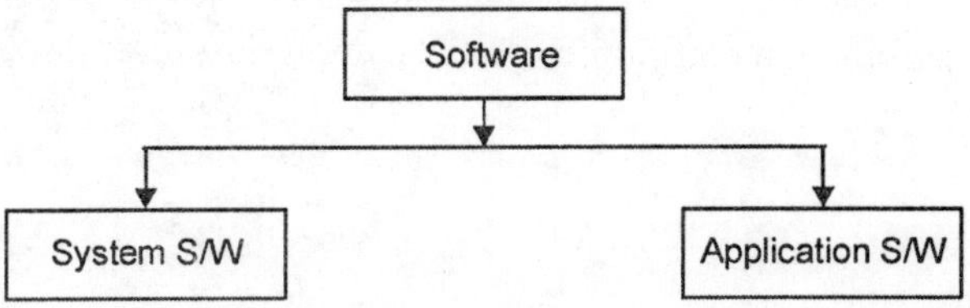

1. ***System S/W.*** The system S/W are generally used to create the environment for the development and execution of application S/W. These programs are required to make the computer system operational; the computer cannot function without these programs. Therefore, they are known as system S/W. Most of these programs are written and developed by the manufactures, operating systems and compilers are the *e.g.*, of system S/W are windows vista, windows (95, 98, 2000, XP), Unix, Lynux.

System S/W is closer to the hardware and performs low-level tasks.

2. ***Application S/W.*** The application S/W are written by the programmer to solve any real world problem. For example., writing a program of report generation, queries, preparation of report are all application programs. These programs are written in either higher level languages or using 4 GLS. The application program may be altered, modified as per the change in the requirement by the programmer.

They uses the services of the system S/W and is considered to perform high-level tasks, such as calculating the total sales for a region or printing pay-slips. For example — Photoshop, tally, MS-Office, Window Media Player.

EXERCISES

1. Explain different types of ROM devices.
2. Explain the role of hard disk in a computer system. Draw the internal design of a hard disk.
3. What is cache memory? Compare various parameters of cache memory, main memory, auxiliary storage devices.
4. Draw the block diagram of a digital computer. Explain its each block in detail giving suitable examples.
5. Explain the difference between microprocessor and microcomputer.
6. Differentiate between static and Dynamic RAM.
7. Explain the hierarchy of memories used in computer system. Compare the characteristic of all the memories shown in the hierarchy.
8. What is a digitizer? Is it an input device or an output device? Justify your answer.
9. Explain the difference between magnetic and optical storage.
10. Explain the difference between firmware and Humanware.

4

PROGRAMMING LANGUAGE, CLASSIFICATION AND METHODOLOGY

4.1 COMPUTER LANGUAGE

A computer program is basically a set of instructions which when executed by the computer, do a specific task. These instructions are written using various syntax and rules. Programming language provides the set of rules/syntax/ Instruction format in which the various instruction are written. The program can be written in many languages.

4.2 GENERATION OF LANGUAGES

1. Machine Language.
2. Assembly Language.
3. High level Language.

4.2.1 Machine Language (Ist Generation)

Binary instruction are written is a sequence of O's and I's. Any program written using these binary instructions is said to have been written in machine language. The machine language for every processor is different. The machine level instructions may be divided into 2 parts: The first part is called the operation code or OP code while the second part presents the binary data or list of operands.

Computer programs are written in machine language as it is the language which a processor understands and it executes only those programs written in this language. However, writing a program in machine language is very difficult as for every task the machine codes are to be searched or remembered. The advantage of machine language code is that a processor can execute it without any translation.

4.2.2 Assembly Language (2nd Generation)

The programming would become easier and it would be similar to understand the code if it is written using letters and digits and carries some meaningful identifier. These issues are addressed in assembly language which uses mnemonic, that is meaningful names which makes assembly language programing easier then machine language. The processors understands the machine language and therefore, assembly language programs have to be converted into machine language. This task is done by the assembler.

Assembly language and machine language are also known as lower level languages.

These languages are dependent on the processor or are processor specific.

The *advantage* of assembly language over machine language is that it is more convenient for the programming to write programs in assembly language.

The *disadvantage* of assembly language is that this language is machine or processor specific.

4.2.3 High Level Language (3rd Generation)

High level languages are machine independent. It is not necessary for the programmer to know the rigorous details of the architecture of a processor to write programs in these languages.

COBOL, BASIC, PASCAL, ADA, C are all high level languages. Each language provides its own construct/syntax and set of statements. The programs written in any of these languages can be executed on any machine. Writing programs in High level languages is more convenient as they provide the construct and set of statements which are easy to use and meaningful.

```
10 Let A = 20
20 Let B = 30
30 C = A + B
40 PRINT C
50 END
```

The program written in a high-level language needs to be translated into the language which a machine understand. Therefore all programs developed in high level languages have to be translated into lower level (machine language) before they are executed. This translation of program from high level language to low level language is done by the S/W called Compiler and Interpreters.

These are procedural languages.

e.g.,—BASIC, COBOL, FORTRAN, C, PASCAL.

4.3 INTRODUCTION TO 4GLs

All the 4GLs languages are based on the concept of using database. Structured Query language (SQL) and Query by Example (QBE) considered fourth generation languages. These languages are used to gather the data from a database with visual interface like Visual Basic (VB). Examples of 4GL products are Oracle, Ingres, Informix, Sybase, DB2 etc. They provide an extremely simplified interface for programmers to create powerful applications with minimum efforts. usually, a 4GL is data-centric, meaning it is mainly concerned with data accessing and manipulation. Most of the 4GL languages are used for developing large and complex software systems. These languages use automated report generator, menus etc.

4.4 COMPARISON OF LANGUAGES

Machine Language	*Assembly Language*	*High Level Language*
1. Programs are not easy to understand.	Are less Understandable	Easy to understand.
2. Programs are not portable.	Not portable	Programs are portable.
3. Debugging in most difficult.	Debugging is more complex.	Debugging is easier.
4. Difficult to write large programs.	Not good for large programs	Good for software development.
5. programs are machine dependent.	Programs are machine dependent	Programs and Machine Independent

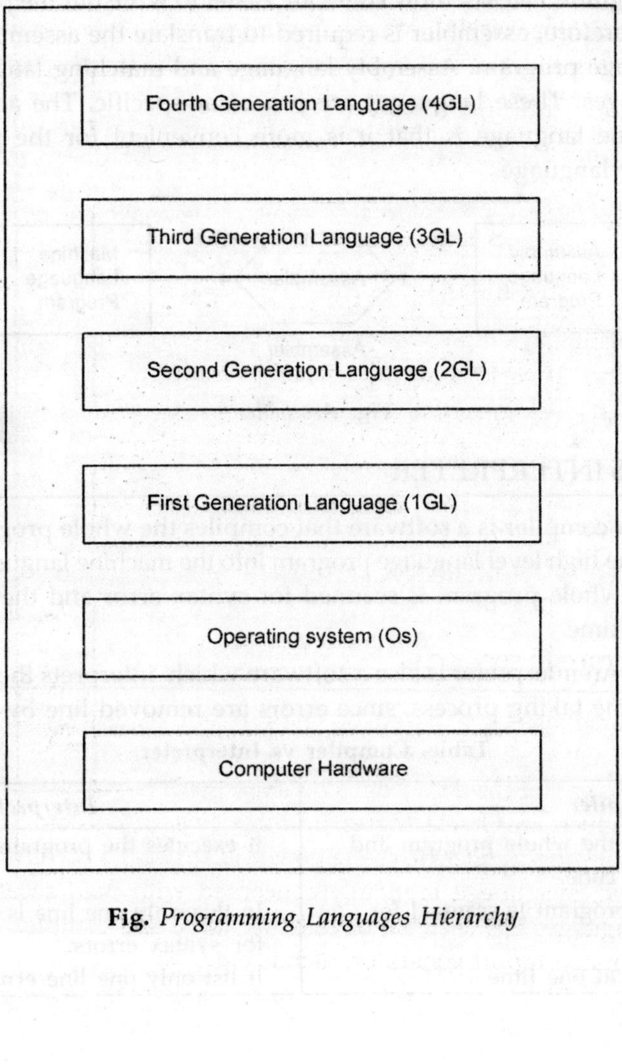

Fig. *Programming Languages Hierarchy*

4.5 TRANSLATOR

A translator is needed for translating a high level language into the corresponding machine language. In fact, even to translate assembly language into machine language, a translator is required. The very reason that translators are required is simple. Computer hardware can understand only machine language instructions. Therefore a program written in a high-level language must firstly be translated into machine language before it can be executed. A program written in a high-level language such as COBOL, or C is called as source program. When a compiler translates it into machine language, it becomes an object program. An object program contains instructions in machine language. It is very important to understand that the object program is just another representation of the same source program. It is required so that a computer can understand it.

4.6 ASSEMBLERS

The assembler is a special program which converts an assembly language program into a machine language program. The assembly codes are easier to write but the processor still executes the machine code. Therefore, assembler is required to translate the assembly language program into a machine language program. Assembly language and matching language are also known as lower level languages. These languages are processor specific. The advantage of assembly language over machine language is that it is more convenient for the programmer to write programs in assembly language.

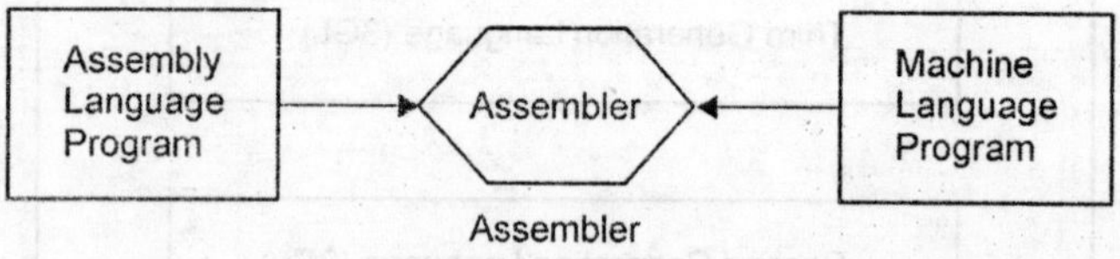

Fig. *Assembler*

4.7 COMPILER VS INTERPRETER

- **Compiler.** A compiler is a software that compiles the whole program at a one time *i.e.,* it converts the high level language program into the machine language. In the compilation process the whole program is scanned for syntax error and the compiler lists all the error at one time.
- **Interpreter.** An interpreter is also a software which interprets the program line by line. Thus it is time taking process, since errors are removed line by line.

Table. Compiler vs Interpreter

Compiler	*Interpreter*
1. The compiler takes the whole program and generate the object code.	It executes the program line by line.
2. In this, the whole program is scanned for syntax errors.	In this only one line is checked at a time for syntax errors.
3. It list all the errors at one time.	It list only one line errors at a time.

4. The execution time is faster.	The execution time is slower.
5. The debugging of a program is difficult in the compilation process because all the errors. are listed at every compilation attempt.	Here debugging is easier because errors are reported line by line.

4.8 FLOW CHART

A flow chart is a pictorial representation of an algorithm in which the steps are drawn in the from of different shapes of boxes and the logical flow is indicated by inter connecting arrows. The boxes present operations and the arrows represent the sequence in which the operations are implemented. The primary purpose of the flow chart is to help the programmer in understanding the logic of the program. Therefore, it is always not necessary to include all the required steps in detail. Flow charts outline the general procedure, since they provide an alternative, visual way of representing the information flow in a program, program developers often find them very valuable.

Symbols	*Symbols Name*	*Symbols*	*Symbols Name*
	Start/stop	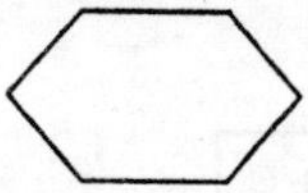	Repeatation
	I/O	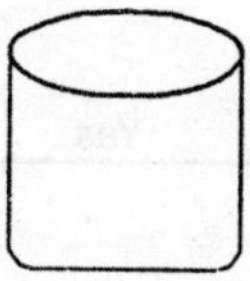	Magnetic disk
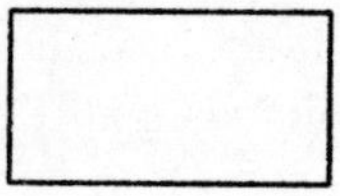	Processing	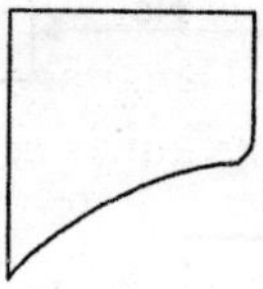	Document
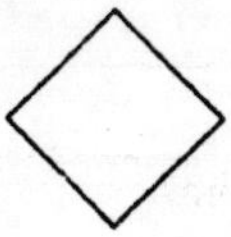	Decision Making		Internal storage

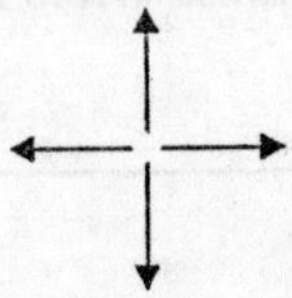	Connections		
	Continuation		

Fig.

1. **Flowchart to find Largest of three Numbers.**

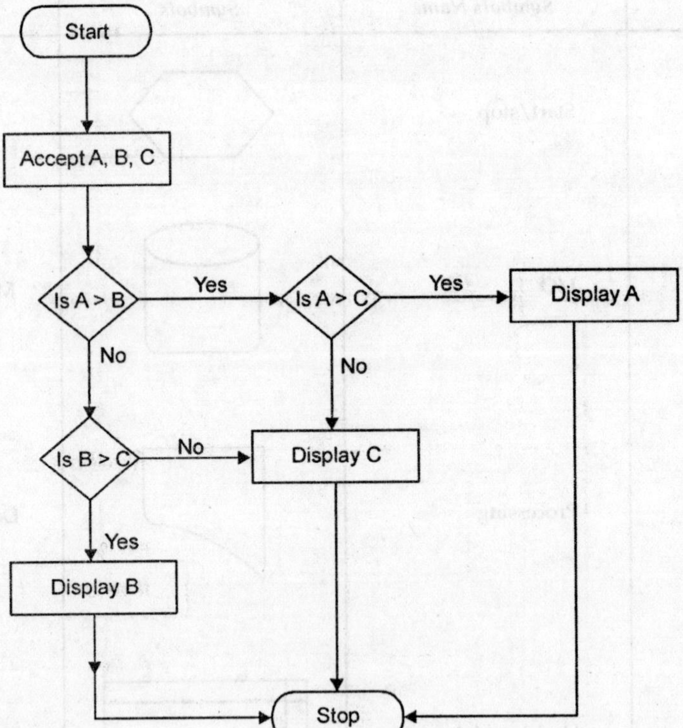

Fig.

2. **Flowcharts: (2) Accept 2 Number and Print their Sum.**

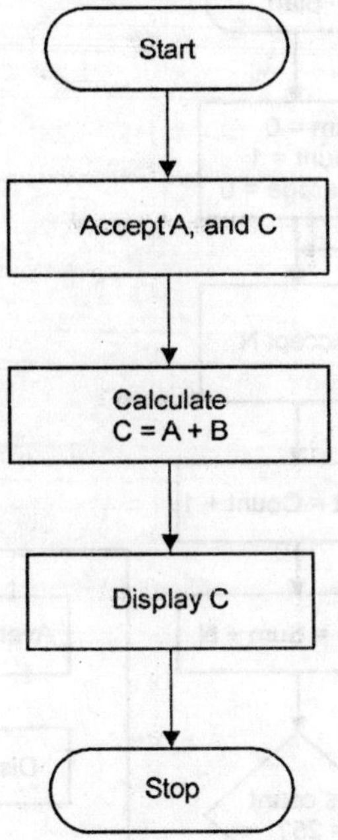

Fig.

3. To Print all odd Numbers b/w and 100.

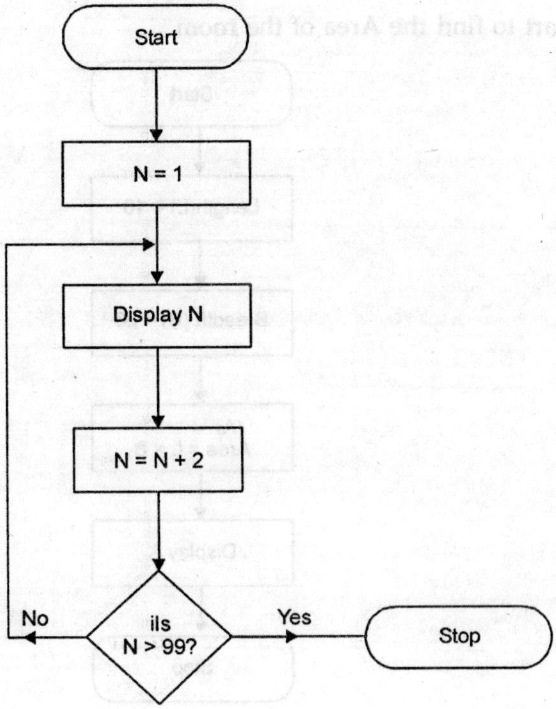

Fig.

4. Flowchart to accept 25 numbers and find their average.

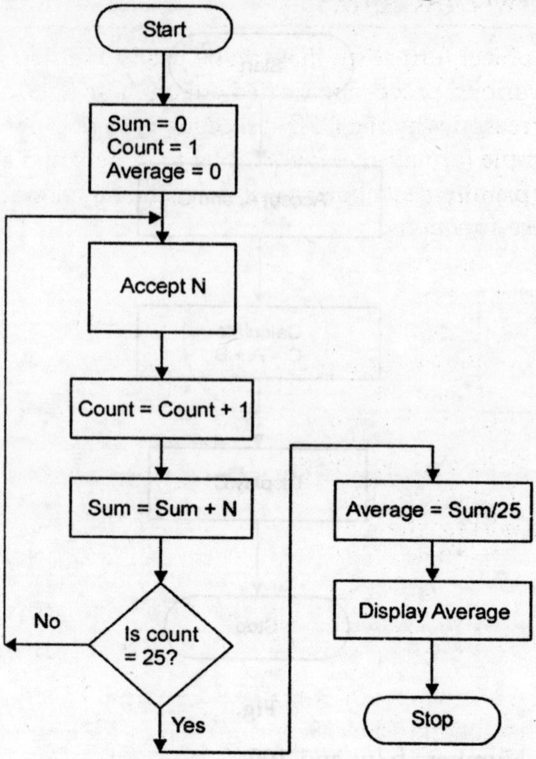

Fig.

5. Flowchart to find the Area of the room

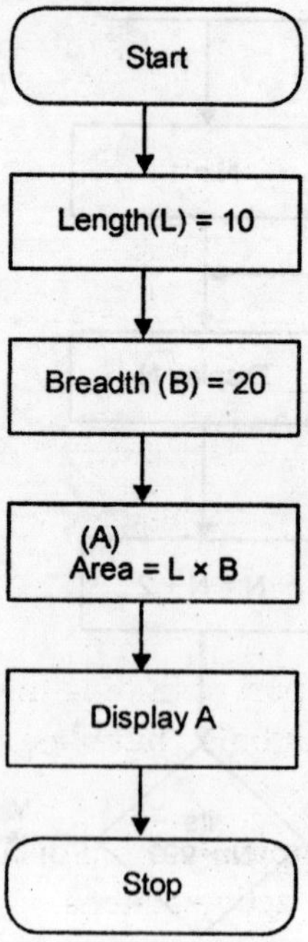

Fig.

4.9 DFD: DATA FLOW DIAGRAMS

DFD is a simple graphical formalism that can be used to represent a system in terms of the input data to the system various, processing carried out on these data, and the O/P data generated by the system. The main reason why the DFD technique is so popular is probably because of the fact that DFD is a very simple formalism—It is simpler to understand and use. A DFD model uses a very limited number of primitive symbols to represent the functions performed by a system and the data flow among these functions.

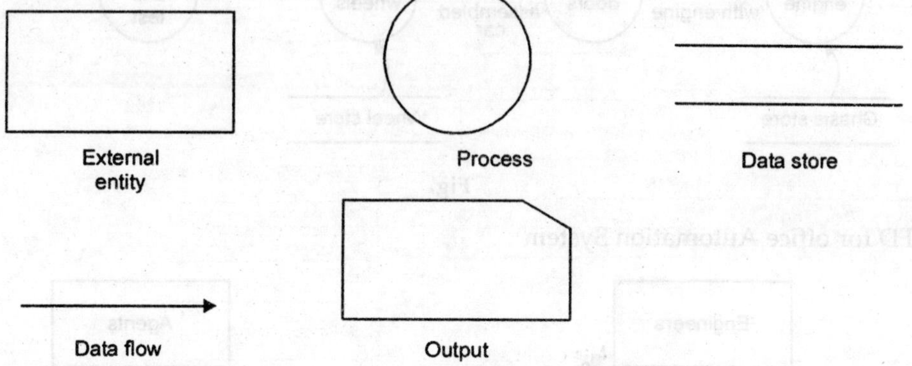

Fig.

1. *e.g.*, of DFD for Results and Rank Determination in an Exam.

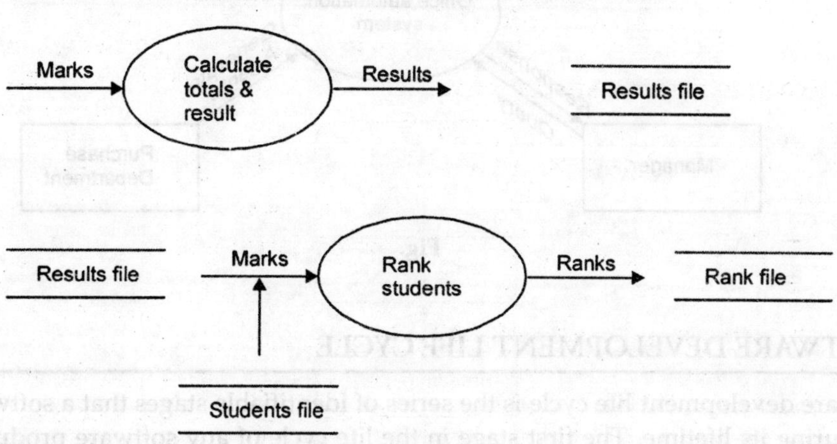

Fig.

■ **Terms used in DFDs:**

(*i*) ***Process.*** It involves the main part of finding the desired results. It is represented by the circle. It is also called as bubble. Bubbles are annotated with the names of the corresponding processes.

(*ii*) ***Data Store.*** A data store is typically a file or a database table. It represents an object, which does not perform any active actions.

(*iii*) ***Data flow.*** A data flow is the heart of a DFD. It represents the actual flow of data within the DFD. It connects the O/P of an object or a process to the I/P of another one.

(*iv*) ***Output Symbol.*** It is used when a hard copy is produced and the user of the copies cannot be clearly specified or there are several users of the output.

2. DFD Model of a car assembly plant

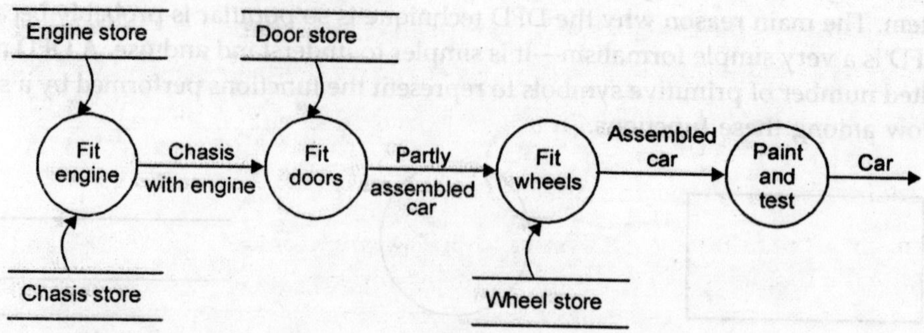

Fig.

3. DFD for office Automation System

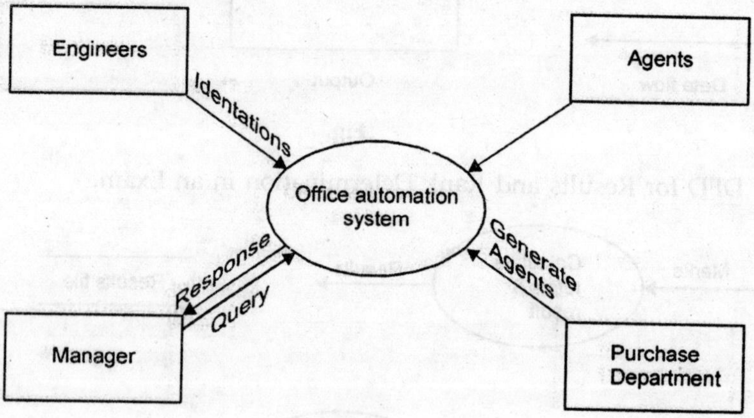

Fig.

4.10 SOFTWARE DEVELOPMENT LIFE CYCLE

A software development life cycle is the series of identifiable stages that a software product undergoes during its lifetime. The first stage in the life cycle of any software product is usually the (1) **Feasibility study stage.** Commonly, the subsequent stages are: (2) **Requirements analysis** and **specification** (3) **Design** (4) **Coding** (5) **Testing** and (6) **Maintenance.** Each of these stages is called a life cycle phase.

4.10.1 Feasibility Study

The main aim of the feasibility study activity is to determine whether it would be financially and technically feasible to develop the product. The feasibility study activity involves the analysis of the problem and collection of all relevant information relating to the product such as the different data items which would be input to the system, the processing required to be carried out on these data, the output data required to be produced by the system, as well as various consrints on the behaviour of the system.

- An abstract problem is defined.
- Formulation of the different solution strategies.
- Analysis of alternative solution strategies to compare their benefits and shortcomings.
- Determination of technical and economic viability.

4.10.2 Requirement Analysis and Specification

The aim of the requirement analysis and specification phase is to understand the exact requirements of the customer and to document them properly. This phase consists of two distinct activities namely requirement gathering and Analysis and requirement specification.

Requirement Gathering and Analysis

The goal of the requirement gathering activity is to collect all relevant information from the customer regarding the product to be developed with a view to clearly understanding the customer requirement and weeding out the incompleteness and inconsistencies in these requirements.

The requirement analysis activity is begun by collecting all relevant data regarding the product to be developed from the users of the product and from the customer through interviews and discussions.

Requirement Specification

The customer requirements identified during the requirement gathering and analysis activity are organized into a SRS document. The important components of this document are the functional requirements the nonfunctional requirements, and goals of implementation. The SRS document normally serves as a contract between the development team and the customer. Any future dispute between the customer and the developers can be settled by examining the SRS document. It is therefore, an important document which must be thoroughly understood by the developer team, and reviewed jointly with the customer.

4.10.3 Design

The goal of the design phase is to transform the requirements specified in the SRS document into a structure that is suitable for implementation in some programming language. In technical terms, during the design phase the software architecture is derived from the SRS document. Two distinctly different design approaches are available; the traditional design approach and the object oriented design approach.

Traditional Design Approach

The traditional design approach is currently being used by many software development houses. It consists of two different activities: first a structured analysis of the requirement specification is carried out where the detailed structure of the problem is examined. This is followed by a structured design activity. During structured design, the results of structured analysis are transformed into the software design.

Object-oriented Design Approach

Object-oriented design (OOD), is a relatively new technique. In this technique, various objects that occur in the problem domain and the solution domain are first identified and the different relationship that exist among these objects are identified. The OOD approach has several benefits such as lower development time and effect and better maintainability of the product.

4.10.4 Coding

The purpose of the coding of software development is to translate the software design into source code. Each component of the design is implemented as a program module. The end-product of this phase is a set of programs modules that have been individually tested. To enable the engineers to write good quality programs, every software development organisation normally formulates its own coding standards that suits itself. A coding standard addresses issues such as the standard ways of laying out the program codes, the templat for laying out the function and module headers, commenting guidelines, variable and function naming convertions, the maximum number of source lines permitted in each module and so forth.

4.10.5 Testing

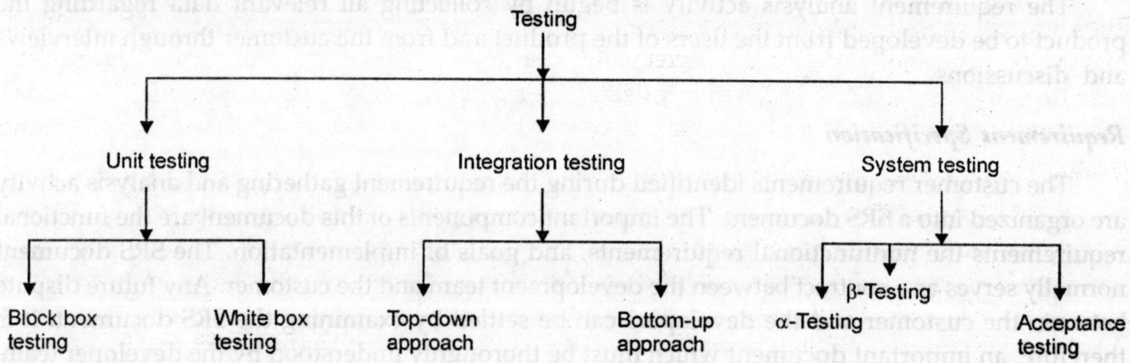

Fig. *Testing Classification*

Unit Testing

In unit testing each module is tested to determine the correct working of all the individual modules. It involves testing each module in isolation as this is the most efficient way to debug the errors. In Unit testing, a module is tested in isolation. Therefore unit testing is also called as isolation testing. The module is tested against general test conditions. There are two ways of code checked called code walk-through and code inspection. Code walk-through is an informal technique for analyzing the quality of code. There a team checks whether the programmer has followed the various rules and guidelines of the software company in writing the code. Whereas code inspection is a formal process where the code for a module is checked in terms of the commonly made errors. Unit testing is carried out in two ways: Black-box testing and white box testing.

(a) ***Black-Box Testing.*** Black box testing of a module is done without bothering about the internal architecture of the module. The test cases are developed in line of SPS document and the behaviour of the module is observed.

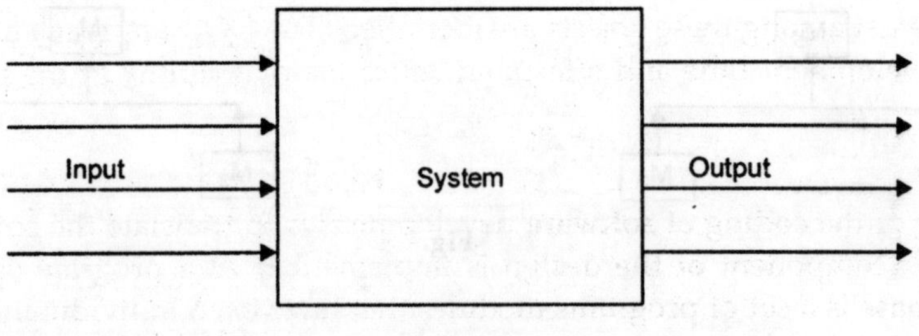

Fig.

(b) ***White-Box Testing.*** It mainly focuses on the internal architecture of the module. The test cases are developed to find the bugs and errors in the code written for the module.

Integration Testing

Integration of different modules is undertaken once they have been coded and unit tested. During the integration and system testing phase, the modules are integrated in a planned manner. The different modules making up a software product are almost never integrated in one shot. Integration is normally carried out incremental over a number of steps. During each integration step, the partially integrated system is tested and a set of previously planned modules are added to it. Finally, when all the modules have been successfully integrated and tested system testing is carried out.

It is of two types:

(i) Top-down Approach

(ii) Bottom-up Approach

(i) ***Top-down Approach.*** In this type of approach various modules developed are integrated according to a certain plan and the test cases are executed to check whether the various modules work as a single entity.

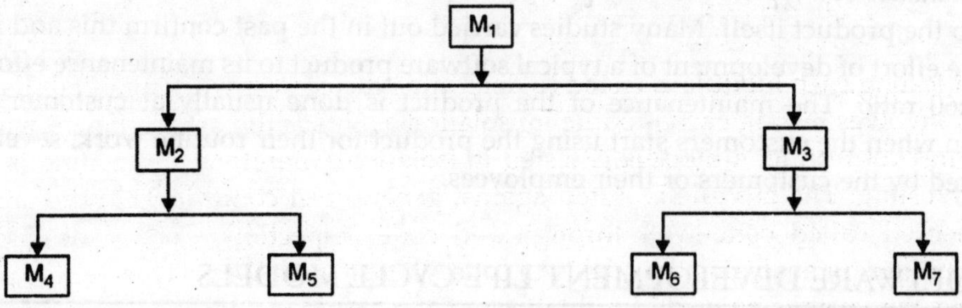

Fig.

(ii) ***Bottom-up Approach.*** In this type of approach small-small modules are integrated to form a big module. At each level each modules are tested and then they are integrated to form larger modules, and finally the build the original module or the main module.

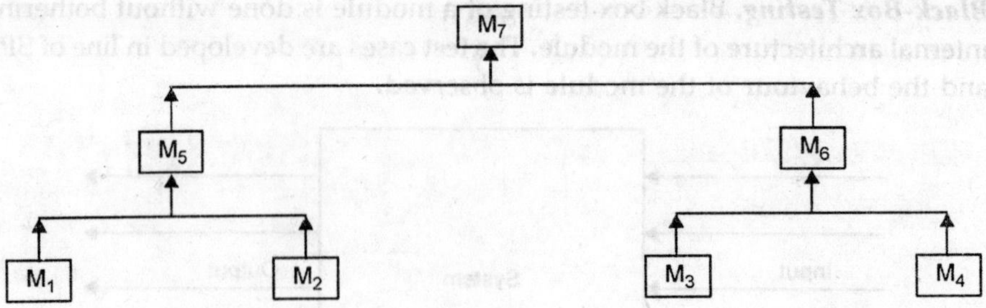

Fig.

System Testing

The goal system testing is to ensure that the developed system conforms to its requirements laid out in the SRS document. This is the final test and performed after all developings all the modules according to the requirements.

System testing usually consists of three different kinds of testing activities:

(*i*) Alpha (α) Testing
(*ii*) Beta (β) Testing
(*iii*) Acceptance Testing

(*i*) **α-Testing**–It is the system testing performed by the development team at the developers site. The software product containing all the modules are intermarried and test cases are executed. It the product is successful, then the next phase of testing is performed.

(*ii*) **β-Testing**–It is the system testing performed by a group of friendly customers in the presence of the software development team.

(*iii*) **Acceptance Teting**–It the system testing performed by the customer himself after the product delivery to determine whether to accept or reject the delivered product.

4.10.6 Maintenance and Implementation

Maintenance of a typical software product requires much more effort than the effort necessary to develop the product itself. Many studies carried out in the past confirm this and indicate that the relative effort of development of a typical software product to its maintenance effort is roughly in the 40:60 ratio. The maintenance of the product is done usually at customer's site. After installation when the customers start using the product for their routine work, several problems are reported by the customers or their employees.

4.11 SOFTWARE DEVELOPMENT LIFE CYCLE MODELS

A software life cycle model is a descriptive and diagramatic representation of the S/W life cycle. A life cycle model represents all the activities required to make a S/W product transit through its life cycles phases. It also captures the order in which these activities are to be undertaken. In other words, a life cycle model maps the different activities performed on a S/W product from its inception to retirement.

There are seven types of Models:

1. Build and Fix Model.
2. Waterfall Model.
3. Iterative Water Fall Model.
4. Evolutionary Model.
5. Prototype Model.
6. Spiral Model.
7. Rapid Action Development Model.

4.11.1 Build and Fix Model

This is an adhoc approach and not well defined. Basically, it is a simple two-phase model. The first phase is to write code and the next phase is to fix. Fixing in this context may be error connection or addition of further functionality. Although this approach may work well on small programming but this model is totally unsatisfactory for software of any reasonable size. Code soon becomes unfixable and unenhancable. There is no room for design or any aspect of development process to be carried out in a structured or detailed way. The cost of the development using this approach is actually very high as compared to the cost of a properly specified and carefully designed product.

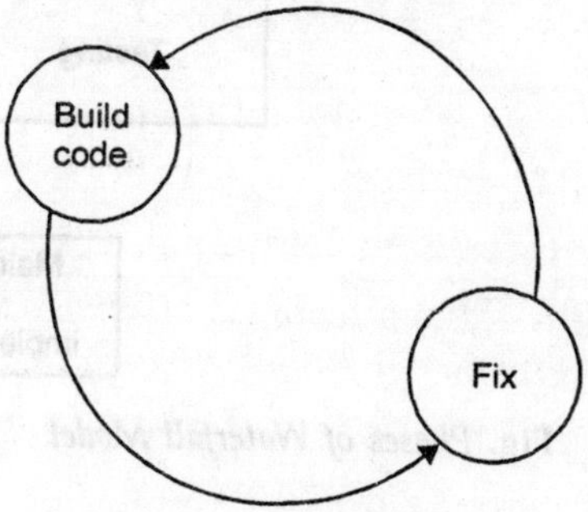

Fig. *Build and Fix Model*

4.11.2 Waterfall Model

The waterfall model is intuitively the most obvious way to develop software. It is not a practical model in the sense that it cannot be used in actual software development projects. Thus, this model is said to be theoretical way of developing software.

The waterfall model divides the life cycle into the sixs phases. The name of this model is justified by its diagramatic representation which resembles as cascade of waterfalls. The different phases of this model are: Feasibility study, requirement analysis and specification, design, coding testing and maintenance. The different phases starting from the feasibility study to the system testing phase are known as the development phases. The part of the life cycle model between the feasibility study and product testing and delivery is known as the development part. At the end of the development part of the life cycle the product becomes ready to be delivered to the customer. The maintenance phase commences after completion of the development phases. Each phase of the life cycle has well-defined starting and ending criteria which typically need to be documented in the form of test description.

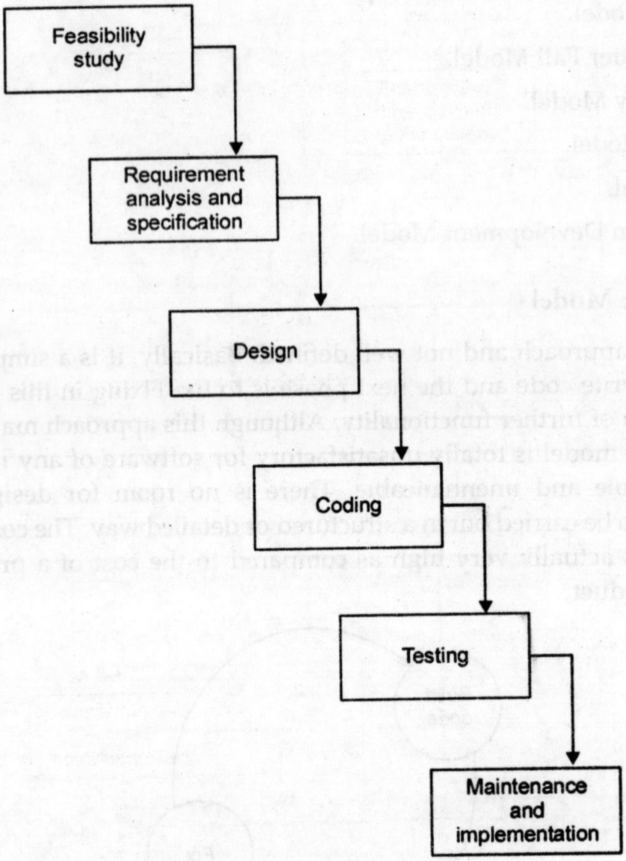

Fig. *Phases of Waterfall Model*

Drawback of Waterfall Model

The waterfall model is an idealistic one, since it assumes that no development error is ever committed by the engineers during any of the life cycle phases. However, in practical development environments, the engineers do commit a large number of errors in almost every phase of the life cycle. So there are no feedback paths in waterfall model from every phase to its preceding phases for the connection of the errors committed during a phase that are detected in later Phases.

4.11.3 Iterative Waterfall Model

The Iterative waterfall model removes the drawback of waterfall model by providing a feedback paths from every phase to its preceding phases to allow for the correction of the errors committed during a phase that are detected in later phases. Though errors are inevitable in almost every phase of development, it is desirable to detect these errors in the same phase in which they occur. However, it may not always be possible to detect all errors in the same phase in which they occur, nevertheless, the errors should be detected as early as possible.

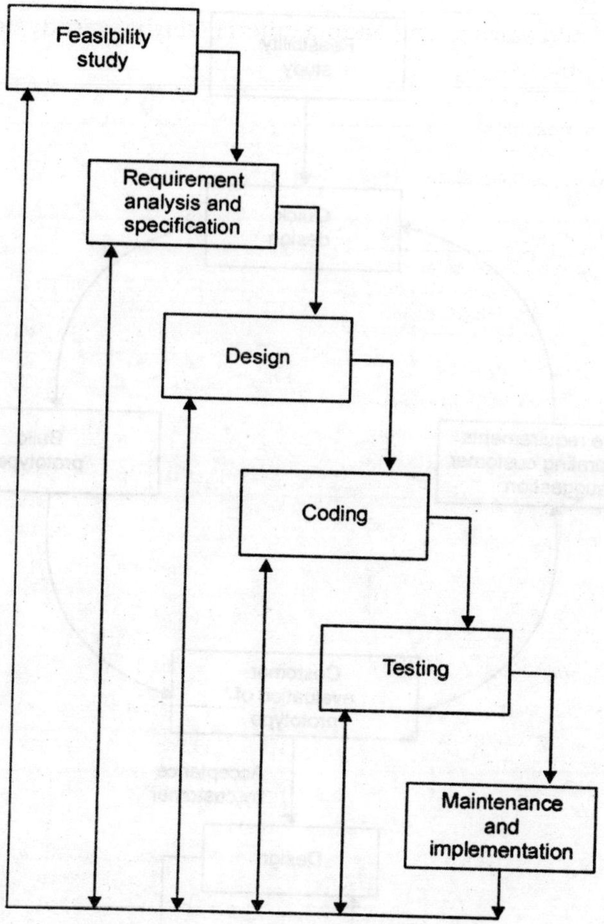

Fig. *Stages of Iterative Waterfall Model*

4.11.4 Prototype Model

The prototyping model suggests that before carrying out the development of the actual software, a working prototype of the system should be built. A prototype is a toy implementation of the system. A prototype usually exhibits limited functional capabilities, low reliability, and inefficient performance compared to the actual software. A prototype is usually built using several shortcuts. This is a valuable mechanism for gaining better understanding of the customer's needs. In this model, product development starts with an initial requirements gathering phase. A quick design is carried out and the prototype is built. The developed prototype is submitted to the customer for his evaluation. Based on the customer feedback, the requirements are refined and the prototype is suitably modified. This cycle of obtaining customer feedback and modifying the prototype continues till the customer approves the prototype. The actual system is developed using the iterative waterfall approach. However, in this model of development, the requirements analysis and specification phase becomes redundant as the working prototype approved by the customer becomes an animated requirements specification.

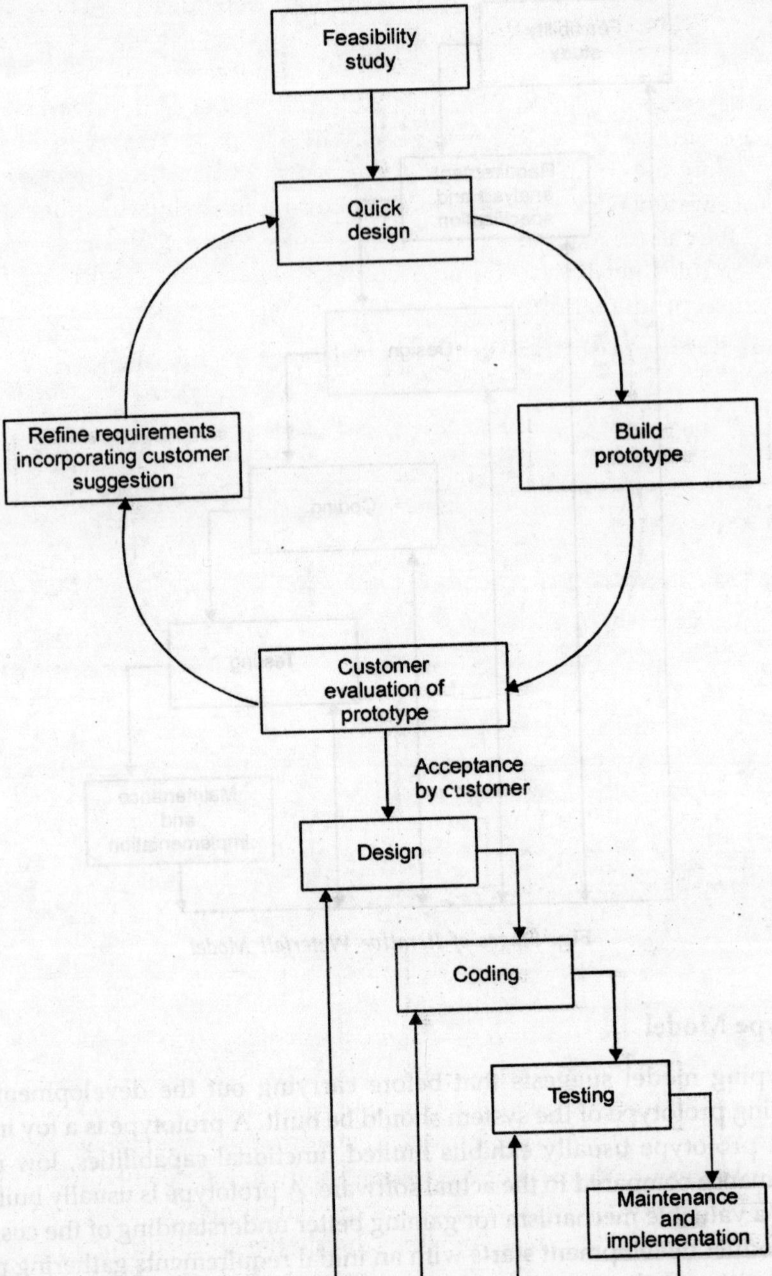

Fig. *Stages of Prototype Model*

4.11.5 Evolutionary Model

This life cycle model is also referred to as the successive versions model and sometimes as the incremental model. In this life cycle model, the software is first broken down into several modules which can be incrementally constructed and delivered. The development team first develops the core modules of the system. This initial product skeleton is refined into increasing levels of capability by adding new functionalities in successive versions. Each evolutionary version may be developed using an iterative waterfall model of development. This model has several advantages. In this model, the user get a chance to experiment with a partially developed software much before the complete version of the system is released. Therefore, the evolutionary model helps to accurately elicit user requirements during the delivery of the different versions of the software, and the change requests therefore after delivery of the complete software are minimized. Also, the core modules get tested thoroughly, thereby reducing chances of errors in the core modules of the final product. Further, this model obviates the need to commit large resources in one go for development of the system.

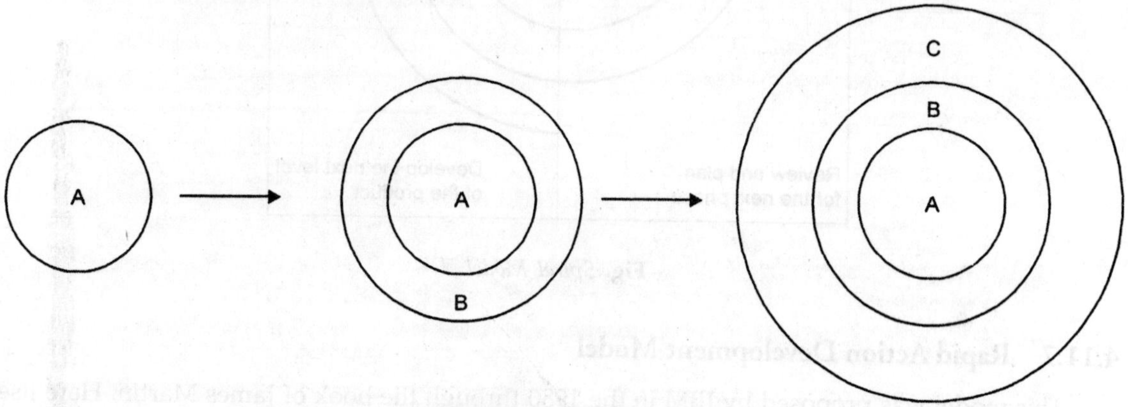

Fig. *Stages of Evolutionary Model*

4.11.6 Spiral Model

The diagramatic representation of spiral model appears like a spiral with many loops. The exact number of loops in the spiral is not fixed. Each loop of the spiral represents a phase of the software process. This model is much more flexible as compared to the other models, since the exact number of phases through which the product is developed in this model is not fixed. It may vary from one project to another. Each phase in this model is split into four sectors (or quadrant). The first quadrant identifies the objectives of the phase and the alternative solutions possible for the phase under consideration. During the second quadrant the alternative solutions are evaluated to select the best solution possible. For the chosen solution, the potential risks are identified and dealt with by developing an appropriate prototype. Third quadrant consist of developing and verifying the next level of the product. Activities during the fourth quadrant cancer reviewing the results of the stages traversed so far with the customer and planing the next iteration around the spiral. With each iteration around the spiral, progressively a more complete version of the software gets built. Usually, after several iterations along the spiral, all risks are resolved and the software is ready for development. The radius of the spiral at any point represents the cost incurred in the project till then, and the angular dimension represents the progress made in the current phase. In the spiral model of development, the project team must decide how exactly to structure the project into phases. Normally, projects start by using some generic model and then adding extra phases whenever some specialrisks are identified later during the project. Possibly the most distinguishing feature of this model is its ability to handle risks.

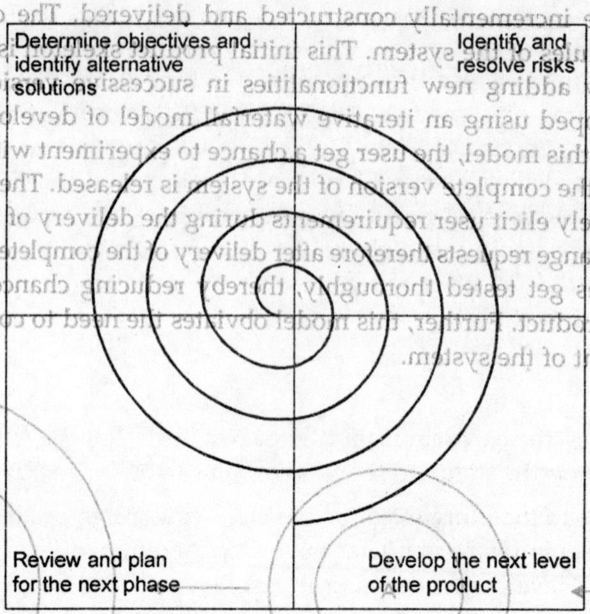

Fig. *Spiral Model*

4.11.7 Rapid Action Development Model

This model was proposed by IBM in the 1980 through the book of James Martin. Here user involvement is essential from requirement phase to delivery of the product. The continuous user participation ensures the involvement of user's expectations and perspective in requirements elicitation, analysis and design of the system. The process is started with building a rapid prototype and is given to user for evaluation. The user feedback is obtained and prototype is refined. The process continues, till the requirements are finalised. There are four phases in this model: With active participation of users.

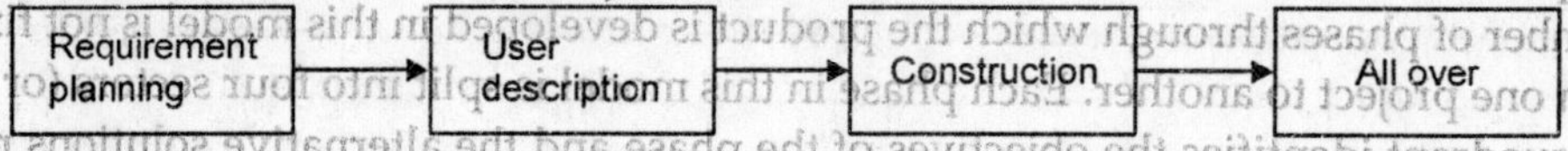

Fig. *RAD Model*

4.12 SOFTWARE QUALITY ASSURANCE (SQA)

Traditionally, a quality product is defined in terms of its fitness of purpose. That is, a quality product does exactly what the users want it to do. For software products, the fitness of purpose is usually interpreted in terms of satisfaction of the requirements laid down in the SRS document. The motivation of SQA is the enable the S/W industry to develop high quality software products and adhere to the standard S/W development practices.

It is of two types:

(*i*) ISO (Inter National Standards Organisation)

(*ii*) SEI-CMM

4.12.1 Definition of ISO

ISO is a consortium of 63 countries established to formulate and foster standardization. ISO published its 9000 series of standards in 1987. ISO 9000 certification series as reference for contract between independent parties. The ISO 9000 standard specifies the guidelines for maintaining a quality system. The ISO standard mainly addresses operational aspects and organizational aspects such as responsibilities, reporting, etc. In a nutshell, ISO 9000 specifies a set of guidelines for repeatable and high quality product development. It is important to realize that ISO 9000 standard is a set of guidelines for the production process and is not directly concerned with the product itself.

4.12.2 Types of ISO

ISO 9001: Applies to the organization engaged in design, development, production and servicing of goods. This is the standard that is applicable to most S/W development organizations.

ISO 9002: Applies to those organization which do not design products but are only involved in production. *e.g.*, Steel industries and car manufacturing industries. Therefore, ISO 9002 is not applicable to software development organisations.

ISO 9003: Applies to those organisation involved only in installation and testing of the products.

4.12.3 Importance of ISO

There is a mad scramble among software development organizations for obtaining ISO certification due to the following benefits it offers:

- Confidence of customers in an organization increases when the organization qualifies for ISO 9001 certification. This is especially true in the international market.
- ISO 9000 requires a well-documented software production process to be in place. A well-documented software production process contributes to repeatable and higher quality of the developed software.
- ISO 9000 makes the development process focused, efficient and cost-effective.
- ISO 9000 certifiecation points out the weak points of an organization and recommends remedial action.
- ISO 9000 sets the basic framework for the development of an optimal process and TQM (Total Quality Management).

4.13 SEI-CMM STANDARDS

4.13.1 Concepts of CMM

Software Engineering Institute capability Maturity Model (SEI-CMM) was proposed by SEI of the Carnegie Mellon University , USA. SEI-CMM is a reference model for inducting the software process maturity into different levels. It can be used to predict the most likely outcome to be expected from the next project that the organisation undertakes. CMM can be used in two ways: capability evaluation and software process assessment. Capability evaluation and software process assessment differ in motivation, objective and the final use of the result. It is basically a model for juding the maturity of the S/W processes of an organization and for identifying the key practices that are required to increase the maturity of these processes. SEI CMM classifies S/W development industries into the five maturity levels.

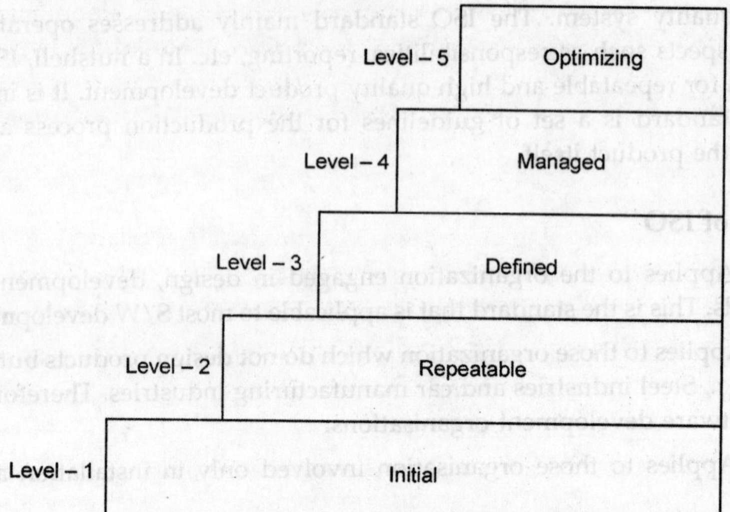

Fig. SEI-CMM Levels

4.13.2 Levels of CMM

Initial (Level 1)—The S/W company where the S/W development activities are adhoc and processes are not defined and not documented.

- Success depends on individual efforts —It is called chaotic level.

Repeatable (Level-2)—At this level, the basic project management practices such as tracking cost and schedule are established. Size and cost estimation techniques like function points analysis, CO COMO, etc. are used. In these companies, the previous efforts done towards success of S/W project may be repeated.

Defined (Level 3)—At this level, the processes for both management and development activities are defined and documented. The processes though defined, the process and the product qualities are not measured. ISO 9000 aims at achieving this level.

Managed (Level 4)—At this level, the focus is on S/W metrics (G: hoc). It these companies, the S/W processes are not only defined but are also controllable. These companies use modern cost estimation, effort estimation techniques.

Optimizing (Level 5)—At this stage the process and the product metrices are collected. At this level the S/W companies, perform error analysis and process monitoring for continuous process improvement. These companies analyze the innovation and new technologies and intend to optimize the current processes in the industry.

Both SEI-CMM Level certification and ISO certification have become a must for a S/W organization in this global erq.

e.g.,:—SEI-Level 5 and Level 4

WIPRO, TCS, Infosys, Infotech, CMC etc.

4.14 COMPARISON BETWEEN ISO AND SEI-CMM

- SEI-CMM goes beyond quality assurance and prepares an organization to ultimately achieve TQM. In fact ISO 9001 aims at level 3 of SEI-CMM model.
- ISO 9000 is awarded by an international standards body. Therefore, ISO 9000 certification. Can be quoted by an organization in official documents. In communications with external parties, and in tender quotations. However, SEI-CMM assessment is purely for internal use.
- SEI-CMM was developed specifically for software industry and therefore addresses many issues which are specific to software industry alone.

EXERCISES

1. Differentiate between High level Language and fourth generation Language.
2. Differentiate between compiler and Interpreter.
3. Differentiate between a program and an algorithm. Draw a flowchart to show whether a given number is positive or negative.
4. What do you understand by software development life cycle? List various stages of waterfall model.
5. Explain in detail different testing techniques used for testing a software.
6. Explain CMM standards for IT industry.
7. What is SRS? Differentiate between debugging and testing.
8. What do you mean by quality assurance? Write a short note on ISO 9000.
9. Write short notes on Data flow diagram.
10. What is the drawback of waterfall model? Flow it is removed in iterative waterfall model.

5

DIGITAL FUNDAMENTAL

5.1 VARIOUS CODES

There are various codes that are handled by a computer.

5.1.1 BCD (Binary Coded Decimal)

BCD code is one of the early memory codes. It is the simplest binary code to represent a decimal number. If a decimal number consists of two or more than two digits, each decimal digit is individually represented by its 4-bits binary equivalent (8421 code).

BCD is a 6-bit code and it was developed by IBM. Soon they realized that with 6 bits, only 2^6; *i.e.*, 64 symbols could be represented.

Difference between Binary Equivalent number and BCD coded number:

- Binary equivalent of a decimal No. 13 = 1101
- But BCD code of a No. 13 = <u>0001</u> <u>0011</u>

  36 = <u>0011</u> <u>0110</u>

5.1.2 Excess-3 Code

In Excess–3 code 3 is added to the individual digit of a decimal number, and then their BCD equivalents are written

For example:

(*i*) 4 → (0111) **Ans.** 7

$$\begin{array}{r} 4 \\ +\ 3 \\ \hline 7 \end{array}$$

(*ii*)

$$\begin{array}{r} 2\,2 \\ +\ 3\,3 \\ \hline 5\,5 \end{array}$$

(0101 0101) **Ans.**

(*iii*)

$$\begin{array}{r} 2\,5\,3 \\ +\ 3\,3\,3 \\ \hline 5\,8\,6 \end{array}$$

Ans. (0101 1000 0110) in excess 3 codes

(iv)

$$\begin{array}{r} 9\quad 9 \\ +\ 3\quad 3 \\ \hline 12\ 12 \end{array}$$

(1100 1100) **Ans.**

5.1.3 EBCDIC (Extended Binary Coded Decimal Interchange Code)

EBCDIC is a 8-bit code used in its main frame series of computers. It is the standard character code for large computer

For example, A → 11000001

B → 11000010

C → 11000011

5.1.4 ASCII (American Standard Code for Information Interchange)

It is the world's most widely used coding standard. In this scheme, 7 bits are used per symbol, thus allowing for 128 symbols to be represented.

Sometimes an 8 bit is also added and this bit is either 0 or 1 or used as parity bit.

A → 65

B → 66

5.1.5 Gray Code

The Gray code is a binary code. The binary bits are arranged in such a way that only one binary bit changes at a time when we make a change from any number to the next. It is also known as reflected code.

Fog example,

$(1\ 1\ 0\ 1)_2 = (1011)_{Gray}$

(write whatever is MSB 0 or 1)

1011

From Binary to Gray

$(1101)_2$

↓

(1011) Gray

From Gray to Binary

(1 0 1 1) Gray code

1 1 0 1

$(1101)_2$

5.1.6 Floating Numbers Representation

A number which has both an integer part as well as a fractional part is called real number or Floating point number. A real number may be either positive or negative.

The real number 546.98 can be written as 5.4698×10^2. This representation is known as scientific form of representation.

The General representation for a floating-point number is expressed as

$$\boxed{N = M \times R^e}$$

Where M → Mantissa

R → Radix of the number system

e → Exponent

5.2 NUMBER SYSTEM AND CONVERSION

There are 4 types of Number System:

1. Decimal Number System $(0-9)_{10}$
2. Binary Number System $(0, 1)_2$
3. Octal Number System $(0-7)_8$
4. Hexadecimal Number System $\left(0-9 \text{ and } \overset{10}{A}, \overset{11}{B}, \overset{12}{C}, \overset{13}{D}, \overset{14}{E}, \overset{15}{F},\right)_{16}$

5.2.1 Decimal Number System

The decimal Number system uses ten digits (0, 1, 2, 3, 4, 5, 6, 7, 8, 9). It there is said to have a base of ten. Since the base in decimal number system is 10, the number 4563 is written as $(4563)_{10}$.

$$\begin{aligned} 4563 &= 4 \times 10^3 + 5 \times 10^2 + 6 \times 10^1 + 3 \times 10^0 \; (10^0 = 1) \\ &= 4000 + 500 + 60 + 3 \times 1 \\ &= 4563. \end{aligned}$$

5.2.2 Binary Number System

This system uses only two digits and thus it is known as the binary number system. These numbers are 0 and 1. Any number represented in the binary number system is a string of 0 and 1's. Hence this system has a base of 2.

$$\begin{aligned} 1001 &= 1 \times 2^3 + 0 \times 2^2 + 0 \times 2^1 + 1 \times 2^0 \quad (2^0 = 1) \\ &= 8 + 0 + 0 + 1 = 9 \end{aligned}$$

5.2.3 Octal Number System

This system uses eight digits (0, 1, 2, 3, 4, 5, 6, 7). Since the octal number system uses a total eight digits to compose a number, this system is said to have a base of eight. Since the base in octal number system is 8.

$$\begin{aligned} 4563 &= 4 \times 8^3 + 5 \times 8^2 + 6 \times 8^1 + 3 \times 8^0 \\ &= 4 \times 512 + 5 \times 64 + 6 \times 8 + 3 \times 1 \\ &= 2048 + 320 + 48 + 3 = 2419. \end{aligned}$$

8	2419	3
8	302	6
8	37	5
	4	= 4563.

5.2.4 Hexadecimal Number System

This system uses sixteen digits (0, 1, 2, 3, 4, 5, 6, 7, 8, 9 A, B, C, D, E, F), to express a number. Thus it is said to have a base of sixteen

$$45AB = 4 \times 16^3 + 5 \times 16^2 + 10 \times 16^1 + 11 \times 16^0$$

Number Conversion

Binary to Decimal

$$\begin{aligned} 11001 &= 1 \times 2^4 + 1 \times 2^3 + 0 \times 2^2 + 0 \times 2^1 + 1 \times 2^0 \\ &= 1 \times 16 + 1 \times 8 + 0 + 0 + 1 \\ &= 16 + 8 + 1 \\ &= 25. \end{aligned}$$

Hence decimal equivalent number is 25.

Decimal to Binary Fraction Number

.40

.40 × 2	= 0.8	0
.8 × 2	= 1.6	1
.6 × 2	= 1.2	1
.2 × 2	= .4	0
.4 × 2	= .8	0

$$(.40)_{10} = (.01100)_2$$

Decimal to Binary

25

2	25	1
2	12	0
2	6	0
2	3	1
	1	

$$(25)_{10} = (11001)_2$$

$$1 \times 2^4 + 1 \times 2^3 + 1 \times 2^0$$

$$= 16 + 8 + 1 = 25.$$

Hexadecimal to Binary

Convert 45A4 to binary

Hexadecimal	4	5	A	4
Each digit equivalent	0100	0101	1100	0100
Equivalent binary	0100010111000100			

Binary to Hexadecimal

Binary	0001	0100	0100	1101
Binary	0001	0100	0100	1101
	1	4	4	D

Equivalent Hexanumber = 144 D

Binary Addition

0 + 0 = 0
0 + 1 = 1
1 + 0 = 1
1 + 1 = 1 0 sum
carry

e.g.,

```
 111010
 + 1001
 111010
```

```
  1 1 1 = 7
   + 10 = 2
   1001 = 9
 7 +  2 = 9
```

Binary Subtraction

0 − 0 = 0
1 − 0 = 1
1 − 1 = 0
* 0 − 1 = 1 1 Borrow
subtraction

e.g.,

```
  101  −  5          1010 → 10
 − 11  −  3         −0101 →  5
   10     2          0101    5
```

Binary Multiplication

0 × 0 = 0
1 × 0 = 0
0 × 1 = 0
1 × 1 = 1

Hexadecimal to a Decimal Number

$$(3AB)_{16} = 3 \times 16^2 + A \times 16^1 + B \times 16^0$$
$$= 3 \times 256 + 10 \times 16 + 11 \times 1$$
$$= 768 + 160 + 11$$
$$= (939)_{10}$$
$$(3AB)_{16} = (939)_{10}$$

Octal Number to Decimal Number

$$(46)_8 = 4 \times 8^1 + 6 \times 8^0$$
$$= 32 + 6$$
$$= (38)_{10}$$
$$(46)_8 = (38)_{10}$$

Decimal to Octal

$$(45)_{10} = (55)_8$$

8 | 38 6   8 | 45 5
4   5

$$(38)_{10} = (46)_8$$

Binary to Octal

e.g., $(11011100)_2$ = 011 011 100

↓ ↓ ↓

3 3 4

$= (334)_8$

e.g., 1101011.110101 **Fraction Part**

1101011 .110101

001 101 011 110 101

↓ ↓ ↓ ↓ ↓

1 5 3 6 5

= 153

$(1101011.110101)_2 = (153.65)_8$ **Ans.**

Octal to Hexa/Hexa to Octal

Hexa to Octal

$(E\ 8A)_{16} = (\quad)_8$

111 0 10 00 1 010 (group by 3 bits)

111 010 001 010

7 2 1 2

$= (7212)_8$

Octal to Hexa

$(752)_8 = (\quad)_{16}$

111 101 010 (group by 4 bits)

0001 1110 1010

1 E A

$= (1EA)_{16}.$

5.3 COMPLEMENTS FORM

5.3.1 I's Complement

1's complement of a binary number may be formed by simply changing each 1 to a 0 and each 0 to a1.

For example, 10011 1.1.1.1.1

1's comp. = 01100 1's con = 00000

5.3.2 2's Complement

2's Complement of a binary number is equal to the is complement of the number plus one.

∴ 2's compl. = 1's comp + 1.

For example, 0101 1101

= 1010 = 0010

+ 1 + 1

2's comp. 1011 2's 0011

5.3.3 SUB using 1's and 2's Complement

- ***1's Complement Method***

Steps:

- First check the length of both are same or not if not then add 0's.
- Take 1's complement of subtrahend. (The no which U want to subtract).
- Add this to the minuend. (number from which U want to subtract)
- If there is a carry in last then add it.
- If there is no carry then take 1's complement of result and place a minus sign in front of it. Now the result is in negative form.

1. Subtract 111_2 from 1110_2

1110

0111→ is complement

2. Subtract $1110_2 - 1011_2$

```
  1110
 +1000
 10110
  └─→1
  0111 Result
```

1's complement

```
  1110
 +0100
 10010
  └─→1
  0011
```

3. Subtract 1100 from 1010

or 1010 – 1100

1's comp.

```
  1010
  0011
  1101
```

Number carry so again is complement – (0010) Result.

■ *2nd Complement Method*

Steps:

- Chick wheather the length is same or not, if less add 0's.
- Take 2's complement of subtrahend.
- Add this 2's complement to the minuend.
- If there is a carry then dropt, this is then final answer.
- If there is number carry in result then take 2's complement and place a minus sign this is the final result, which is neg.

1. Subtract $(1011)_2$ –(101)

```
  1011
 -1010
 10101 Same
  └──→1
  0110
```

1011

0101 2's complement → 1010 +1 = 1011

1011–1011

carry 10110 answer = $(0110)_2$.

2. 10010 – 10011

2's Complement 10011 → 01100 + 1 = 01101

```
  10010   number carry so 2's Complement
 -01101
  11111
```

00000 + 1 = $-(00001)_2$ Result.

5.4 LOGIC GATES

The fundamental units for performing digital operations are called logic gates. These gates allow the Input signal to be processed in logical way. There are 3 basics gates.

1. OR, 2. AND, 3. NOT

5.4.1 OR Gate

There may be two or more than two Input signals at the OR Gate and only one output is there

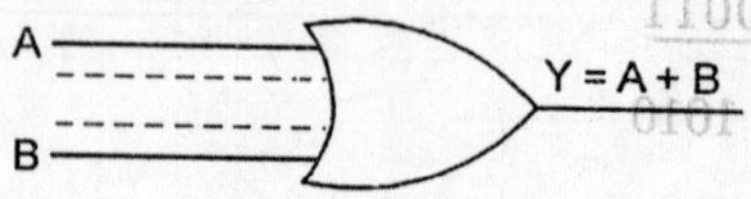

Fig. *Ckt Diagram*

Truth table:

A	B	Y
0	0	0
0	1	1
1	0	1
1	1	1

Y = A + B **Algebraic Expression.**

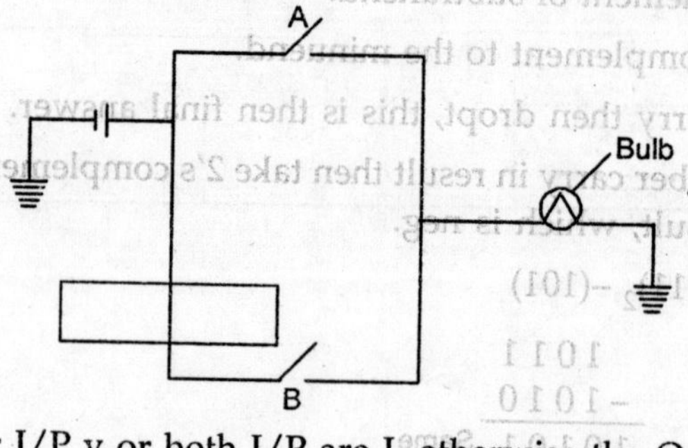

The O/P is 1, if I/P x or I/P y or both I/P are I, otherwise the O/P is O.

5.4.2 AND Gate

There may be two or more than two input signal and only one output.

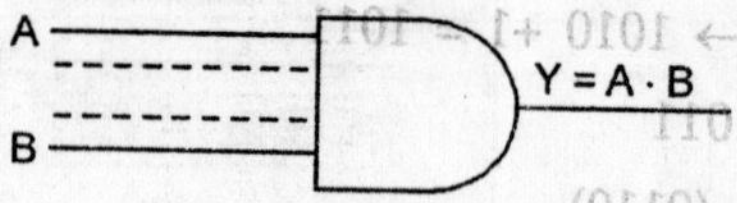

Y = A . B

A	B	Y
0	0	0
0	1	0
1	0	0
1	1	1

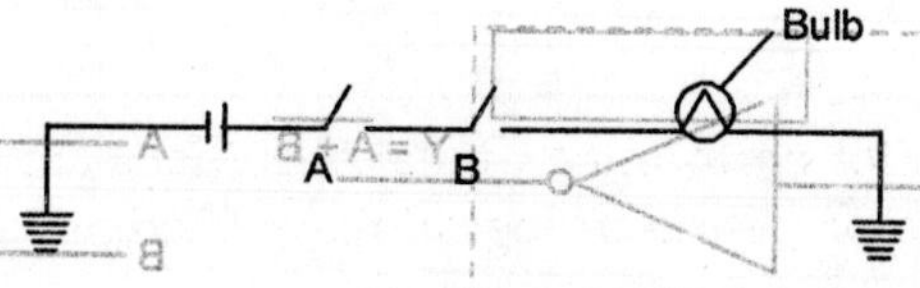

If any I/P is Low, then its output is low and when both I/P is high then O/P is high.

5.4.3 NOT Gate

It is also known as inverter. It has one input and only one O/P. Status of the signal at I/P (High or low) in inverted by the NOT gate. It produces the NOT, or complement function.

$$Y = \overline{A}$$

A	Y = $\overline{x}$
0	1
1	0

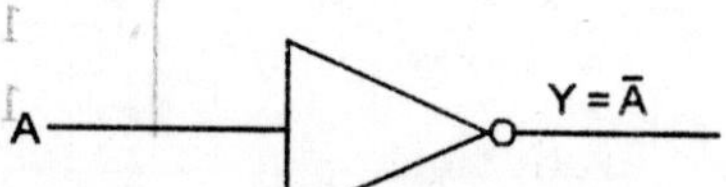

5.4.4 NAND Gate

A NAND gate is functionally equivalent to combinations of AND and NOT gate in series. It is also called as universal gate because other logic operations can be realized using only NAND gates. A universal operations is one that can be used to implement the three basic logic operations AND, OR and NOT.

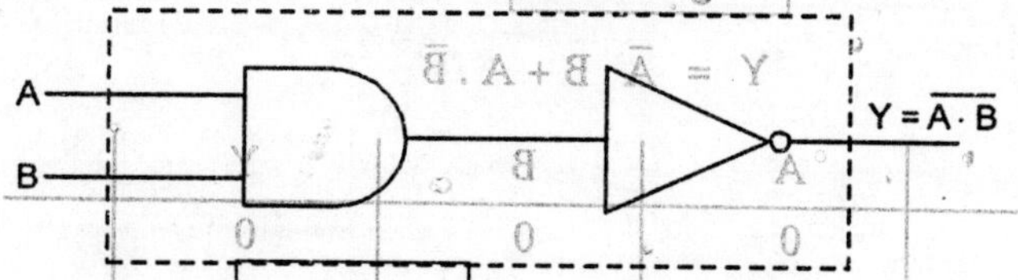

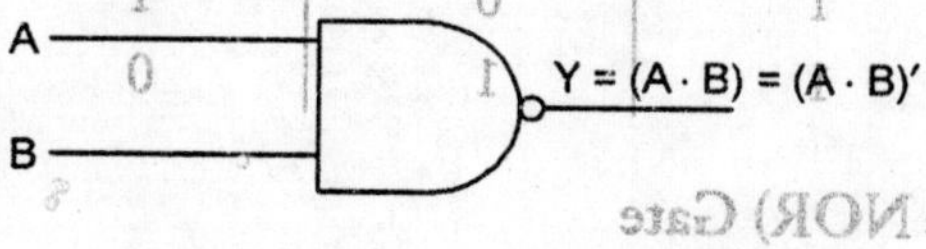

$Y = \overline{A \,.\, B}$ Algebraic Exp.

A	B	Y
0	0	1
0	1	1
1	0	1
1	1	0

5.4.5 NOR Gate

A NOR gate is functionally equivalent to combinations of OR and NOT gate in series. It is represented as:

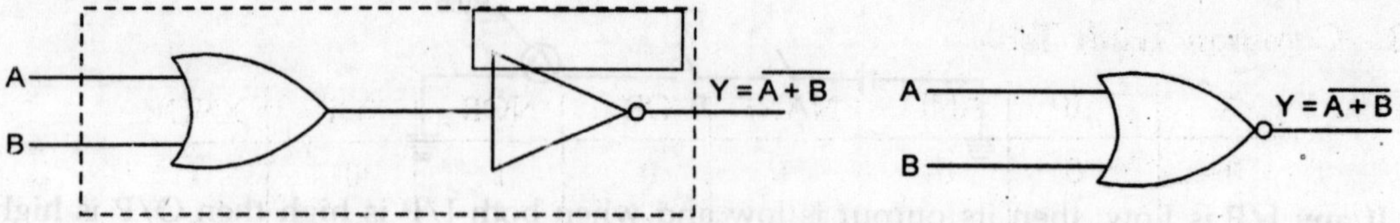

$$Y = \overline{A+B}$$

A	B	Y
0	0	1
0	1	0
1	0	0
1	1	0

5.4.6 EX-OR (Exclusive OR) Gate

The O/P of the Ex-OR Gate is high if the I/P lines are at different levels. If the I/P lines are at the same level, then the O/P is low.

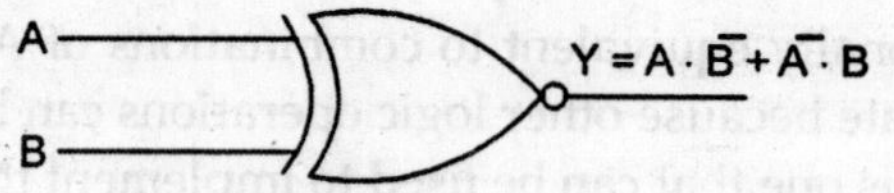

$$Y = \overline{A \oplus B}$$

$$Y = \overline{A}\,.\,B + A\,.\,\overline{B}$$

A	B	Y
0	0	0
0	1	1
1	0	1
1	1	0

5.4.7 Ex-NOR (Exclusive NOR) Gate

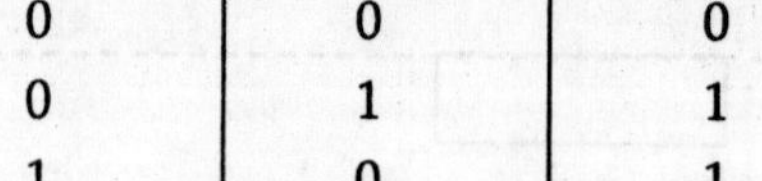

$$Y = \overline{A \oplus B}$$

$$Y = A\,.\,B + \overline{A}\,.\,\overline{B}$$

A	B	Y
0	0	1
0	1	0
1	0	0
1	1	1

5.4.8 Common Truth Table

A	B	AND	NAND	OR	NOR	XOR	XNOR
0	0	0	1	0	1	0	1
0	1	0	1	1	0	1	0
1	0	0	1	1	0	1	0
1	1	1	0	1	0	0	1

5.4.9 Realization with NAND Gates

(i) NOT Gate

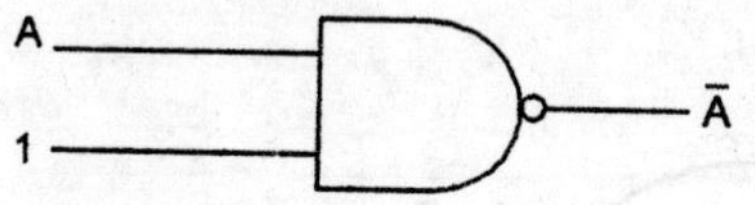

$\bar{A} = \overline{A.1}$ - A NAND 1 (1 is a constt.)

(ii) AND Gate

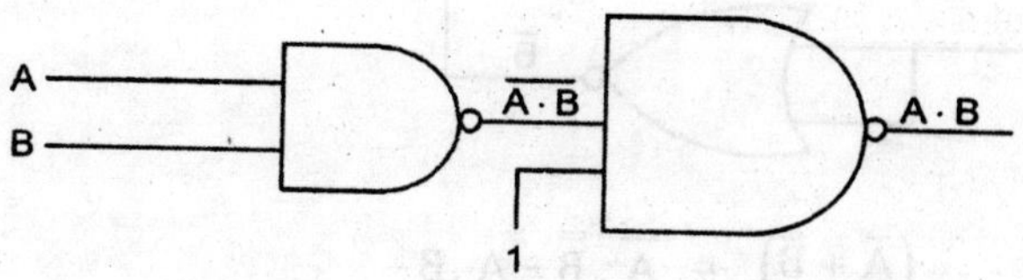

$$\overline{\overline{A.B}} = A.B$$

(iii) OR Gate

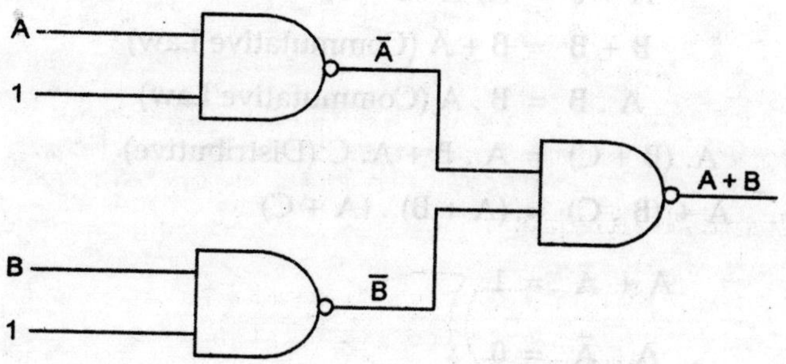

$A + B = \overline{\bar{A}.\bar{B}}$ (using De Morgan's Theorem)

5.4.10 Realization with NOR Gates

(i) NOT Gate

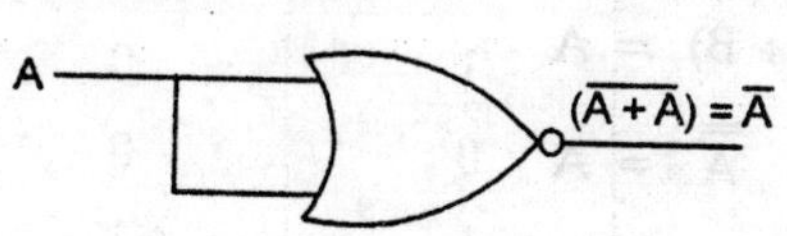

$$\left(\overline{A+A}\right) = \bar{A}$$

(ii) OR Gate

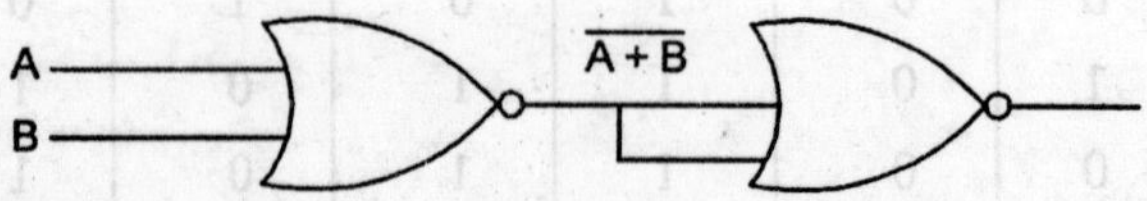

$$\overline{\left(\overline{A+B}\right)+\left(\overline{A+B}\right)} = \overline{\overline{A+B}} = A+B$$

(iii) AND Gate

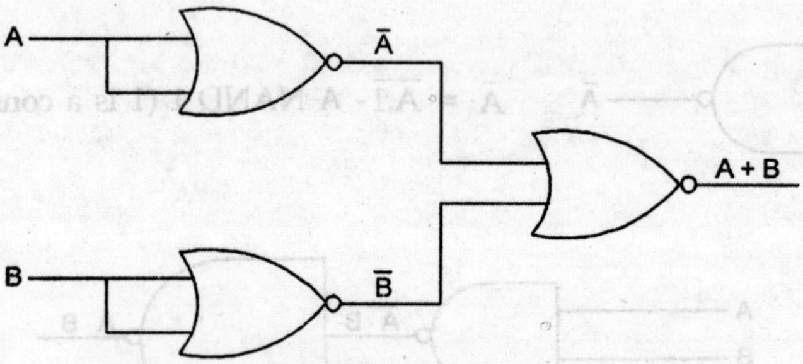

$$\left(\bar{A}+\bar{B}\right) = \bar{\bar{A}} . \bar{\bar{B}} = A . B$$

5.4.11 Boolean Postulates

Identities

$$A + 0 = A, A . 1 = A$$
$$B + B = B + A \text{ (Commutative Law)}$$
$$A . B = B . A \text{ (Commutative Law)}$$
$$A. (B + C) = A . B + A. C \text{ (Distributive)}$$
$$A + (B . C) = (A + B) . (A + C)$$
$$A + \bar{A} = 1$$
$$A . \bar{A} = 0$$
$$A + A = A$$
$$A . A = A$$
$$A + 1 = 1$$
$$A . 0 = 0$$
$$A + A . B = A$$
$$A . (A + B) = A$$
$$\bar{\bar{A}} = A$$

$$A + \bar{A} \cdot B = A + B$$

$$A \cdot (\bar{A} + B) = A \cdot B$$

$$\left.\begin{aligned} \overline{(A + B)} &= \bar{A} \cdot \bar{B} \\ \overline{A \cdot B} &= \bar{A} + \bar{B} \end{aligned}\right\} \text{De Morgan's Theorem}$$

5.5 FLIP FLOPS

Flip Flops are the basic memory elements capable of storing a bit. A flip flop is a bit stable device which remains in one of two states. The state of a flip flop is changed by the appropriate excitation at the input. The states of a flip flop are called SET and RESET. Since the flip flop remains in one of the states unit an appropriate excitation is applied at input.

SET state : The high stable state, *i.e.,* 1

RESET state: The low stable state, *i.e.,* 0.

The behaviour of a flip flop is represented by two types of tables called characteristic and Excitation Table. The characteristic table shows the possible input signal and cross pending output. The Excitation table of a flip flop shows what excitations are required at the input to get the desired changes.

The eq. are RS, JK, T and D.

All of these FF are build around the basic storage element called latches. There are two types of latches possible called NOR latch and NAND Latch. The NOR latch is built around the NOR gates and NAND latch users NAND gates.

■ NOR Latch

The NOR latch has two I/P lines called R and S. The O/P has two lines called Q and $\bar{Q}$. When the O/P line Q is at high level, it is said to have stored a bit '1', and this state is called SET state. The RESET state is one where the status of the O/P line Q is low (0).

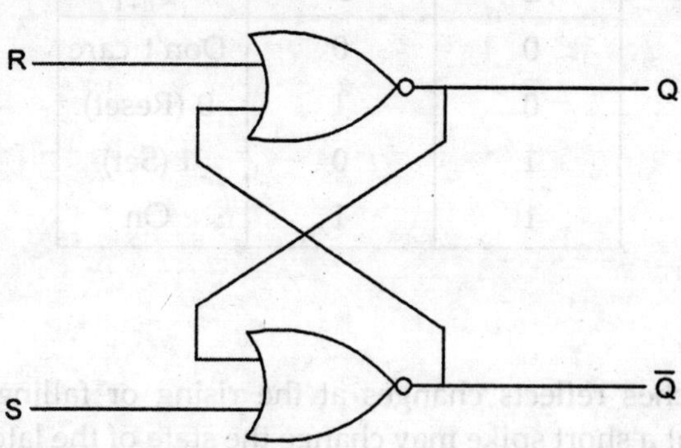

Characteristic Table of NOR Latch:

S	R	Q	
0	0	NC	No change in the state
0	1	0	Reset
1	0	1	Set
1	1	X	Don't care or not allowed.

When both the excitations R and S are placed at high level, the state becomes unstable. This situation is also called Race condition. The FF are so designed that this situation is never allowed to occur.

■ **NAND Latch**

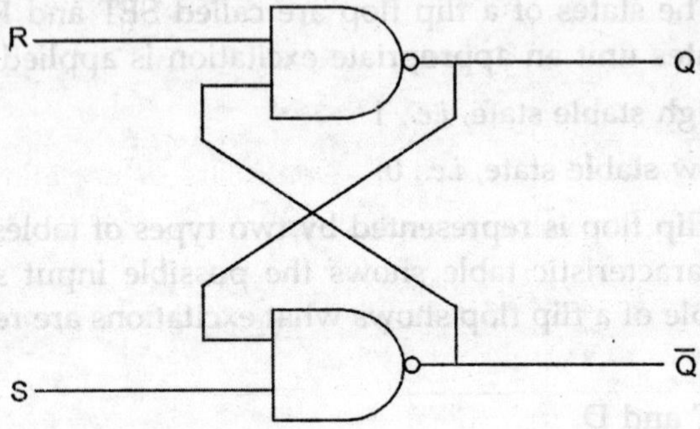

Characteristic Table of NAND Latch:

S	R	Q	
0	0	X	Don't care
0	1	0	Reset
1	0	1	Set
1	1	NC	No change

S	R	Q_{n+1}
0	0	Don't care
0	1	0 (Reset)
1	0	1 (Set)
1	1	On

5.5.1 SR Flip Flop

The state of the latches reflects changes at the rising or falling edge of the signal. The disadvantage of this is that a short spike may change the state of the latch. This is the main reason for using an input conditioning circuit before the latch. SR Input are conditioned and are loaded with the clock. The changes at SR lines are allowed to pass when the clock is high.

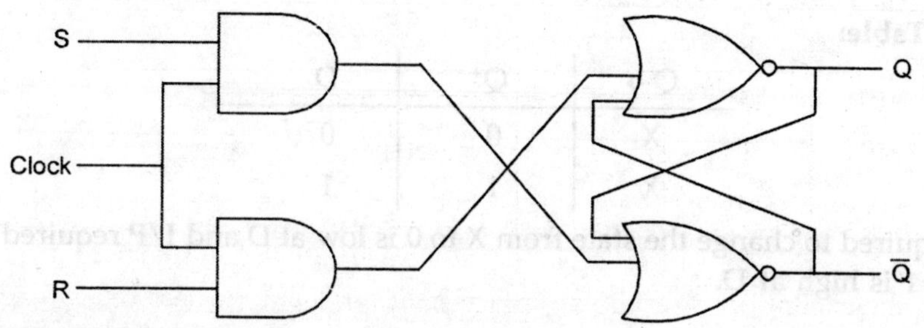

Characteristic Table:

S	R	Q	Description
0	0	NC	No change in state
0	1	0	Reset
1	0	1	set
1	1	X	Don't care or not allowed.

Excitation Table:

Present state Q	Next State Q^+	S	R
0	0	0	X
0	1	1	X
1	0	0	1
1	1	X	0

5.5.2 D-Flip Flop

It may be noted that the clocked D flip flop stores the bit which appears on input line 'D'. Change in the input is allowed only when the clock is high.

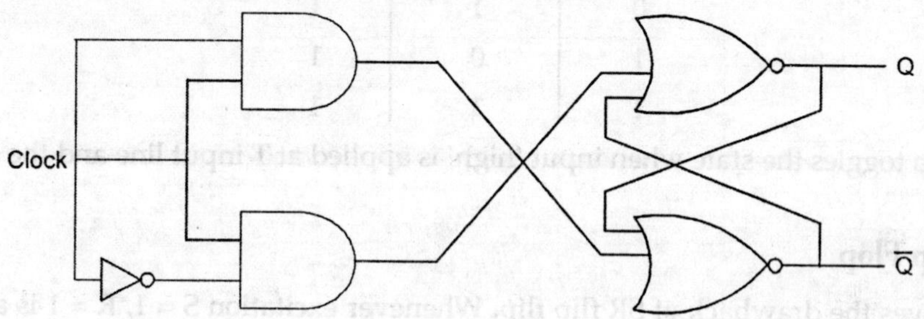

Characteristic Table:

Clock	D	Q
0	X	No Change
1	1	1
1	0	0

Excitation Table:

Q→	Q+	D
X	0	0
X	1	1

The I/P required to change the state from X to 0 is low at D and I/P required to change the state from X to 1 is high at D.

5.5.3 T-Flip Flop

T-Flip Flop is also known as Toggle flip flop. Toggles the state as the Input signal with clock.

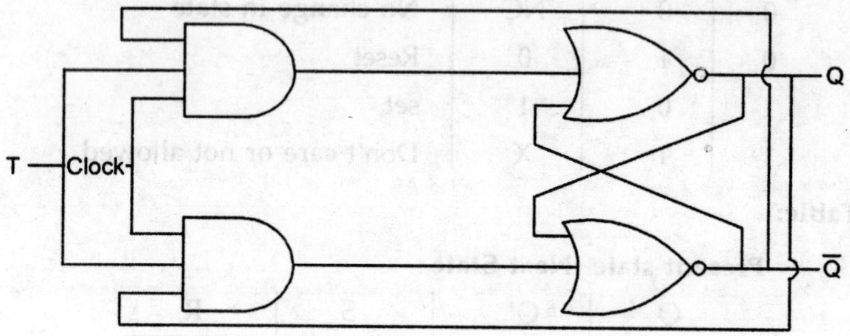

Characteristic Table:

Clock	T	Q
0	X	No change
1	0	No change
1	1	State change 1 → 0, 0 → 1

Excitation Table:

Q→	Q+	T
0	0	0
0	1	1
1	0	1
1	1	1

T-Flip Flop toggles the state when input 'high' is applied at T input line and the clock is high.

5.5.4 JK Flip Flop

This removes the drawback of SR flip flip. Whenever excitation S = 1, R = 1 is applied to SR flip flop, it enters into the race condition and this I/P is considered as undesirable. The Jk FF works similarly as SR FF but when J = 1, K = 1, excitation is applied, the JK FF changes the state or the next state is the complement of the previous one. If the level of Q line before applying J = 1, K = 1, input is low, it converted to high and if it is high, then it is converted to low. The JK FF may be constructed over SR FF.

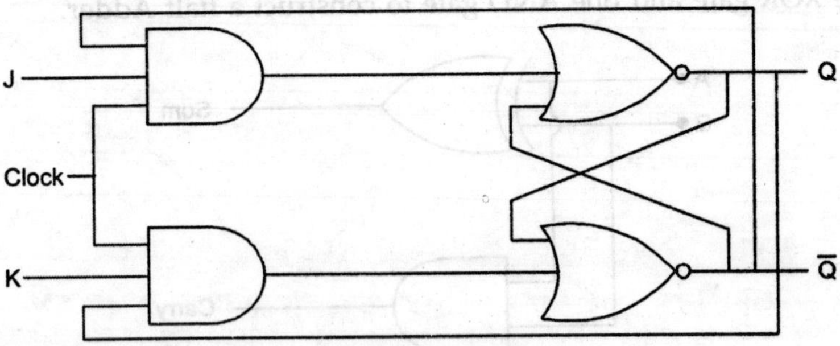

Chartacteristic Table:

Clock	J	K	Q
0	X	X	No Change
1	0	0	No Change
1	0	1	0
1	1	0	1
1	1	1	Toggle {1 → 0, 0 →1}

Excitation Table for JK Flip Flop:

Present state Q	Next state Q+	J	K
0	0	0	X
0	1	1	X
1	0	X	1
1	1	X	0

5.6 ADDER

5.6.1 Half Adder

It is a combinational circuit or connected arrangement of logic gates with a set of Input and Outputs, which perform addition of two bits. The half adder is one step ahead of XOR gate. It uses a XOR gate and an AND gate internally and successfully adds two bits. This takes care of any carry that arises as well.

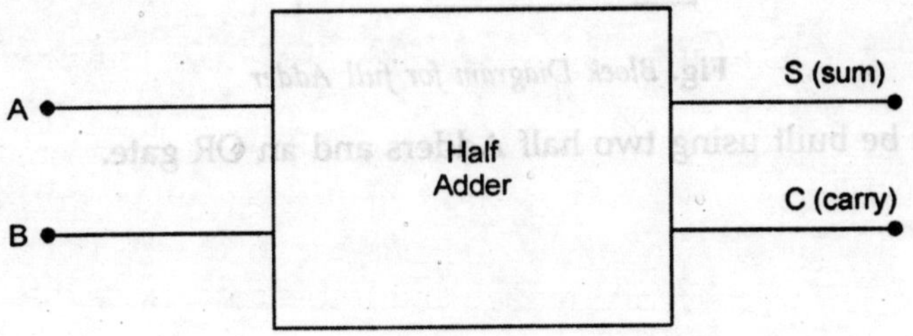

Fig. *Block Diagram of Half Adder*

We need one XOR gate and one AND gate to construct a half Adder.

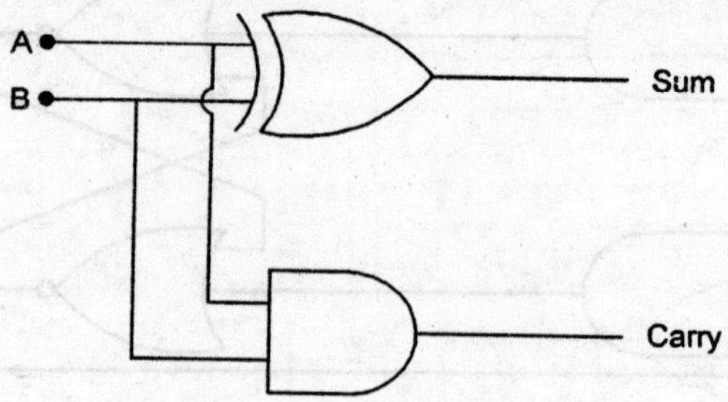

Fig. *Circuit diagram of Half Adder*

Truth Table:

A	B	Sum	Carry
0	0	0	0
0	1	1	0
1	0	1	0
1	1	0	1

Algebraic Expression:

$$\text{Sum} = A \oplus B = \bar{A}.B + A.\bar{B}$$

$$\text{Carry} = A\,.\,B$$

5.6.2 Full Adder

It is a combinational circuit which performs addition of three input bits. Full adder has three input bits—two are avgend bit and third one is the carry bit from the previous addition. Output has two bits: Sum bit and carry bit.

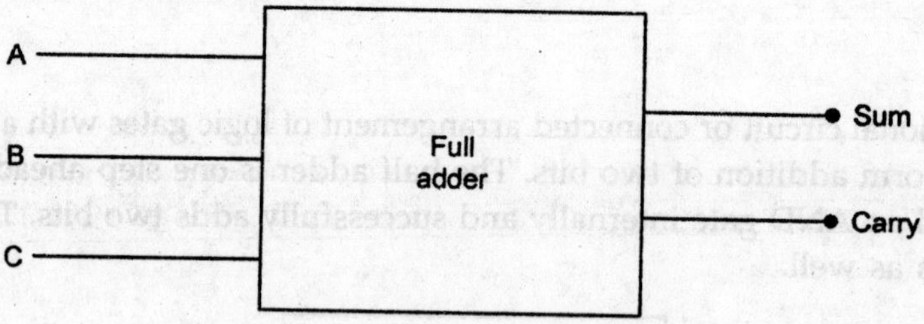

Fig. *Block Diagram for full Adder*

A full Adder can be built using two half Adders and an OR gate.

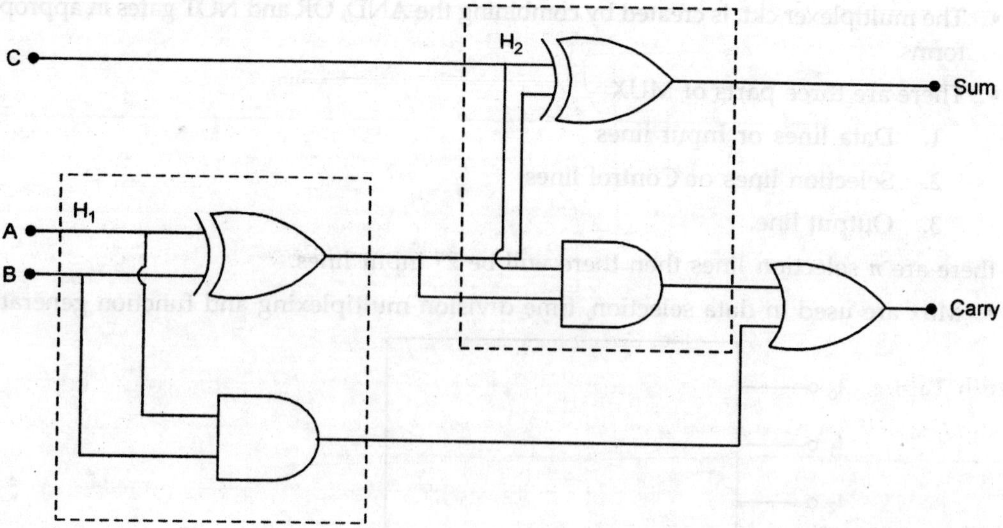

Fig. *Circuit Diagram for Full Adder*

Algebraic Expression:

$$\text{Sum} = A \oplus B \oplus C$$

$$\text{Carry} = AB + BC + AC$$

Truth Table:

A	B	C	Sum	Carry
0	0	0	0	0
0	0	1	1	0
0	1	0	1	0
0	1	1	0	1
1	0	0	1	0
1	0	1	0	1
1	1	0	0	1
1	1	1	1	1

5.7 MULTIPLEXER (MUX)

- It is combinational logic circuit.
- Multiplex means many into one. That cas many inputs, but only one output. We can use control signalling to decide which of the inputs should become the output.
- It's use is in parallel to serial data converter. Where we put the 8-bit input on 8 input lines, and then by using the control signalling mechanism, we can retrieve the 8 bit one after the other in a serial fashion.

- The multiplexer ckt. is created by combining the AND, OR and NOT gates in appropriate forms.
- There are three parts of MUX.
  1. Data lines or Input lines
  2. Selection lines or Control lines
  3. Output line.

If there are n selection lines then there will be 2^n input lines.

- Mux are used in data selection, time division multiplexing and function generation.

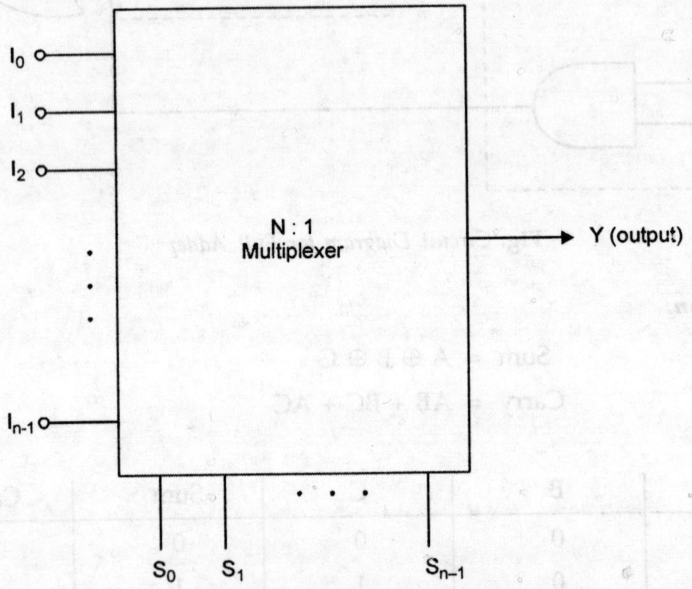

Fig. *Block Diagram of MUX*

e.q. (1) 2 : 1 MUX (2-line to 1-line multiplexer)

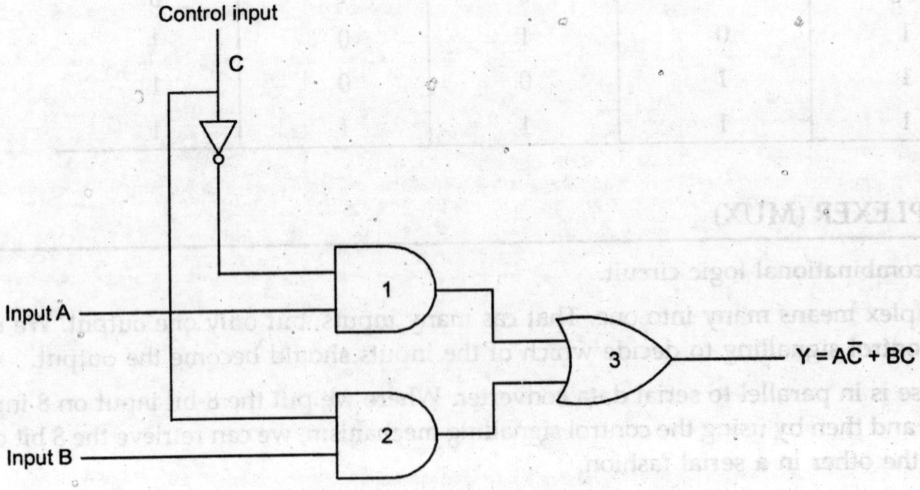

e.q. (2) 4 : 1 Mux

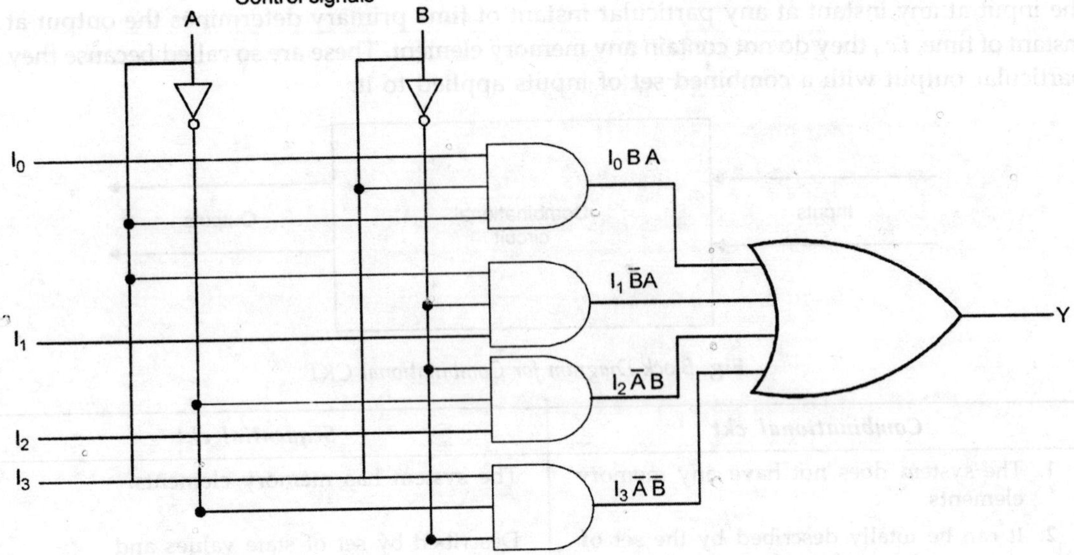

Fig.

5.8 SEQUENTIAL VERSUS COMBINATIONAL CIRCUIT

5.8.1 Sequential Circuit

The sequential circuit are digital circuits containing the memory elements such as flip-flops, or it is an interconnection of flip flops and gates.

Sequential circuits are those circuit whose output depends on the present input as well as the previous history of inputs *i.e.*, these circuits contain at least one memory elements, which can store binary information in it. These are so called as they work in sequence by taking into account the previous input states as well as the present input state.

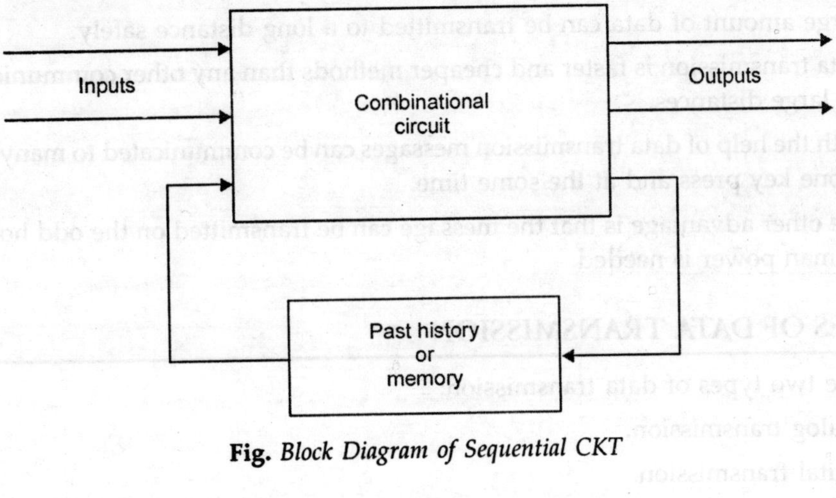

Fig. *Block Diagram of Sequential CKT*

5.8.2 Combinational Circuit

It is a connected arrangement of logic gates with a set of input and output. In these circuit, the input at any instant at any particular instant of time primary determines the output at that instant of time, *i.e.*, they do not contain any memory element. These are so called because they give particular output with a combined set of inputs applied to it.

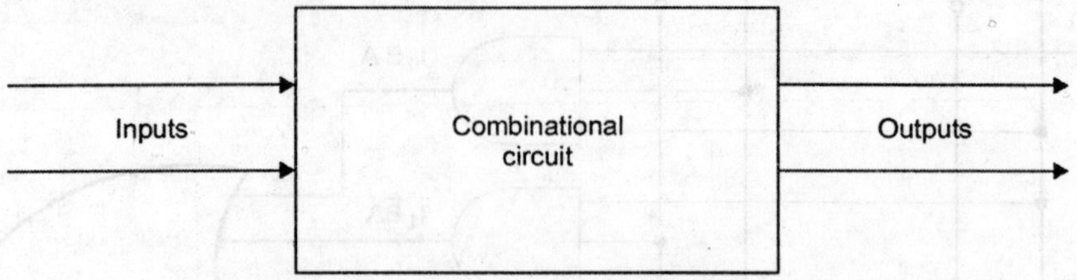

Fig. *Block Diagram for Combinational CKT*

Combinational ckt	*Sequential ckt*
1. The system does not have any memory elements.	The system has memory elements.
2. It can be totally described by the set of output values only.	Described by set of state values and output values.
3. System design is easy.	System design is difficult because of presence of memory element.
4. Speed is faster.	Speed is slower due to delay produced by the memory element.
5. More Hardware required.	Less Hardware is required.
6. It is expensive in cost.	It is cheaper in cost.

5.9 NEED FOR DATA TRANSMISSION OVER DISTANCE

Need for transmitting data over distances is due to the following reasons:

- People want to share resources like computers, printers, business data, personal data sitting over distances.
- Large amount of data can be transmitted to a long distance safely.
- Data transmission is faster and cheaper methods than any other communication media for large distances.
- With the help of data transmission messages can be communicated to many destinations at one key press and at the some time.
- The other advantage is that the message can be transmitted on the odd hours also and no man power is needed.

5.10 TYPES OF DATA TRANSMISSION

There are two types of data transmission:

1. Analog transmission.
2. Digital transmission.

5.10.1 Analog Transmission

Analog signals are continuous electromagnetic waves. These waveforms may be periodic or aperiodic. The amplitude which represents the value of the signal at a particular instant of time, changes continuously with the time in analog signal. There are basically 3 items which defines the analog signal *i.e.*, Amplitude, Frequency and phase angle.

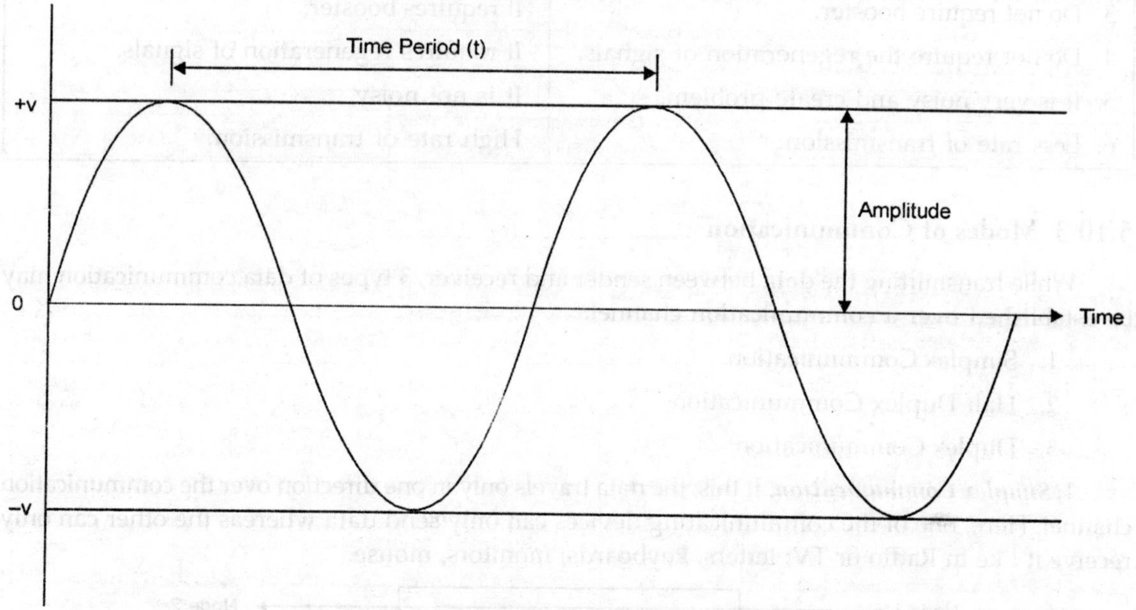

(*i*) ***Amplitude.*** Amplitude can be defined as the maximum displacement gain from the axis. It represents the value of analog signal at a particular instant of time.

(*ii*) **Frequency.** Frequency can be defined as the number of cycles covered per second. It is measured in Hertz (Hz).

(*iii*) ***Phase Angle.*** The phase difference in two signals is the difference of phase when the two waveforms are compared. It is measured in degree.

5.10.2 Digital Transmission

Digital signals are the strings of electronic pulses. A digital signal contains only two discrete values called high or low *i.e.*, 1 or 0 respectively.

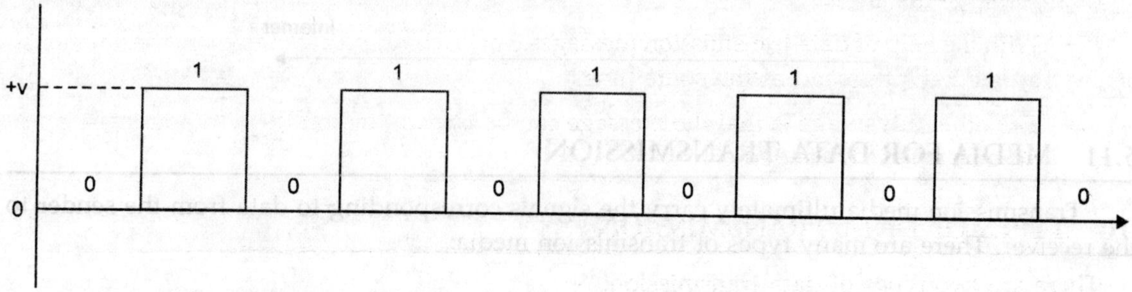

Digital signal format has precise voltages that are not affected by noise or attenuation as compared to analog signals, which are very prone to noise.

Table. Difference between Analog and Digital Signal

Analog Signal	*Digital Signal*
1. Analog signals can travel longer distances.	Digital signal can not travel longer distance.
2. It is more error prone.	It is less error prone.
3. Do not require booster.	It requires booster.
4. Do not require the regeneration of signals.	It requires regeneration of signals.
5. It is very noisy and create problem.	It is not noisy.
6. Less rate of transmission.	High rate of transmission.

5.10.3 Modes of Communication

While transmitting the data between sender and receiver, 3 types of data communication may be established over a communication channel:

1. Simplex Communication
2. Half Duplex Communication
3. Duplex Communication

1. ***Simplex Communication.*** It this, the data travels only in one direction over the communication channel. Here, one of the communicating devices can only send data whereas the other can only receive it like in Radio or TV; letters, keyboards, monitors, mouse.

2. ***Half Duplex Communication.*** It this, the communication channel may be used to communicate the data in both directions but the restriction that at a time, the data may travel in only one direction. *e.g.*,— Talk-back Radio (Walkie-Talkie), Telephone.

3. ***Full Duplex Communication.*** In full duplex mode of transmission data transfer in both the direction from one device to other simultaneously. It means that both the devices (sender and receiver) can transmit the data as well as receive the data at the same time.

e.g., Data transmission in PC's.

5.11 MEDIA FOR DATA TRANSMISSION

Transmission media ultimately carry the signals corresponding to data from the sender to the receiver. There are many types of transmission media:

5.11.1 Twisted Pair Cable

There are two classes of TPC

(i) ***Unshielded TPC.*** This is the most commonly used medium today, due to its usage in the telephone system. This cable can carry both voice as well as data. It consists of two conductors. **PVC or other insulator covers the copper conductors.**

(ii) ***Shielded TPC.*** In 'this' case apart from the insulator, the twisted pair itself is carried by a metal shield and finally by a plastic cover. The metal shield prevents penetration of electromagnetic noise. It also helps eliminate crosstalk. STP is more expensive that UTP.

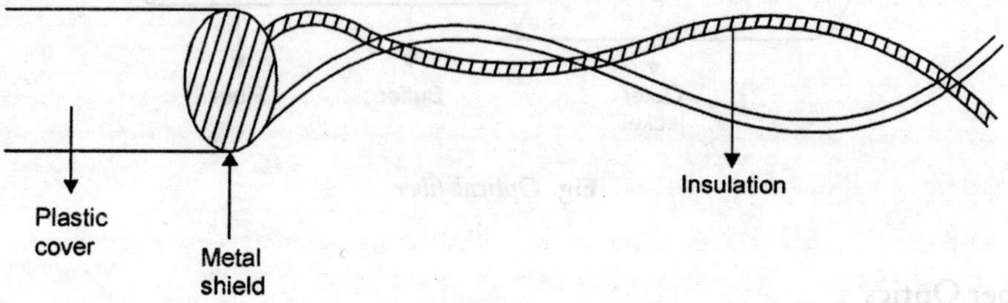

Fig. *STP*

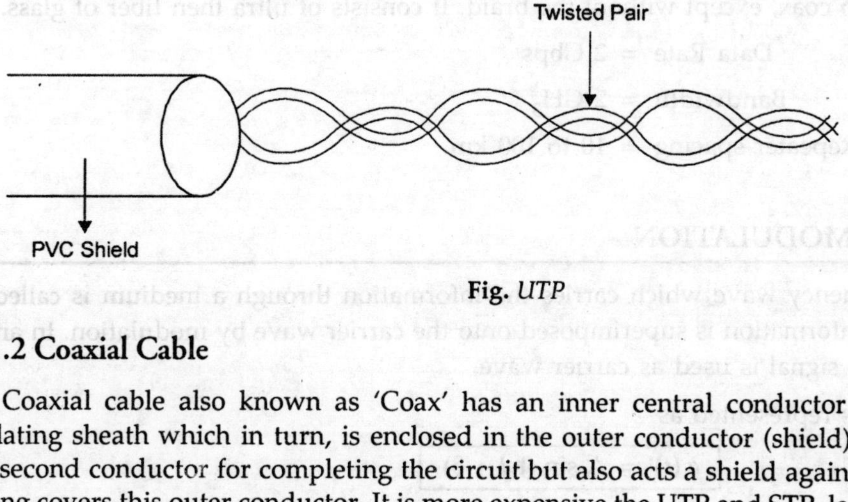

Fig. *UTP*

5.11.2 Coaxial Cable

Coaxial cable also known as 'Coax' has an inner central conductor surrounded by an insulating sheath which in turn, is enclosed in the outer conductor (shield). This acts not only as a second conductor for completing the circuit but also acts a shield against noise. The plastic coating covers this outer conductor. It is more expensive the UTP and STP, less flexible and more reliable and can achieve for higher data rates.

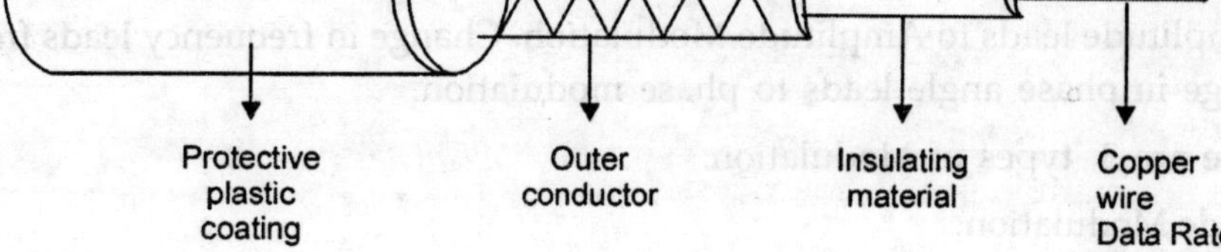

Data Rate : 500 Mbps
Bandwidth = 350 MH_3
R.S. 1 to 10 km

Fig. *Coaxial cable*

5.11.3 Optical Fiber

In case of optical fiber, light is used as a means of signal propagation, instead of electrical signals optical fibers are made up of glass fibers that are enclosed in a plastic jacket. This allows fibers to bend and yet not break. The transmitter at the sender's end of the optical fibre uses a light emitting diode (LED) or laser to emit pulses of light across the fibre. A receiver on the other end makes use of a light sensitive transistor to detect the absence or presence of light to indicate 0 or 1.

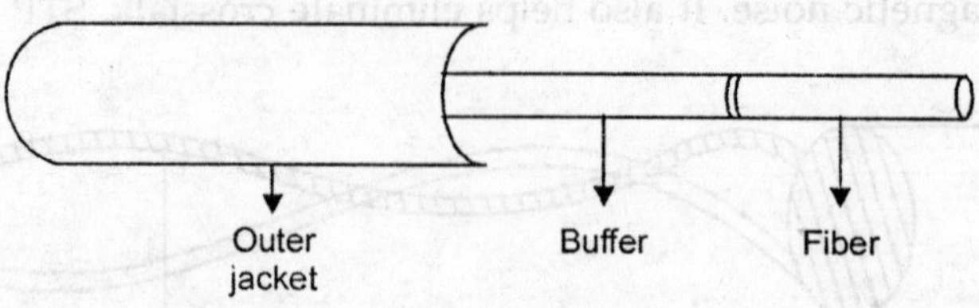

Fig. *Optical fiber*

5.11.4 Fiber Optics

In fiber optics, semiconductor lasers transmit information in the form of light. Fiber optics cables are similar to coax, except without the braid. It consists of ultra then fiber of glass.

Data Rate = 2 Gbps

Bandwidth = $2\ GH_3$

Repeater spacing = 10 to 100 km.

5.12 ANALOG MODULATION

The high frequency wave which carries the information through a medium is called the carrier wave. The information is superimposed onto the carrier wave by modulation. In analog modulation, analog signal is used as carrier wave.

Carrier wave is represented as

$$a(t) = A \sin(wt + \delta)$$

$w = 2\pi f,\ \delta \rightarrow$ phase

where $A \rightarrow$ amplitude

$w = 2\pi f,\ f \rightarrow$ frequency $\delta \rightarrow$ phase angle

Change in Amplitude leads to Amplitude Modulation. Change in frequency leads frequency modulation. Change in phase angle leads to phase modulation.

Basically there are 3 types of Modulation:

1. Amplitude Modulation.
2. Frequency Modulation.
3. Phase Modulation.

5.12.1 Amplitude Modulation

If the amplitude of the carrier wave is changed according to the varying amplitude of waveform, then this process is called amplitude modulation. The AM wave is transmitted over the transmitting end, and at the receiving end, the reverse procedure is adopted to detach the input wave from the AM wave. This process is called. *"demodulation"*.

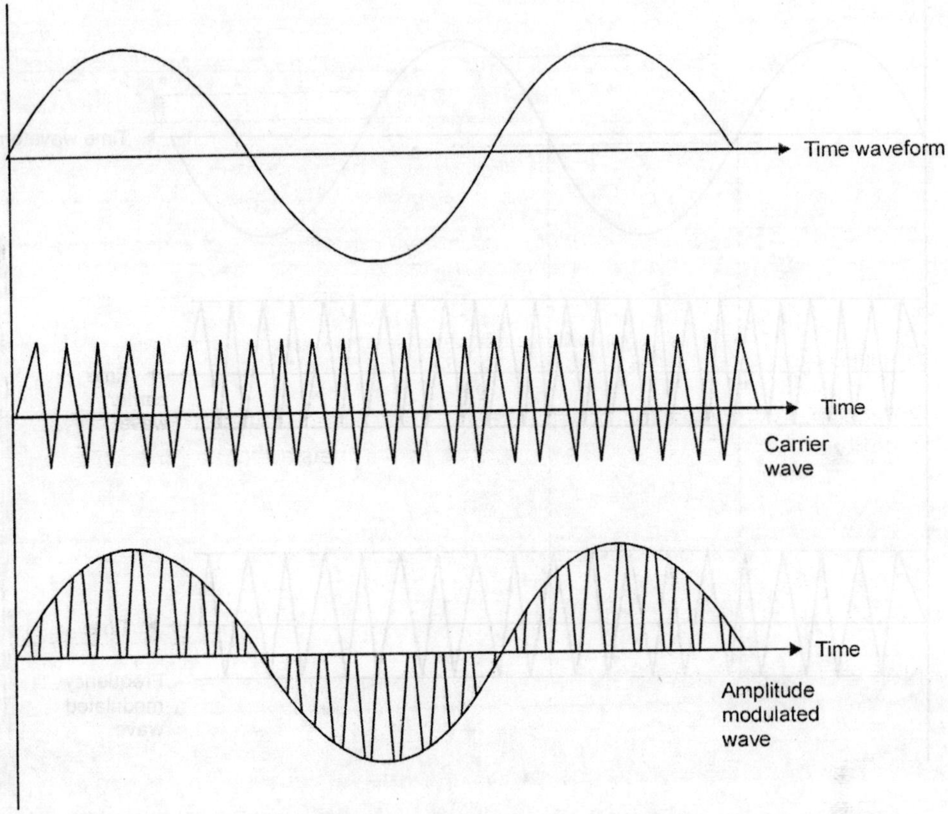

Fig.

- Simple to design.
- Frequency is constt, Amplitude varies.
- Noise spikes at transmission medium interface with the carrier signal.

5.12.2 Frequency Modulation

Here, the frequency of the carrier wave is modified in proportion to the modulating signal. The frequency of the carrier wave is increased according to the increase in the amplitude of the input waveform.

- Amplitude of the carrier remains constant, and frequency varies.
- Signal is always present.
- Loss of signal easily detected.

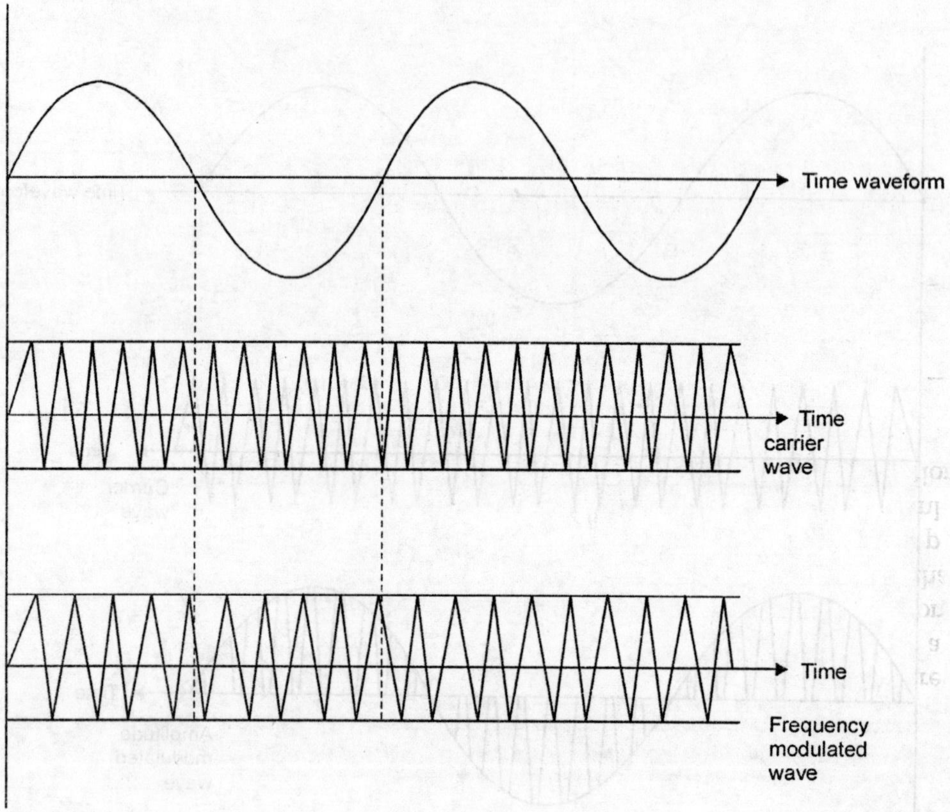

Fig.

5.12.3 Phase Modulation

In this type of modulation, the phase of the carrier wave is varied in accordance with the variations in the input waveform. The phase angle of the carrier wave is changed in terms of the corresponding changes in the amplitude of the input waveform.

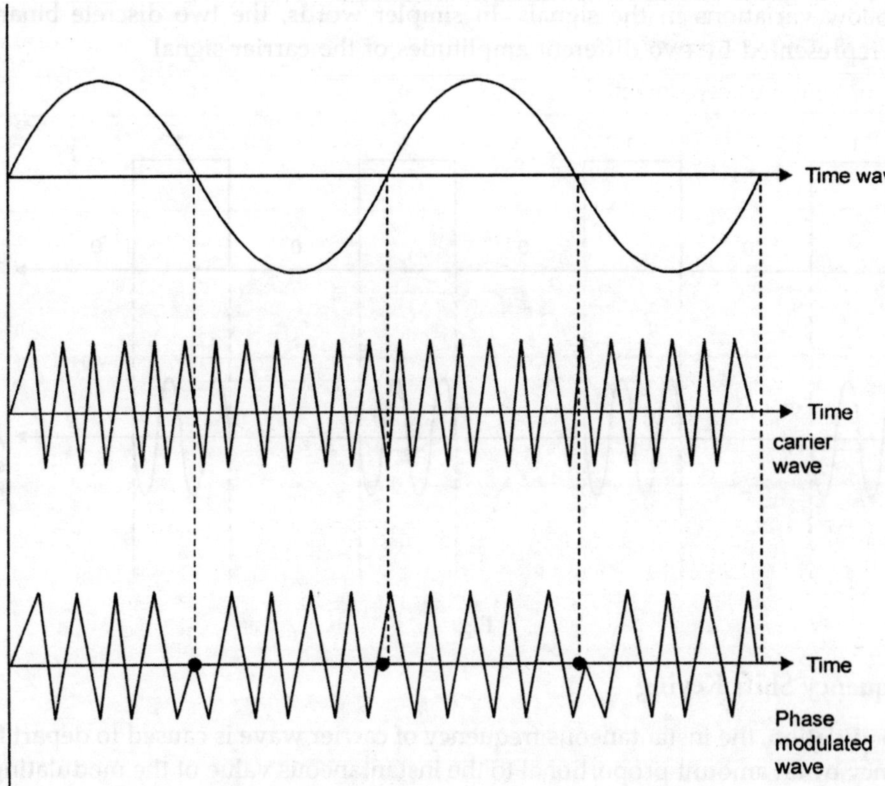

Fig.

The modulated carrier wave is lagying the carrier wave when the modulating frequency is positive and when the modulating frequency is negative, the modulated carrier wave is leading the carrier wave.

5.13 DIGITAL MODULATION

In digital modulation techniques, varying properties such as amplitude frequency or phase of a second signal transmits the digital signals. The sinusoidal carrier wave is used for transmission of digital signals.

There are three types of Digital Modulation:

1. Amplitude Shift Keying (ASK)
2. Frequency Shift Keying (FSK)
3. Phase Shift Keying (PSK)

5.13.1 Amplitude Shift Keying

In this modulation, the amplitude of a carrier wave is varied in accordance with a characteristic of the modulating signal. The frequency of the carrier remains the some. Only the amplitude changes to follow variations in the signals. In simpler words, the two discrete binary digits (0 and 1) are represented by two different amplitudes of the carrier signal.

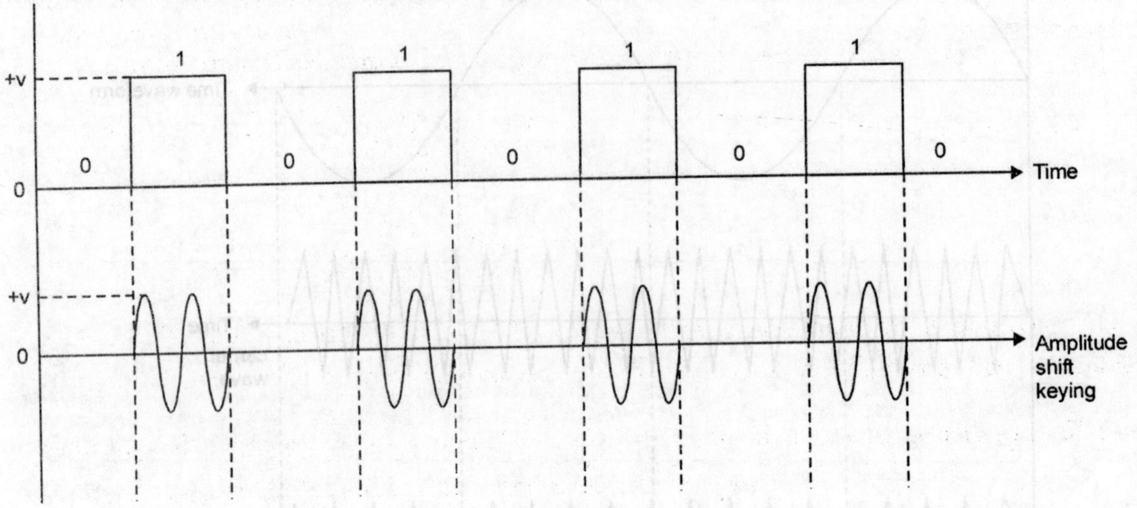

Fig.

5.13.2 Frequency Shift Keying

In this modulation, the instantaneous frequency of carrier wave is caused to depart from the centre frequency by an amount proportional to the instantaneous value of the modulating signal. In simple words frequency modulation is the method of impressing modulating signal onto 9 lamer signal wave by varying its instantaneous frequency rather than its amplitude. In this modulation technique, we keep the amplitude and the phase of the carrier signals unaltered. We assign a certain frequency f_1 to denote 1 and f_0 to denote 0.

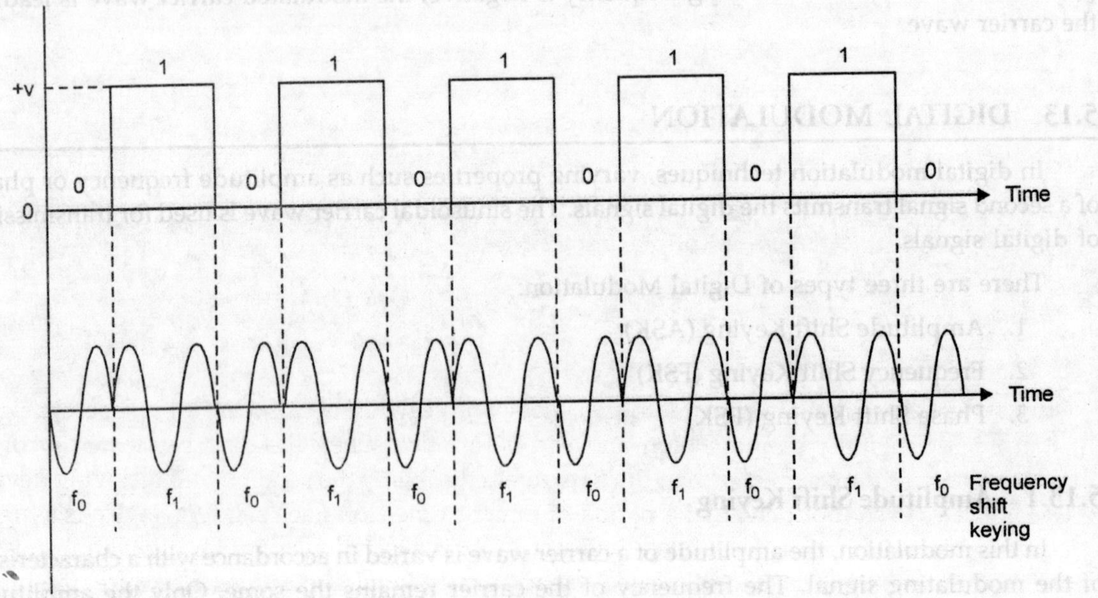

Fig.

5.13.3 Phase Shift Keying

In PSK, we keep the amplitude and the frequency of the carrier signal unchanged and only change the phase to denote 0s and 1s. In this, we change the timing of the carrier wave abruptly to encode data.

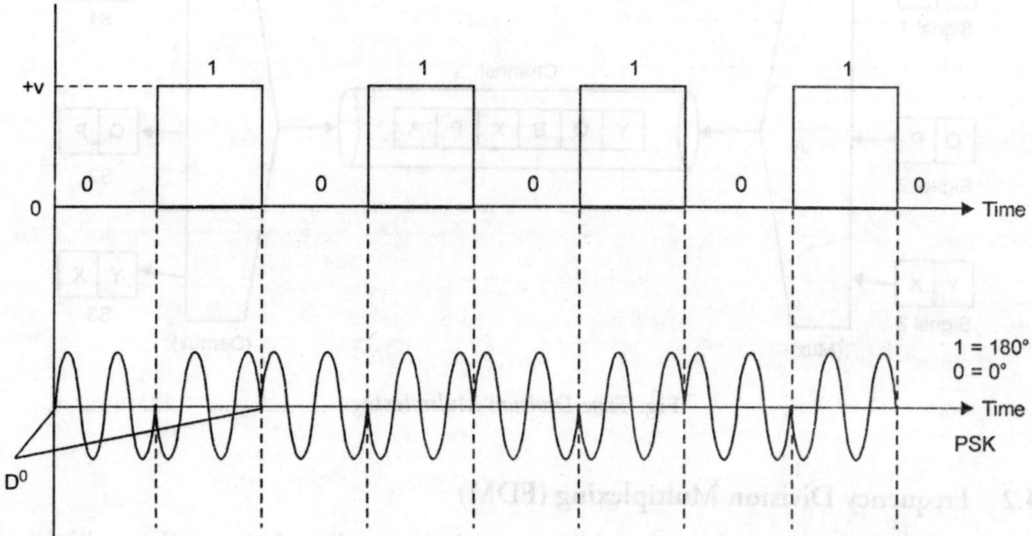

Fig.

5.14 MULTIPLEXING OF SIGNALS

Multiplexing is a technique used for sending several signals simultaneously over a common medium. Multiplexing divides the physical line or a medium into logical segments called channels. In multiplexing, different channels carry data simultaneously over the same physical medium. Hardware equipment called multiplexer (MUX) combines the inputs from different sources, and loads them on different channels of a medium. The mux is responsible for both multiplexing and demultiplexing. Therefore, it has to be present at both the ends of a medium. Multiplexing allows us to add new channels in the same existing telephone line without having to install a new line.

They are basically two types:

1. Frequency Division Multiplexing (FDM)
2. Time Division Multiplexing (TDM)

5.14.1 Time Division Multiplexing (TDM)

TDM divides the main signal into time-slots, with each time-slot carrying a separate signal. It is used for digital communication and can be applied when the data rate capacity of the transmission medium is greater than the data rate required by the sending and receiving devices. TDM allocates each input channel a period of time or time-slot. Each sending device is assigned the transmission path for a predefined time-slot. TDM is a technique used for digital transmission only. In this case, the time slice allocated to each source would be different because, the time is allocated to a source node until it completes transmission and each node may want different amount of data to be transmitted.

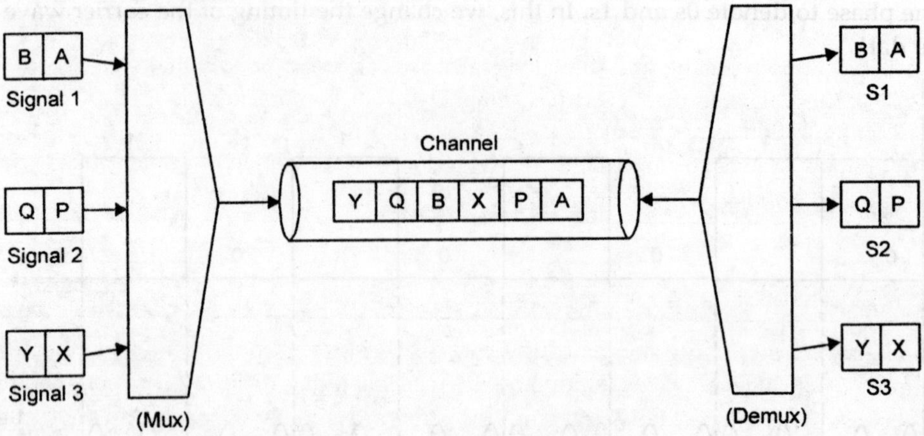

Fig. *Time Division Multiplexing*

5.14.2 Frequency Division Multiplexing (FDM)

FDM is used when the bandwidth of the transmission medium between the multiplexer and demultiplexer is much greater than the requirements from any one stream being multiplexed. FDM is usually used for broadband analog transmissions. In this techniques, signals from each sending device is modulated using carrier waves with different frequencies. These modulated signals are then combined into a single composite signal that is transported over the common medium. Each modulated signal acts as a channel. One of the most common examples of FDM is the transmission of radio stations.

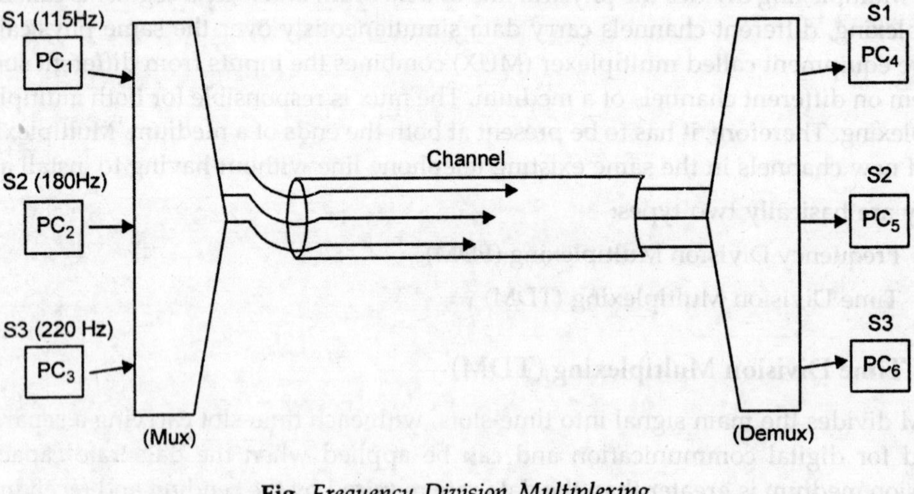

Fig. *Frequency Division Multiplexing*

Table. Difference between FDM and TDM

FDM	*TDM*
1. Cost is less.	Cost is high.
2. Used in both analog and digital signals.	Used in only digital signals.
3. FDM less flexible than TDM (*i.e.*, channel configuration is not easy)	It is more flexible.
4. Simplex system to implement	Not simpler to implement.
5. Not so popular when compared to TDM.	It is more popular.

5.15 SWITCHING

On a network, switching means routing traffic by setting up temporary connection between two or more network points. This is done by devices located at different locations on the network, called switches. In a switched network, some switches are directly connected to the communicating devices while others are used for routing or forwarding information. These are basically two types:

1. Circuit switching
2. Packet switching

5.15.1 Circuit Switching

Circuit switching technique creates a fixed bandwidth channel, called a circuit, between the source and the destination *i.e.*, there exist at least one dedicated path between sender and receiver. This circuit is reserved exclusively for a particular information flow and no other flow can use it. Other circuits are isolated from each other, and thus their environment is well controlled. The path taken by data between its source and destination is determined by the circuit on which it is

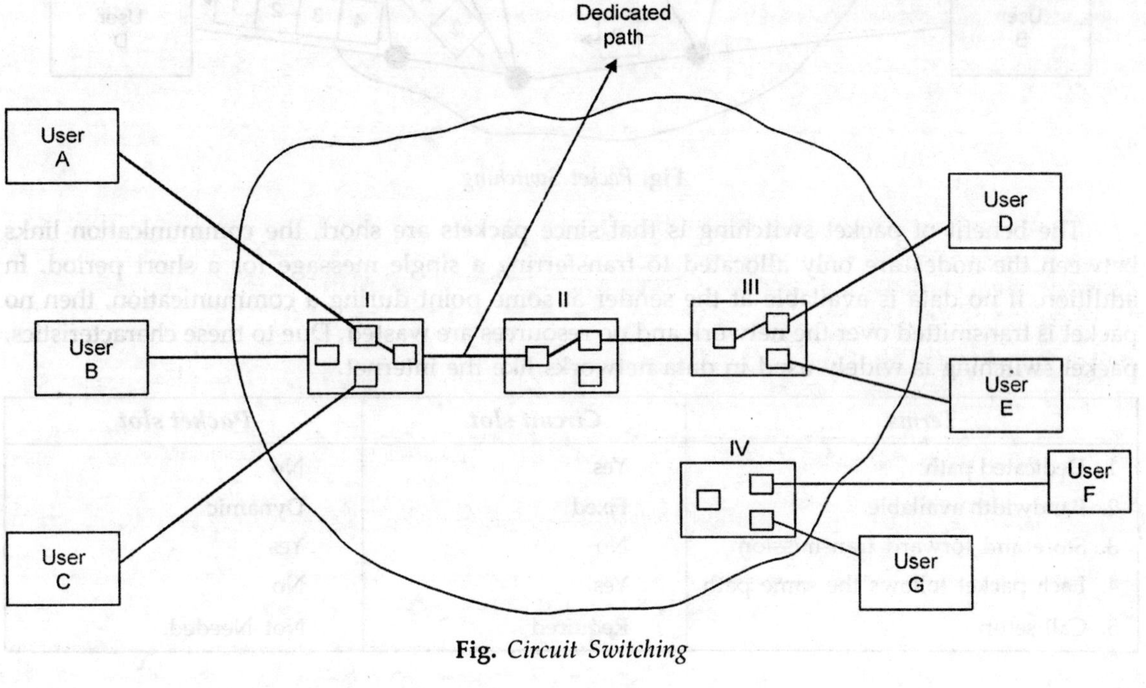

Fig. *Circuit Switching*

flowing and does not change during the lifetime of the connection. The circuit is terminated when the connection is closed. Therefore, this method is called circuit switching.

e.g., Public Switched Telephone Network (PSTN)

In circuit switching data is transmitted with no delay. This method is simple and requires no special facilities. Therefore it is well suited for low speed data transmission.

5.15.2 Packet Switching

Packet switching introduces the idea of breaking data into packets, which are discrete units of potentially variable length blocks of data. Apart from data, these packets also contain a header with control information like the destination address, priority of the message, and so on. These packets are passed by the source point to its local packet switching exchange. If the channel is not free, then the packet is placed in a queue until the channel becomes free. As each packet is received at each transitional PSE along the route, it is forwarded on the appropriate link mixed with other packets. At the destination PSE, the packet is finally passed to its destination.

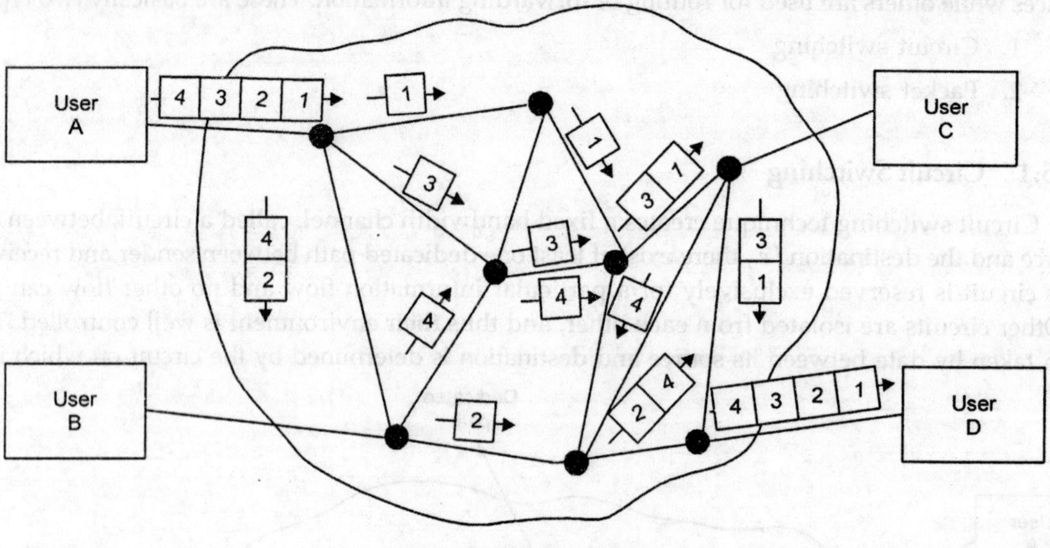

Fig. *Packet Switching*

The benefit of packet switching is that since packets are short, the communication links between the nodes are only allocated to transferring a single message for a short period. In addition, if no data is available at the sender at some point during a communication, then no packet is transmitted over the network and no resources are wasted. Due to these characteristics, packet switching is widely used in data networks like the internet.

Terms	*Circuit slot*	*Packet slot*
1. Dedicated path	Yes	No
2. Bandwidth available	Fixed	Dynamic
3. Store and forward transmission	No	Yes
4. Each packet follows the same path	Yes	No
5. Call setup	Required	Not Needed.

EXERCISES

1. What are flip-flops? What are the problems in SR flip-flops? Explain by using the characteristics table for SR flip-flop.
2. Define BCD code. What is the disadvantage of using BCD code? How do we remove this problem as BCD code Weighted code?
3. What do you mean by digital modulation? Explain briefly the various digital modulation techniques.
4. Differentiate between FDM and TDM.
5. Convert the following:
   (*i*) FFFF hexadecimal to Decimal format.
   (*ii*) Decimal 31.54 to Binary format.
   (*iii*) Binary 11.0001 to Decimal format.
   (*iv*) Decimal 15 to Gray code format.
   (*v*) Hexadecimal 7F2 to Octal format.
6. What are NAND gates, why it is called a universal gate?
7. Draw a full adder using two half adder. Also give truth table.
8. Explain why multiplexer is used with an example.
9. Find the binary sum and convert it into octal format.

(*i*)	(*ii*)
11001011	1000011
+ 10110110	+ 0111110
________	________

6

DATA COMMUNICATION AND NETWORK

6.1 COMPUTER NETWORK

Computer Network is a collection of two or more computers, which are connected together to share information and resources. The main purpose of computer networking is 'sharing'. When two computers are linked together using a cable that allows them to share data, it is known as networked environment, the computers and other devices are connected together through a cable. This is called network and the concept of connected computers sharing resources is called networking.

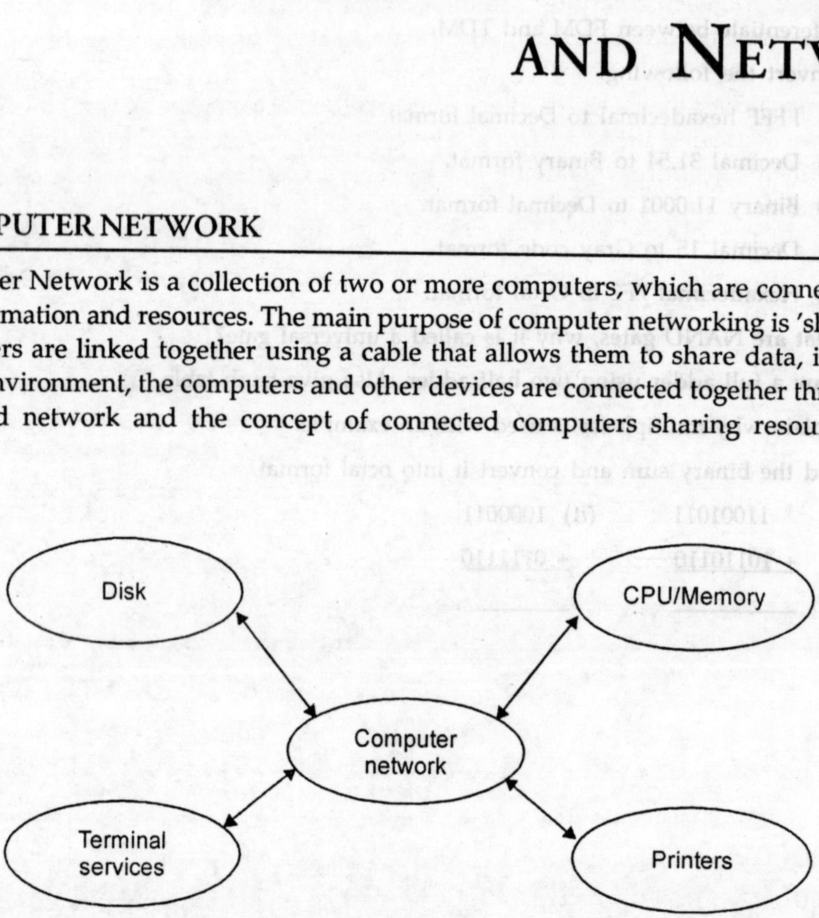

Advantages of Computer Network

- Resource Sharing
- Enhanced Performance
- Improved Reliability
- Modular Expandability

6.2 TYPES OF COMPUTER NETWORK

Based on the arrangements of computer there are two types of computer networks:

1. Client server Network
2. Peer-to peer Network

6.2.1 Client Server Network

It this network, each computer is either a client or a server, to complete a particular task, these exists a centralised host computer known as server and a user's individual workstation known as client. In simple words client requests a service from the server and the server responds by providing that service. Client/server network centralises functions and applications in one or more dedicated file servers. The servers provide access to resources, while the clients have access to the resources available on the servers. A typical example of client-server is sending an email.

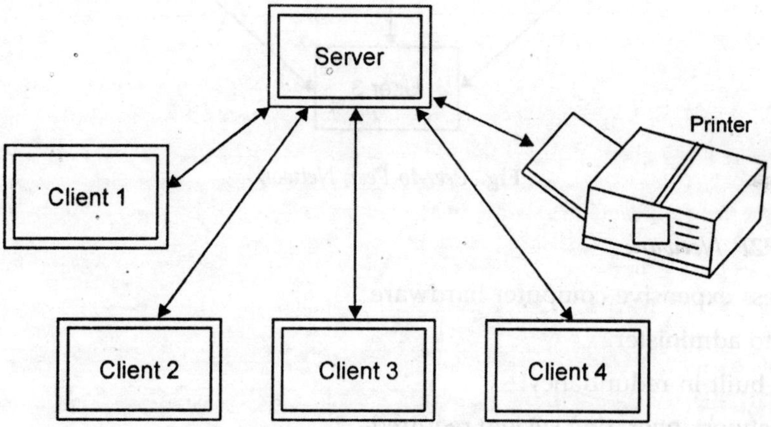

Fig. *Client-Server Network*

Advantages of client-server Network

- It is very secure network.
- Better performance.
- Centralized Backup.
- It is very reliable.

Disadvantages

- Required professional Administration.
- More hardware intensive.

6.2.2 Peer-to-Peer Network

A peer-to-peer (or P2P computer network does not rely on dedicated servers for communication instead it uses direct connection between clients (peer). A pure P2P network does not have the notion of clients or servers, but only equal peer nodes that simultaneously function as both 'clients' and 'servers' to other nodes on the network *i.e.*, every node is able to initiate or complete any supported transaction with the other connected node. The upper limit of the number of nodes that can function as both clients and servers on a P2P network is between 10 and 25. P2P networks have been designed primarily for small to medium local area networks. These networks have gained widespread popularity on the internet.

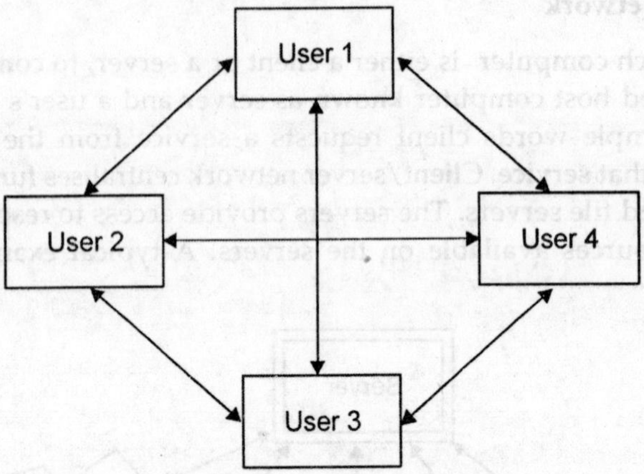

Fig. *Peer-to-Peer Network*

Advantages of P2P Network

- Use less expensive computer hardware
- Easy to administer.
- More built in redundancy.
- No Network operating system required.

Disadvantages

- Not very secure.
- Hard to take backup.
- Might hurt user's performance.
- Hard to maintain version control.

6.3 INTRODUCTION TO LAN, WAN AND MAN

6.3.1 Local Area Network (LAN)

A LAN is a computer network that covers only a small geographical area ranging from 100 metres to 1 kms, such as an office, home or buildings. They are privately owned. In a LAN, computers connected have a network operating system installed onto them. On most LANs, cables are used to connect the computers. Generally LAN offers a bandwidth of 100 Mbps.

For example,–Computers in a Lab.

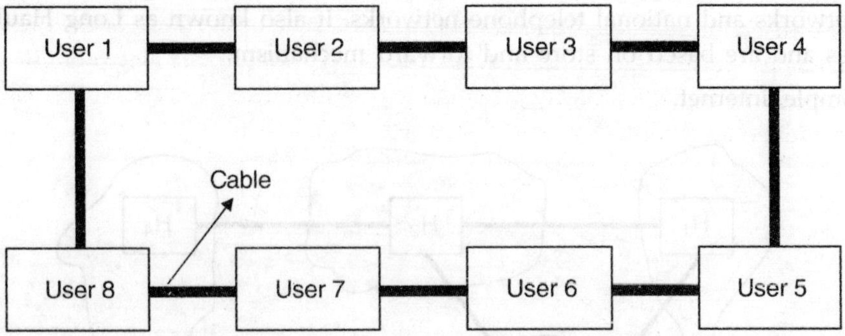

Fig. *Local Areal Network*

6.3.2 Metropolitan Area Network (MAN)

A MAN is a network of computers spread over a 'metropolitan' area such as a city and its suburbs. The range of MAN lies between 5 to 50 KMs. As the name suggests, this sort of network is usually reserved for metropolitan areas where the city bridges its local area networks with a series of back bones, making one large network for the entire city. It uses high speed data transfer medium like fiber optics.

For example, Cable Television Network.

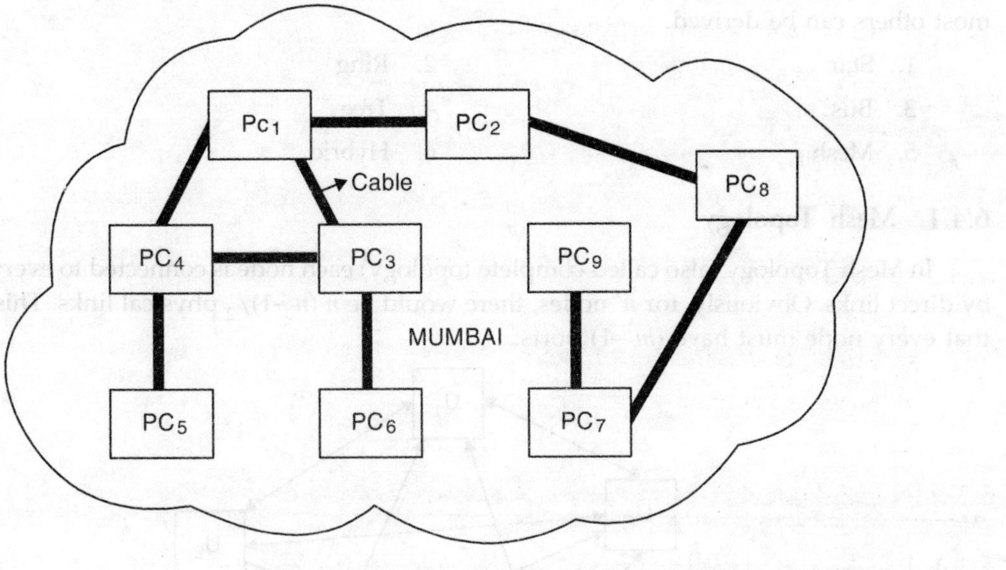

Fig. *Metropolitan Area Network*

6.3.3 Wide Area Network (WAN)

A WAN, is a system of inter connecting many computers over a large geographical area such as cities, states, countries or even the whole world. These kinds of networks use telephone lines, satellites links, and other long-range communications technologies to connect. Such networks are designed to serve an area of hundreds or thousands of miles such as public and private packet switching networks and national telephone networks. It also known as Long Haul Network. It uses switches and are based on store and forward mechanism.

For example, internet.

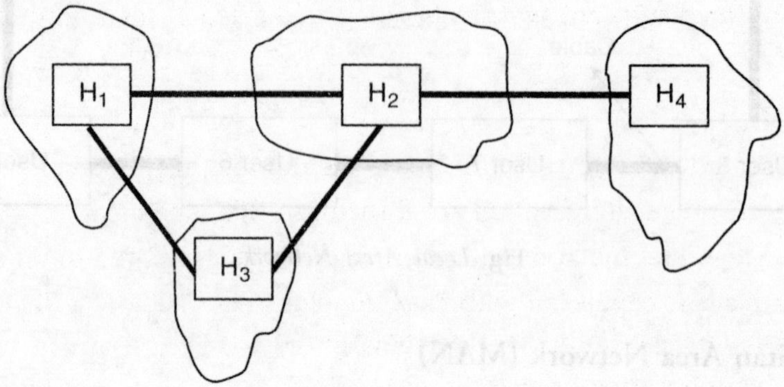

Fig. *Wide Area Network*

6.4 NETWORK TOPOLOGIES

Network Topologies refers to the connection of different computers and deals with problem of how best various computers can be interconnected. There are six basic topologies from which most others can be derived.

1. Star
2. Ring
3. Bus
4. Tree
5. Mesh
6. Hybrid.

6.4.1 Mesh Topology

In Mesh Topology (also called complete topology) each node is connected to every other node by direct links. Obviously, for *n'* nodes, there would be $n\ (n-1)/_2$ physical links. This also means that every node must have $(m-1)$ ports.

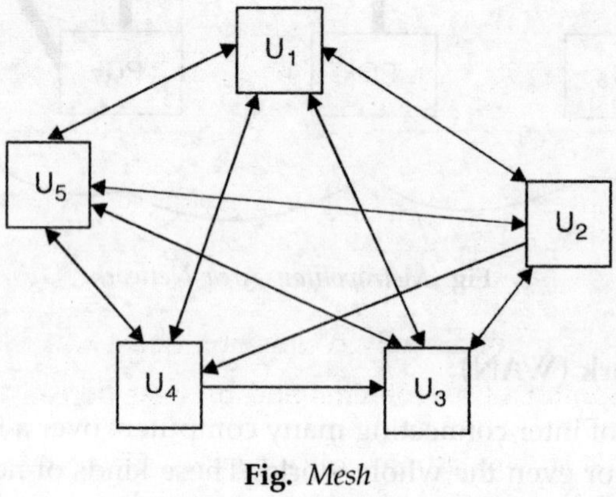

Fig. *Mesh*

Advantages

- The Mesh topology does not give traffic congestion problems, due to the dedicated link.
- Point to point links make fault identification and fault isolation easy in this topology.
- It is also robust in nature, *i.e,* fone link is down, all the rest of the Network can still continue.
- When any message sent or travels along dedicated P line, only intended recipient sees it.

Disadvantages

- The use of dedicated links will increase the number of I/O ports.
- Installation and reconfiguration are difficult in this topology.
- The cable length is much more in this topology as compared to others.

Question: A college is connected with mesh topology consisting of 8 devices. Calculate the total number of table links and number of ports required.

Number to units = $n\ (n - 1)/2 = 28$

Number: Port = $(m - 1) = 7$

6.4.2 Star Topology

In the star topology, the various computers are attached to a single point. The center of the star Network is called Hub. The function of the Hub is to facilitate the communication between the two computers. It receives the required from the computer sending the data and delivers the data to the destination computer.

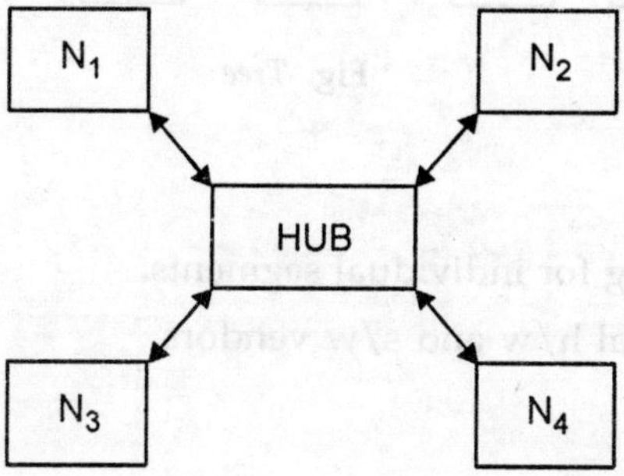

Fig. *Star*

Advantages

- It is less expensive than mesh topology.
- It is easy to install and re-configure.
- Less Cabling is required.
- Moves and deletions involves only connection between the device and the hub.
- Hub is used to monitor link problems and by pass defective links.

Disadvantages

- Two terminals/devices can't interact directly, *i.e.*, they have to go via central controller Hub.
- The Network dependence on the main computer is more *i.e.*, if the central computer (Hub) breakdown the entire Network stops functioning.

6.4.3 Tree Topology

Tree Topology can be derived from the star topology. The tree topology requires the computers to be linked in a hierarichal way. Nodes in a tree are linked to a control hub that controls the traffic to the Network. In this case, every node is connected to some hub. However, only a few nodes are connected directly to the central hub. Tree Topology is a collection of several bus topology Network with a common bus.

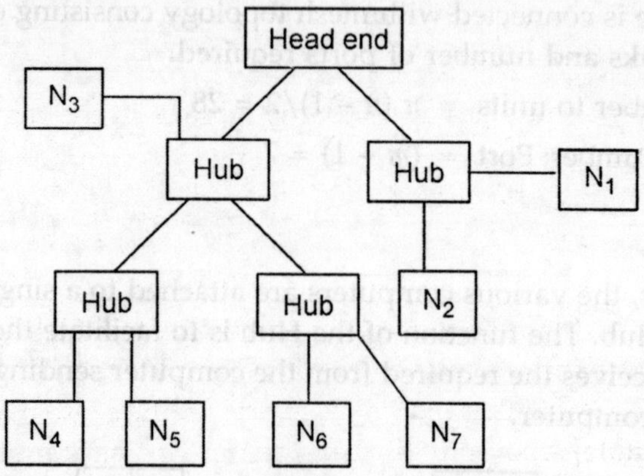

Fig. *Tree*

Advantages

- Point-to-point wiring for individual segments.
- Supported by several h/w and s/w vendors.

Disadvantages

- Overall length of each segment is limited by the type of cabling used.
- If the backbone line breaks, the entire segment goes down.
- More difficult to configure and wire than other topologies.

6.4.4 Bus Topology

In bus topology, the bus is used as a carrier for data packets. The computer communicates by sending various packets and each packet contains the address of destination. Packets are traversed along the bus and all the computers on the N/W have access to the bus. The common bus is used by all computers as a medium for communication.

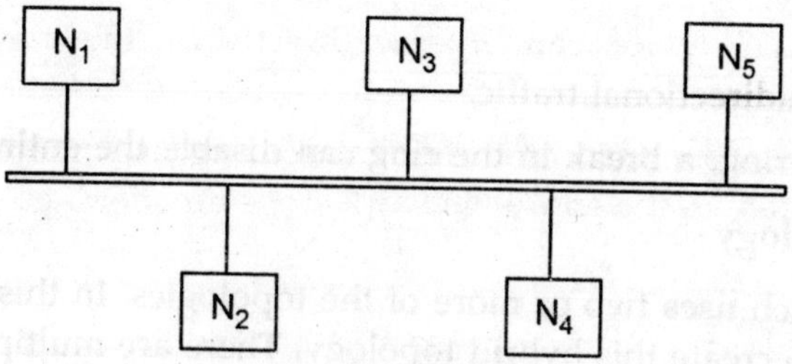

Fig. *Bus Topology*

Advantages

- Easy to install. Easy to connect a computer or peripheral to a linear bus.
- Only the backbone cable stretches through the entire facility.

Disadvantages

- Entire Network shuts down if there is a break in the main cable.
- Difficult to identify the problem if the entire Network shuts down.
- Not meant to be used as a stand alone solution in a large building.

6.4.5 Ring Topology

In Ring Topology, each node is directly connected to only its two adjacent neighbours. In this the computers on the Network form a logical ring. The ring represents a cable which connects all the computers. It may be noted that the ring is logical, in the sense that the first computer connects to the second one by cable, second to third and so on. The last computer in the Network connect to first one by cable, there by forming a logical ring. If a node wants to send something to a distant node on a ring, it has to go through many intermediate nodes, which act like repeaters, reproducing the incoming bit stream with full signals on the outgoing line.

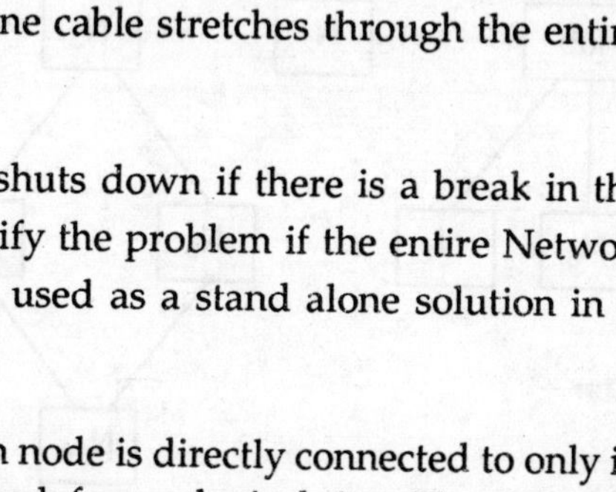

Fig. *Ring Topology*

Advantages

- A ring is relatively easy to install and re-configure. Each device is linked only to its immediate neighbours.
- To add or delete a device requires moving only two connections.
- Fault isolation is simplified.

Disadvantages

- Supports unidirectional traffic.
- In a simple ring, a break in the ring can disable the entire Network.

6.4.6 Hybrid Topology

It is the one, which uses two or more of the topologies. In this case, the bus, star and ring topologies are used to create this hybrid topology. There are multiple ways in which this could be created.

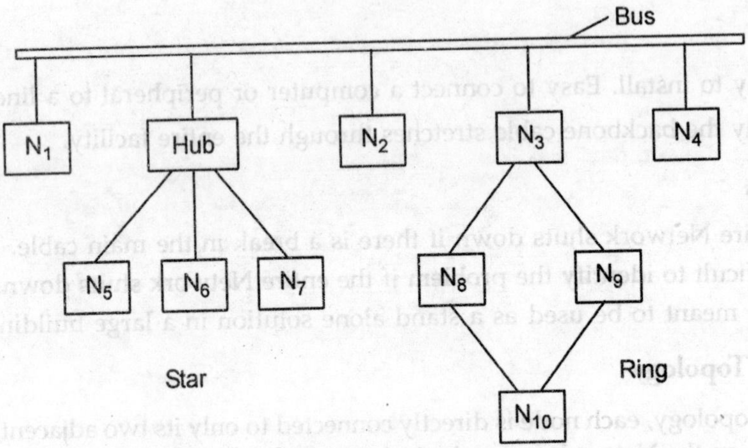

Fig. *Hybrid Topology*

6.5 BASIC CONCEPTS IN COMPUTER NETWORK

Networks are becoming more complicated and more pervasive everyday. Terms likes switch, router, gateways, and hubs have become part of our everyday language.

6.5.1 Network Interface Card (NIC)

NIC is the first contact between a machine and the network. It connects clients, servers and pheripherals to the network through a port. Most network interfaces comes on small circuit board that can be inserted onto one of the computer motherboard's slots. Each N/C is associated with a unique address called its Media Access Control (MAC) address. The MAC address helps in sending information to its intended destination. N/C are a major factor in determining the speed and performance of a network.

1. ***Repeater.*** A repeater is the most basic device on a network. Signals that carry information within a network can travel a fixed distance before attenuation endangers the integrity of the data. A repeater installed on the link receives signal, regenerates it and sends the refreshed copy back to the link. Repeaters are most commonly used to extend a network cable. Without the repeater, the signal will be too weak for the computers on each end to reliably understand.

2. ***Hub.*** A hub is a small box like, that connects individual devices on a network so that they can communicate with one another. The hub operates by gathering the signals from individual network devices, optionally amplifying the signals, and then sending them onto all other connected devices. A hub can be thought of as the centre of a by cycle well, where the spokes meet. Hub is mostly used to connect multiple machines to the same LAN.

3. ***Switch.*** A switch is a multi-port bridge. It connects individual devices on a network so that they can communicate with one another. The behaviour of a switch is the some as a bridge. It is capable of inspecting the data packets as they are received, determining the source and destination device of that packet, and forwarding that packet appropriately.

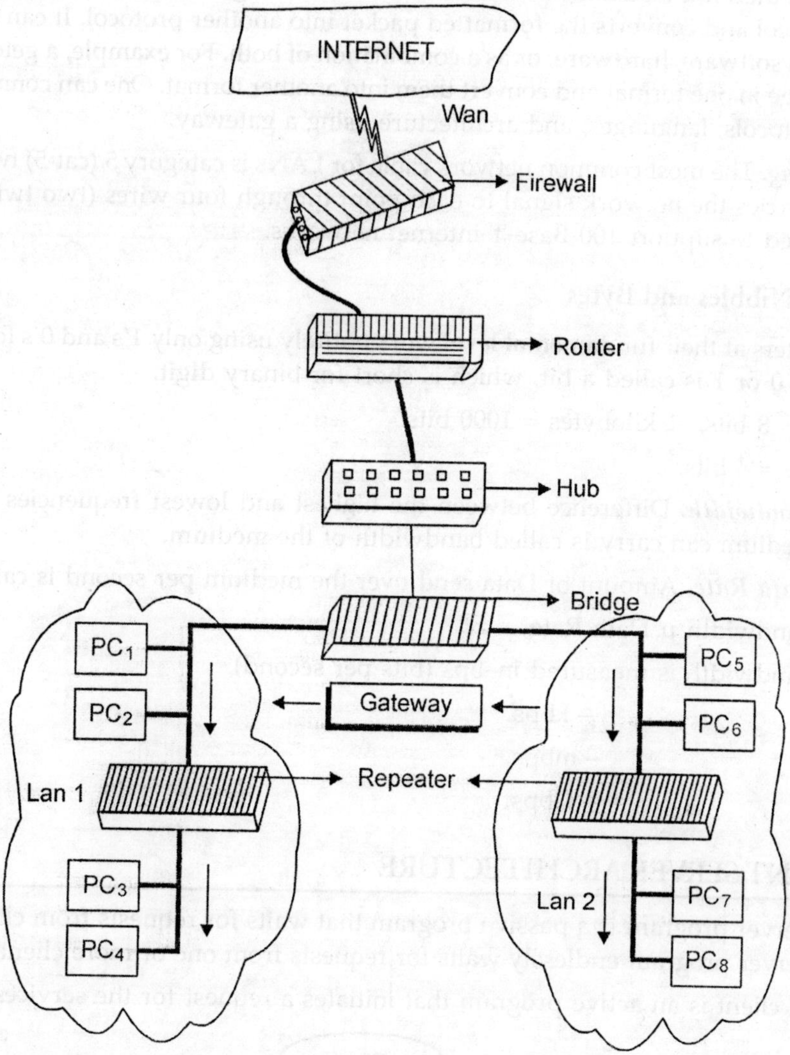

4. ***Bridge.*** A bridge is a device that allows division of a large network into two smaller, more efficient networks. It monitors the information traffic on both sides of the network so that it can pass packets of information to the correct location. A bridge first looks at the MAC address of the sender and creates a mapping between the part and the sender's MAC address . Bridges can be used to connect different types of cabling, or physical topologies.

5. ***Router.*** A router is an essential network device for interconnecting two or more networks. Router's aim is to trace the best route for information to travel. A router creates and/or maintain a table, called a routing table that stores the best routes to certain network destinations. While bridges know the addresses of all computer on each side of the network, routers know the addresses of computers Routers can even listen to the entire network to determine which sections

are the busiest Routers are generally expensive and difficult to configure and maintain. They are critical components of a network, if they fail, the network services will be significantly impaired.

6. *Gateway.* A gateway is an internet working device, which joins two different networks protocols together. It is also known as protocol converter. A gateway accepts the packet formatted for one protocol and converts the formatted packet into another protocol. It can be implemented completely in software, hardware, or as a combination of both. For example, a geteway can receive e-mail message in one format and convert them into another format. One can connect systems with different protocols, languages, and architecture using a gateway.

7. *Cabling.* The most common network cable for LANs is category 5 (cat-5) twisted-pair cable. This cable carries the network signal to each point through four wires (two twisted pairs). Cat-5 cable is used to support 100 Base-T internet networks.

6.5.2 Bits, Nibbles and Bytes

Computers at their fundamental level work entirely using only 1's and 0's for numbers. Each one of these 0 or 1 is called a bit, which is short for binary digit.

1 Byte = 8 bits, 1 kilobytes = 1000 bits.

1 nibble = 4 bits.

1. ***Bandwidth.*** Difference between the highest and lowest frequencies of signals that a medium can carry is called bandwidth of the medium.
2. ***Data Rate.*** Amount of Data send over the medium per second is called Data rate

   Bandwidth μ Data Rate

   Bandwidth is measured in–bps (bits per second)

   – kbps.

   – mbps.

   – Gbps.

6.6 CLIENT SERVER ARCHITECTURE

- Server program is a passive program that waits for requests from clients. Therefore, a server program endlessly waits for requests from one or more clients.
- A client is an active program that initiates a request for the services of that server.

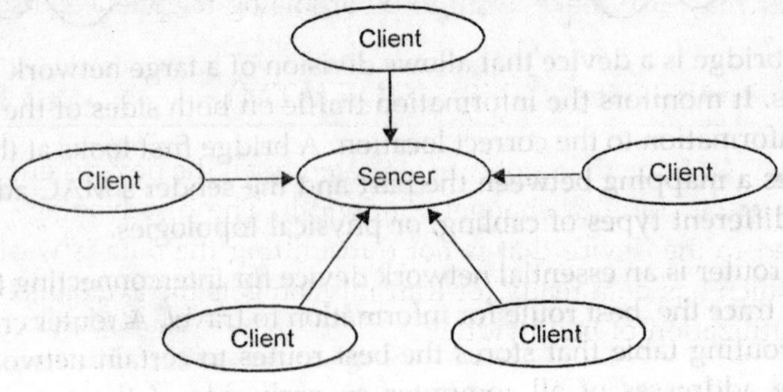

C-S Model

- Processes that need some services are called clients and processes that provides the services are called servers.
- The client sends the request to the server sound server replies back to the clients and sends the result after performing the required processing.

6.7 INTEGRATED SERVICE DIGITAL NETWORK (ISDN)

ISDN is the most powerful tool for various services such as voice, images and video and multimedia data communication over the telephone network. ISDN may be viewed as a logical extension to the digitalization of telephone network and has become very common in the western countries. In India, too the various mail network service provides such as DOT, VSNL and MTNL are providing this service to users. In ISDN the voice, image, video and multimedia data is transmitted over the telephone line in digital form.

6.7.1 ISDN Services

- High speed data transmissions at 64 kbps.
- High quality voice transmission at 64 kbps.
- Desktop video conferencing using a single ISDN lines.
- High quality conferencing on dial-up basis between any two ISDN users by three ISDN lines.

6.7.2 Types of ISDN

The ISDN works in two modes:

(*i*) BRI (Basic Rate Interface) local ISP users.

(*ii*) PRI (Primary Rate Interface) Used for ISDN compatible EPABX etc.

ISDN Versus Analog Telephone Line:

- In Normal telephone line, the user can make a voice call and the voice data is transmitted in analog form, which is normally vulnerable to distortions. In ISDN, the multimedia data *i.e,* voice data or image graphics is transmitted, over the telephone lines in digital form.
- In ISDN the user may establish two independent calls to other users over the telephone pair of existing telephone line. In normal telephony, one call is possible at one time.
- ISDN user may also make a call to other analog telephone subscribers.

6.8 ASYNCHRONOUS TRANSFER MODE (ATM)

In synchronous TDM, the time slots are allocated to all the devices one by one. Therefore all the devices get an equal share of channel bandwidth. The disadvantage in STDM is that the bandwidth allocated to the device that is not transmitting the data is wasted. In asynchronous TDM, the device which has data ready for transmission gets the available bandwidth. Therefore making optimum utilization of bandwidth.

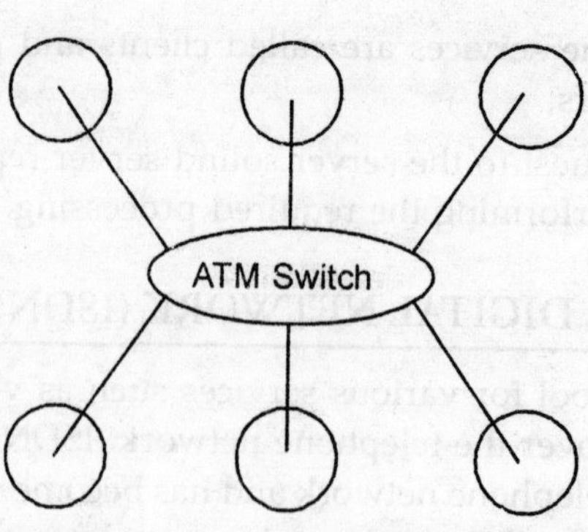

6.8.1 ATM

ATM scheme is widely used for data communication in telecommunication Network. ATM Network user an ATM switch which receives the request for data transfer from different computers. The ATM switch facilitates the data transfer in asynchronous mode. Various computers are connected to the ATM switch. The ATM switch connects the sender's and receiver's computers and transfers the packets to destination at a high speed.

6.9 TOKEN BASED PROTOCOL

1. Token Bus protocol
2. Token Ring Protocol
3. Slotted Ring Protocol

6.9.1 Token Bus Protocol

This protocol is also commonly used for the N/W based on the bus topology. In this case, the devices connected to the bus form a logical ring. This protocol uses a control packet called "token". The token is circulated in the logical ring and passes from one node to another. The device holding the token becomes the owner of the bus for the period it continues to hold the token. The holder of the token may transmit the data. Holder of token may poll another device and may send the requests.

6.9.2 Token Ring Protocol

This protocol is widely used in the ring N/W for access control. The protocol employs a token which is circulated in the logical ring.

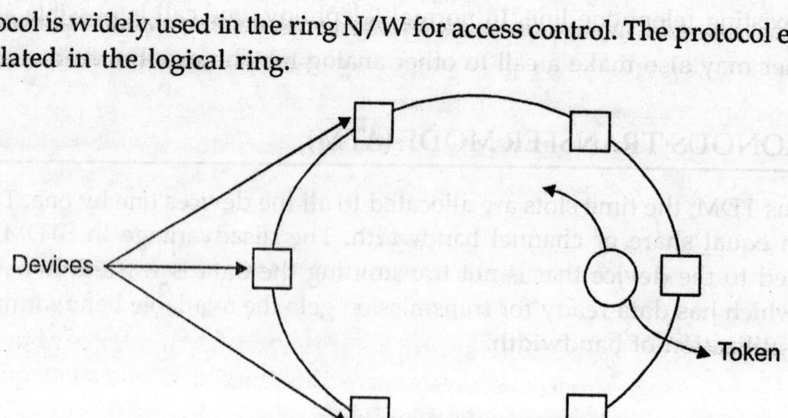

Fig. *Token Ring protocol*

The advantage of this protocol is that it utilizes the bandwidth of the medium to full benefit. The disadvantage of this protocol is its complexity.

6.9.3 Slotted Ring Protocol

Slotted ring protocol is used in ring N/W. Unlike token ring protocol, there are several fixed length slots continuously travelling in the logical ring.

6.10 CSMA/CD

6.10.1 Carrier Sense Multiple Access with Collision Detection

The CSMA/CD protocol is most widely used for access control on bus topology. The access of common medium (bus) is available to all the modes on the N/W. The node which wants to communicate to another node senses the medium and if there is no data in transit, it places the data on the bus and the destination node receives the data.

The advantage of this protocol is its simplicity while the major disadvantage of this protocol is that under heavy load, the performance degrades drastically.

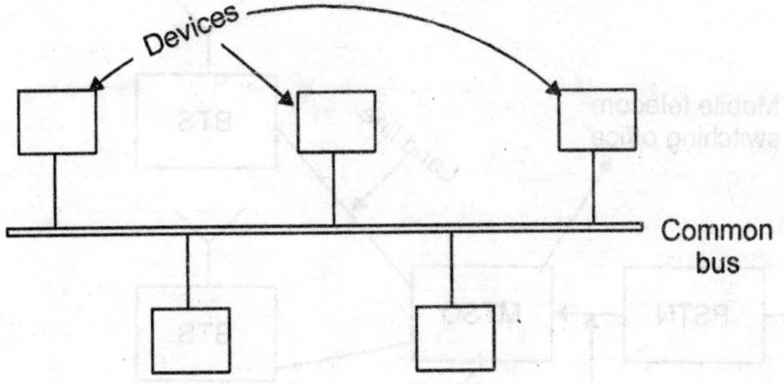

Fig. *CSMA/CD Protocol*

6.11 MOBILE COMMUNICATION

The mobile communication also known as wireless communication transport electromagnetic waves without using a physical conductor. The signals propagate through air. The primary objective of this system is to allow customers to use their own personal phones while they are on the move. The handset is small enough to go into their pockets and a customer will be connected to a communication system anywhere any time.

There are two cellular communication technologies, which are both popular and coexist.

1. GSM (Global System for Mobile Communication) used in Europe, Far East and in India by BSNL, Airtel, Hutch, Spice etc.
2. CDMA (Code Division Multiple Access) popular in U.S.A Japan, India by Reliance and Tata Telecom.

Both GSM and CDMA, use so-called spread spectrum wireless technology but the modulation methods are different. As the modulation system are different the mobile telephones use different technologies, and they are not interchangeable.

6.11.1 GSM

In GSM mobile phone system the region to be covered by the service is divided into hexagonal cells which are typically 5 km diameter. The size depends on the density of traffic and would be larger in sparsely populated Areas. At the center of each hexagonal cell is a Base Transceiver station (BS), which sends and receives calls to/from mobile phones within its range. The cell shape is hexagonal as the distance b/w center of neighbouring hexagons is consult. This property is useful to ensure easy hand-off, *i.e.*, transfer of control of a mobile phone from one cell to an appropriate adjacent cell when the user of the mobile phone moves.

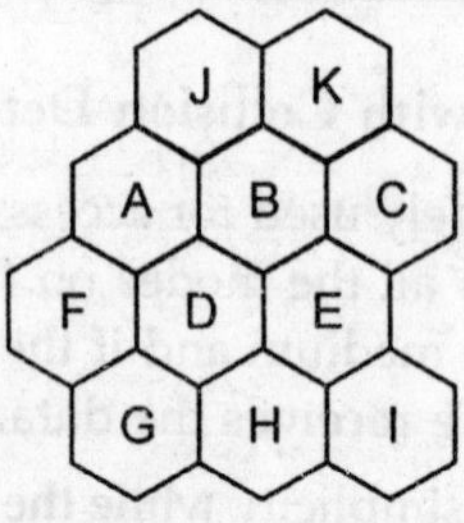

Fig. *Cellular Structure*

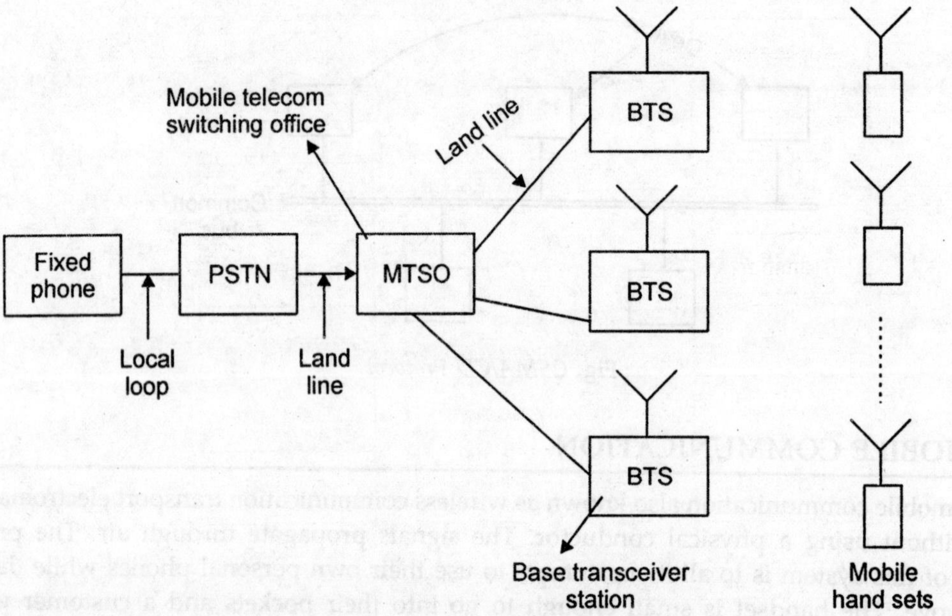

Fig. *Architecture of Mobile Communication System*

6.11.2 CDMA (Code Division Multiple Access Systems)

By CDMA very high bandwidth input signals may be sent. However in practice synchronization of bits in sent signal and received signal is not perfect. Lack of synchronization reflects itself as noise. Thus effective useful bandwidth is lower than the width of the spectrum.

CDMA can also support many more users in a cell compared to GSM. The cell size is also very large 30 to 50 km radius. The major disadvantage of CDMA is the complexity of the technology which requires more expensive mobile hand phones, Base station and MTSO.

6.12 ISO OSI REFERENCE MODEL

International standards organization (ISO) has proposed open system interconnection (OSI) reference model which provides a frame work for data communication protocols. An open system is referred to as set of protocols, which allows the communication to take place between two independent computer systems. OSI model addresses the problem of interconnection of different computer and associated devices.

The OSI reference model has seven layers each performing a well-defined function. The purpose of classification of layers in OSI model to define specific protocol, function, independent design and testing of components for a particular class of a problem.

1. ***Physical Layer:*** The main function of this layer is to send the data bit stream over a communication Network. The design issues in this layer confirm that the bit sent by the sender is received in original.
2. ***Data link:*** The function of this layer is to recover from the transmission errors. Data link layer takes care of the spend mismatch between Senders and receivers. Any disparity in the speed of sending a data and receiving it is taken care by data link layer.

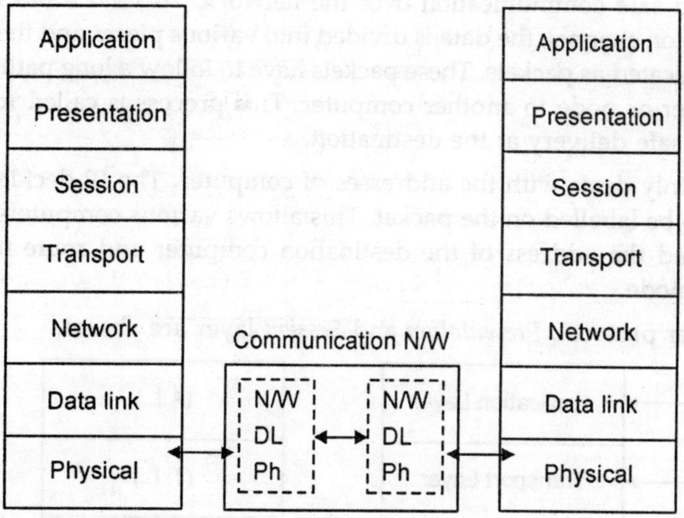

Fig. *OSI Reference Model*

3. ***N/W Layer:*** It is mainly concerned with routing and congestion control. This layer decides which outbound communication channel must be used to reduce the congestion. It also decides the optimal path for routing of a packet.
4. ***Transport Layer:*** It's role is to receive the data from the session layer and divide it into pieces in order to pass it to the N/W Layer. A major function of this layer is to hide the details of communication N/W and provide a N/W independent device-to-device communication.
5. ***Session Layer:*** This layer establishes a session for communication b/w the two hosts. Establishing a connection involves authentication of the hosts, who wants to communicate as well as authentication of transportation service.

6. ***Presentation Layer:*** This layer serves as an interface b/w the application and the communication N/W. Typical function of the layer is to code the data into mutually agreed formats. The presentation layer performs the compression of data and forms a sequence of symbols according to the standard format.
7. ***Application Layer:*** The major role of an application layer is to provide the facility to use the other layers. It contains several protocols that are generally needed to perform a job. The contents of the Application determined by the user themselves.

6.13 TCP/IP

6.13.1 Transmission Control Protocol/Internet Protocol

TCP/IP is the protocol which defines the rules and algorith for data communication b/w different computers. To establish a link between two or more computers it is required to define the address of the computer. This address must be unique. TCP/IP is divided into two set of protocols one is called TCP and other is IP or Internet Protocol.

1. ***TCP:*** It deals with packets over network. The packets are small pieces of data meant for effective and safe communication over the network. To send a block of data over a communication channel, the data is divided into various pieces and these pieces of data are communicated as packets. These packets have to follow a long path, traversing from one computer or node to another computer. This process is called routing. TCP also ensures the safe delivery at the destination.

2. ***IP:*** This mainly deals with the addresses of computer. The IP decides the address of computer to be labelled on the packet. This allows various computers or intermediate nodes to read the address of the destination computer and route the packet to the destination node.

   It is a 5 layer protocol. *Presentation* and *Session* layer are absent.

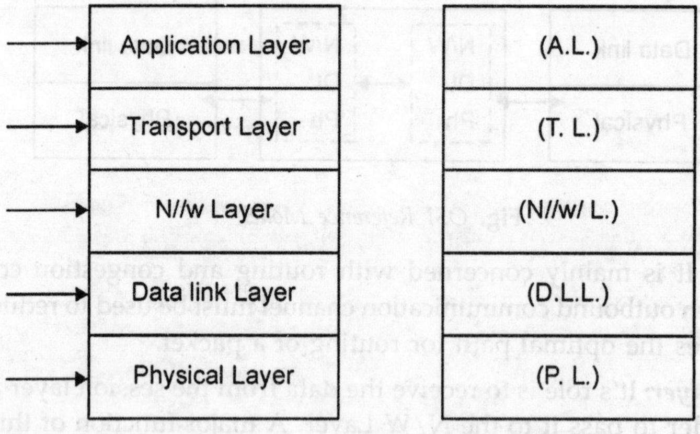

1. ***Physical Layer:*** It deals with Hardware levels, voltages etc.
2. ***Data link Layer:*** It covers who can send data and when etc.
3. ***Network Layer:*** It concerns with the format of data grams as defined in the internet protocol.

4. ***Transport Layer:*** It ensures the communication between the sender and the receiver is reliable, error free and in sequence.
5. ***Application layer:*** This layer allows an end user to non various applications on the internet and use the internet in different ways. These are:
   - File Transfer Protocol (FTP)
   - Simple Mail Transfer Protocol (SMTP)
   - Telenetworking (TELNET)
   - World Wide Web (WWW).

EXERCISES

1. What do you mean by client server architecture? Discuss the pros and cons of it.
2. What do you understand by token based protocols? Explain the working of any such protocol.
3. Give an overview of ISO OSI layers. Also discuss the basic functioning of each layer.
4. What is TCP/IP? Why TCP/IP is so important for internet users?
5. Write short notes on any two:
   (*i*) CSMA/CD
   (*ii*) Network topology
   (*iii*) Client-server Architecture.
6. Explain the role of various network elements in a mobile communication network . Which cell shape is used in it and why?
7. What is computer network? What are the advantages of computer networks? Explain how Local Area Network is different from Wide Area N/W.
8. Write short notes on ATM and ISDN.
9. Explain LAN, MAN and WAN.
10. Write short note on Mobile Communications.

7

INTERNET AND WORLD WIDE WEB

7.1 HYPER TEXT MARKUP LANGUAGE (HTML)

HTML is a scripting language in which various information on the web is published. World wide web is a collection of millions of documents written in HTML. Web page is a collection of text, image, graphics arranged in systematic way and provides the information about a subject. The very first page or root page which is encountered first while visiting the website is called the Home page. Web pages are developed using HTML. Files created using HTML originally contained only text. However, these days, HTML allows, graphics, sound and video.

Hyper text. It is ordinary text that has been dressed with extra features, such as formatting, images, multimedia and links to other document. Thus it is more than a simple text.

Markup. It can be termed as the process of taking ordinary text and adding extra symbols. Each symbol used for markup in HTML is a command that tells a browser how to display the text.

Language. This is actually a key point to remember about HTML. Markup languages are a special type of computer language because they are solely concerned with classifying various parts of a document according to their functions. In other words, HTML is used to define the different parts of your document.

Thus, HTML is not really a programming Language. Instead, HTML is markup language that has different goals. HTML has several inherent *e.g.*, including, flexibility, affordable price and independence of M/C of platform. At present many advantages versions of HTML are there *e.g.*, HTML+, HTML 2.0, HTML 3.0, HTML 3.2, HTML 4.0.

7.1.1 HTML Tags

The basic elements in HTML is the 'tag'. You may write text, include table, image, audio, graphic etc., within the tag.

'Tag' defines the way of presentation or combination of all components on the web browser.

Tags

HTML. This tag informs the browser that the file contains HTML-coded information. <HTML> </HTML>.

HEAD. The head tag identifies the first part of the HTML documents that contains the title. The title is shown as part of the browsers window.

TITLE. The title element contains the document's title. The title is typically displayed in the title bar at the top of the browser window, but not inside the window itself.

BODY. This is the largest part of the HTML document. It contains the content of the document.

	Tags
Paragraph	<P> </P>
Heading levels	<h1> and </h1> ..... <h>> and </h>>
Horizontal rule	<hr> and .... </hr>
Line Break	 .... </BR>
Centering	<Center> </Center>
Bold	<B> ..... </B>
Italic	<I> ... </I>
Unumbered list	<UL>.... </UL>
	Numbered list
Underline	<U> ... </U>
Ordered List	<OL> ... </OL>
Table Header	<TH> .... </TH>
Table row	<TR> ... </TR>
Line anchor	<a href = "urt"> and </a> (< *i* → listitem)

e.g., → (B) This is an example </B>.

7.1.2 Program using HTML

This is an example-1

```
<HTML>
<HEAD>
<TITLE>  K  I  ET  </TITLE>
</HEAD>
<BODY>
<H1>  <b>  welcome  to  the  Dep.  </b>  </h1>
<H2>  <b>  courses  Undertaken  </b>  </h2>
<OL>
<li>  B.Tech  (CSE)  </li>
<li>  B.Tech  (I.T)  </li>
<li> MCA </li>
<li>  B.Pharma  </li>
```

```
    <li> MBA </li>
    </OL>
    <h4> To view the course structures click < a href = ''Syllabus.html''>
here </a>
    </BODY>
    </HTML>
```

Example 2, of HTML

```
<HTML>
<HEAD>
<TITLE>
MY FIRST WEB PAGE
</TITLE>
</HEAD>
<BODY>
I am Indian
I love my family
<BODY>
</HTML>
```

7.2 DYNAMIC HTML: IS AN EXTENDED VERSION OF HTML

DHTML has very precise positioning of text and graphics because it allows the content of a web page to change each time a user clicks, drags or points to buttons, pictures or other elements on the page. DHTML gives developers the ability to create web page that looks like a real application.

DHTML is used to create Dynamic web pages. DHTML combines HTML with cascading style sheets (CSS) and scripting language.

7.3 WWW (WORLD WIDE WEB)

WWW is one of the most popular services on the Internet. It can be thought of as a network of millions of servers, hosts and users. It is based on on-line documents containing text, image, video and sound. The documents which contains these items are arranged systematically. The contents stored on www are accessed through an interactive software called web browser. Some examples of web browsers are netscape navigator, and microsoft Internet Explorer. The information contents are displayed on the browser and it requires only a few clicks of the mouse to interact with the browser.

WWW is a distributed hypermedia system. A distributed hypermedia system is one where all information resides on multiple websites or servers.

In summary, we may say that the www is a collection of millions of documents written in HTML.

7.4 WEB BROWSER

The web pages can be viewed by using web browser. "Web page is a collection of text, images, graphics arranged in systematic way and provides the information about a subject". Web browsers are programs which are used in viewing documents or pages written or coded to HTML. Most popular web browsers are MS. Explorer and Netscape Navigator web browsers may be of two types.

GUI based or text based. Graphical user Interface web browsers permit the user to move the mouse and click on the desired item, selecting a hyper text of choice and the appropriate tool bar button.

When you use web browser for net surfing, it acts as a client and connects you to desired server after specifying the URL address (Universal Resource locator). It then takes you to the home page of the server.

7.5 TELNET

Telnet is a protocol or set of tools, which allows you to log on to any computer on the internet. Telnet is a service on the internet which enables an Internet host to become the terminal of remote computer. It is therefore a very strong and powerful facility where are host may get the full command of another machine. After logging in you may use the s/w and other programs stored on the remote computer you logget in. To use telnet you should have access permission usually in the form of an account and password. Telnet is very similar to the Remote login. The following command at prompt may open telnet session . Telnet 144.16.202.14

220.225.19.51 –

It is an IP address of the remote M/C (144.16.200.14). It will then ask you to enter your Id and password in order to the log onto remote M/C.

7.6 FTP (FILE TRANSFER PROTOCOL)

FTP stands for file transfer protocol which means the method of transferring files from a remote host computer to your computer. FTP is an utility for transfer of files from one computer to another permanently. On internet these are thousands of FTP sites from which you may transfer the files to your computer. FTP tools are used to transfer any type of file from one computer to another. Anything which can be stored on the computer may be copied to another destination or vice-versa with FTP. For establish an FTP session > FTP 144.16.202.14.

7.7 GOPHER

Gopher is a service on the internet, which allows users to access resources such as files or text. Gopher is a protocol used for searching and retriening information from remote sites on Internet. It is based on client server architecture just like web browsers. It is the same as the www with the difference that information in it is stored in a hierarchical order. Most educational institutions and universities create Gopher resources like, 4.5.

For example—University directories.

A Gopher menu may always call another Gopher menu. Gopher menu is faster in the sense that it contains the listing only in an indexed manner. The difference b/w web browsing and visiting a Gopher is that in the former, you see the graphical pictures/text etc., While Gopher presents you with a menu.

For accessing by specified its URL gopher://gopher.kent.edu.

7.8 NET SURFING

The ability of users to jump from one site to another site for sake of searching a relevant document or information is called surfing the net.

7.8.1 Services of Nets

1. ***Usenet (users N/W).*** It is a collection of thousands of users called as newsgroup. Each newsgroup is related to a specific topic, such as the game of tennis, and the inflation in Nation. These are called as bulletin boards, or discussion group. The main features of newsgroup is that they are very dynamic in nature.

Newsgroup Name	*Description*
Comp	Computer related description
Sci	Science related description
Soc	Society and cultural issues
news	Related to the usenet system
misc	An other topic

2. ***Mailing List.*** A mailing list is simply a list of e-mail addresses. People can subscribe to mailing lists—i.e., they can become members of mailing lists.
3. ***Internet Relay Chat (IRC).*** The e-mail system is (generally) good for sending long messages that may or may not need immediate attention. However, if we want to communicate with over the internet as if we are talking to that person in real time, then the IRC is a better option. Chatting is one of the most widely used services on the internet and has actually emerged as a very good substitute to expensive. Long distance telephone calls. e.g., Chatting S/W products , yahoo messenger, Rediffbol, indiatimes chat, Microsoft's MSN messenger.
4. ***Online games.*** Multiple people can play a game on the Internet at the same time. In the early days, all such games were text oriented. However, these days, graphical games are mostly popular.
5. ***Videoconferencing.*** In this technique, people remain at their respective location. For e.g, a team of programmer could be sitting in India, and a team of users can be sitting in USA. Both parties have cameras and television like sets at their end. The camera at each end captures the live video of the people and sends it across to the other end. Along with the pictures, the sound is also transmitted.

7.9 SEARCH ENGINES

Search engines are actually websites and they contain links to millions of web pages. All you have to do is to type in the URL of the search engine the document you are searching some popular search engines are:

- www.google.com
- www.Lycos.com
- www.altavista.com
- www.hotbot.com
- www.yahoo.com
- www.webcrawler.com

7.10 E-MAIL

Electronic Mail (E-mail) was created to allow two individuals to communicate using computers. In early days, the e-mail technology allowed one person to type a message and then send it to another person over the internet. It was like posting a card, except that the communication was electronic, instead of a paper.

E-mail Address Format:

User name	@	Domain Name

for e.g:Pramodyadavster@gmail.com

The actual protocol that performs the e-mail operations is called as simple mail transfer protocol (SMTP).

7.10.1 Domain Name

It identifies the general class in which particular websites are grouped. Any two websites may not have the same domain name. Some of the common Domain name are:

- .com — Commercial websites
- .edu — Educational websites
- .gov — Governmental websites
- .org — Organisational websites
- .mil — Military websites
- .net — Networking websites
- .in — India
- .ac — Academics
- .my — Malaysia
- .uk — United Kingdom
- .fr — France.

Some of the most popular free e-mail service providers are:

- www.hotmail.com.

- www.Gmail.com.
- www.Yahoomail.com
- www.Rediffmail.com
- www. Indiatimes.com.

E-mail Facilities

- **Inbox.** The mail are kept in the inbox. Any mail receive are kept (stored) in the inbox.
- **Composing.** When we want to send mail, we have to compose it. When we click compose, then four sub folder *i.e.,*
  TO, BCC, CCC Subject.
- **Attachment.** When we want to send our resume to any organisation, than we attach the resume and send it. We can also attach birthday, Marriage cards etc.
- **Forwarding.** Suppose if we want to send the receive mail to our friends, than we forward these mails.
- **Address Book.** It is book containing the e-mail address of our friends.
- **Creating Signature.** This creates our name, designation and Address. This is by default added in each page, which we are sending.

Internet and IP Address

The internet is a bunch of computers linked together through a network so computer users in different locations can have access to the same information. Most home users make use of the modem, linking their computer to an ISP, through the phone line.

7.10.2 Modem

A modem is a hardware device, which converts digital data into analog signals that can be sent over an analog telephone line and convert the analog signal back into digital data. Thus, when the modem receives the data from a web server via phone system, it reconstitutes the analog signal into digital form so that the computer can understand it. Modems speed are measured in kilobits per second (kbps), modern modem supports 28k to 56k speeds. They are of two types:

1. ***Internal Modem.*** It is a card, which is fitted inside the computer with a lead running directly from the computer to the phone socket.
2. ***External Modem.*** It is a small external box wired between the computer and the phone socket.

7.10.3 Types of Internet Connection

1. ***Dial-up Connection.*** This method uses telephone lines to connect to the internet. It is the most common way that individuals who use home computers connect to the internet. To connect to the internet by using dial up, the user needs to specify a user name, a password, a telephone number. After the connection is established the user can start browsing sites on the internet.
2. ***ISDN Connection.*** It stands for integrated services Digital network and is more common in business and commercial use. It was the first high-speed alternative to regular analog

phone modems. Digital connections have fewer errors in transmission, which means speed of downloading graphics, webpages, sound and so on is increased to four times faster than with dial-up modems.

3. ***Cable Modem Connection.*** A cable modem connects the user to the internet through a cable television line. Cable modems not only provide a faster internet access (10 to 100 times as fast as the dial-up modem), but they also give added interactivity to the television.
4. ***Leased Line Connection.*** This facility provides reliable, high-speed internet access ranging from 2.4 kbps to 45 Mbps. A leased line connection is an affordable way to link two or more sites for a fixed monthly charge. Leased line service provides a consistent amount of bandwidth and is an excellent way to provide data, voice, and video links between sites.
5. ***DSL Connection.*** Digital subscriber line service is provided through the existing phone line, but it works differently than regular analog modem dial-up access. DSL operates over normal telephone lines and it can be used simultaneously with the telephone. DSL can increase the connection speed by as much as ten-fold from a standard dial-up modem.
6. ***Broadband Connection.*** This type of access is good for remote locations, where ISDN, cable or DSL are not available. It gives a decent download speed, but to upload data, the user still needs a regular analog modem to dial in, via a phone line. Satellite connection can be either a two-way services or a one-way service. Satellite connection is expensive but sometimes is the only fast option for people who are beyond the service area of cable and DSL providers.

7.10.4 Universal Resource Locator (URL)

Each web page on the internet is accessed by providing an address. This unique address is called Universal or Uniform Resource Locator.

For example, http://www.kiet.edu
http://www.Gmail.com.

7.10.5 IP Address

IP address is an actual address of a node or computer or server on the internet. It identifies every computer that is connected to the internet. It is a unique number consisting of four positions separated by dots. For example— 108.20.10.20

The relation between computer names and IP address is achieved by Domain Name system.

7.11 ISP (INTERNET SERVICE PROVIDER)

ISP is the agency which enables users to access internet services. The ISP is equipped with all tools and technology to provide you the internet services. The computers at home or at offices have to be connected to the ISP first for accessing the internet. The following are some of the important issues relating to ISPs.

Cost. Lost of accessing the internet is one of the prime factor which should be looked at while selecting an ISP. Generally, different ISPs, offer different schemes and they charge Rs. 500 to 10,000 for providing on internet access for hours ranging from 10 hours to 500 hours. Several ISP provide unlimited internet access.

Connectivity. To get a good and sustainable connectivity of your computer to the ISP, over the telephone line is also a prime factor. It is very common that you get disconnected from your ISP. Due to telephone disturbances.

Dial up region. If you are frequent traveller across the country/regions with your own Laptops, then you should check whether your ISP provides the facility for access the net.

7.11.1 Technical Service Offered by for ISP

Many ISPs provides a help desk for the benefit of users. In case of any technical trouble, you may dial a specific number provided to your ISP.

7.11.2 Personal Disk Space

Your ISP also provide a disk space to your PC for the purpose of keeping your mails. The total size of your mail should not exceed the space reserved for you in the range of 1MB to 10 MB depending on the ISP.

VSNL, a government organisation in India, is considered to be largest internet service provider. It provides the internet access in India through GIAS (Gateway Internet Access Service). Similarly DOT (Department of Telecom) provides this service through DOT internet access service.

7.12 EDI (ELECTRONIC DATA INTERCHANGE)

Refers to the computer-to-computer exchange of structured business information in a standard electronic format. Using EDI the various trading partners can establish links between their computers to exchange the information electronically. EDI may also be define as the transfer of structured data b/w the computer on mutually agreed formats known as EDI formats. The information stored in the source computer in an organisation is converted into EDI format by S/W or programs, and it is received by the recipient computer system for direct usage. The same information may be passed to more than one or all the trading partners depending upon the requirement. The trading partners computers, if so required, may translate the information using s/w programs into a form they can understand.

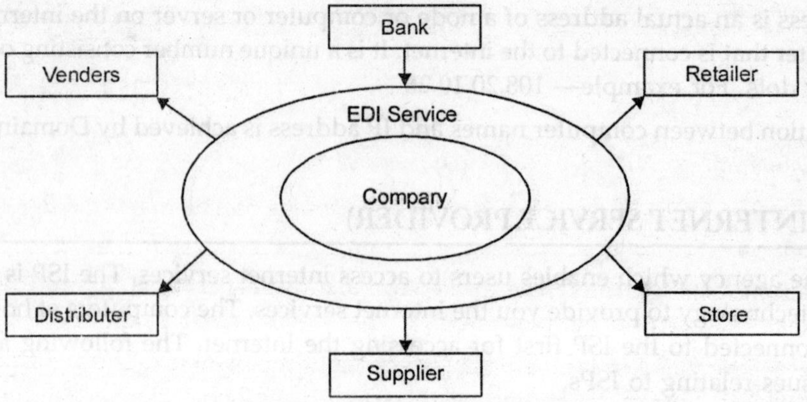

EDI interface is essentially a s/w, which converts or prepares the document into mutually agreed format which is accepted by the computer in partner companies in its original form or without requiring any further processing. Thus EDI interface converts various documents into mutually agreed formats which are automatically accepted by different computers.

7.13 SAFETY OF BUSINESS TRANSACTION ON WEB

A business transaction on the web involves mainly three activities; search of product, price negotiation and delivery of product and payments. There are several ways of making payments on the Internet using credit and debit cards , this is electronic currency, with the newer version of web browsers, transactions can be enerypted. Using secure sockets layer, a protocol that creates a secure connection to the server and protects the information as it travels over the Internet. SSL uses a public key encryption. The documents may be signed by the customers which involves the payment details. These documents are coded in such a way that it is almost impossible for on intruder to decode it. All credit cards companies are promoting an additional security standard called secure Electronic Transactions. This standard encode the credit card numbers in such a way that it can be decoded only by their bankers and credit card companies.

7.14 PUBLIC KEY AND PRIVATE KEY CRYPTOGRAPHY

7.14.1 Cryptography

Cryptography is an essential technique required for communicating over any untrusted medium, which includes any network, particularly the internet. It provides an important tool for protecting information and is used in many aspects of computer security. Cryptography is traditionally associated only with keeping the secrecy of data. However, nowadays these are used to provide many security services, such as electronic signatures and non-modification of data.

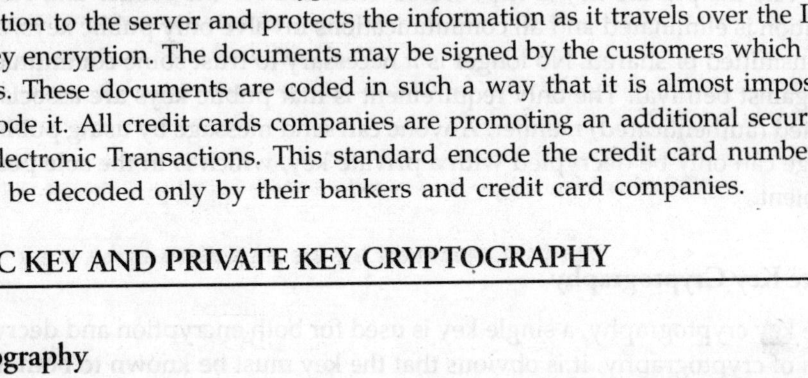

Model of Cryptography

- **Plain text.** This is the original intelligible message or data that is fed into the algorithm as input.
- **Encryption Algorithm.** The encryption algorithm performs various substitutions and transformations on the plain text.
- **Secret key.** The key is a value independent of the plain text The algorithm will produce a different output depending on the specific key being used at the time.

- **Cipher text.** This is the scrambled message produced as output. It depends on the plain text and the secret key. For a given message, two different keys will produce two different cipher text.
- **Decryption Algorithm.** This is essentially the encryption algorithm run in reverse. It takes the cipher text and the secret key and produces the original plain text.

7.14.2 Public Key Cryptography

In this technique, each person gets a pair of keys, one called the public key (used for encryption) and the other called the private key (used for decryption). Each person's public key is published while the private key is kept secret. The need for the sender and receiver to share secret information is eliminated and all communications involve only public keys, and no private key is ever transmitted or shared. No longer is it necessary to trust some communication channel to be secure against betrayal. The only requirement is that public keys are associated with their users in a trusted (authenticated) manner. Anyone can send message by using public information, but the message can only be decrypted with a private key, which is in the sole possession of the intended recipient.

7.14.3 Private Key Cryptography

In private key cryptography, a single key is used for both encryption and decryption of data. With this form of cryptography, it is obvious that the key must be known to both the sender and the receiver. If the key is compromised, the security offered by private key cryptography is severely reduced or eliminated. Private key cryptography assumes that the parties who share a key rely upon each other not to disclose the key and protect it against modification.

The main problem in private key cryptography is getting the sender and receiver to agree on the secret key without anyone else finding out.

EXERCISES

1. What is data encryption? Differentiate between public key and private key cryptography?
2. HTML is a programming language. Justify.
3. What are the factors that influence the selection of an ISP (Internet Service Provider)?
4. What is cryptography? Why do we use it in Internet?
5. What is a domain Name? How does computer resolves IP address corresponding to a domain name?
6. Discuss Gopher, FTP, Telnet, HTTP and E-mail.
7. What is world wide web? How is www related with the term website?
8. Write short note on any two:

   (*i*) Web browser.

   (*ii*) HTML

   (*iii*) FTP.
9. Explain the various tags used in HTML.

8

WEB TECHNOLOGIES

8.1 ELEMENTARY CONCEPTS OF E-COMMERCE

It may be defined as a modern business activity that includes the delivery of information, product and services and payments using electronic medium such as the internet. This medium of business reduces the cost of services, and improves the quality of items and service.

E-commerce is mainly concerned with the business processes prevalent in an organisation. It requires an information base of customers, creation of various information resources and an effective interaction between sellers, buyers, consumers etc. Thus, the major requirements to establish E-commerce activity are the creation of information base, processing capability of information and an effective mechanism for information communication within and outside the organisation.

Advantages of E-Commerce

- ***24/7 Access.*** Online businesses never sleep as opposed to conventional businesses, consumers can access goods and services anytime they want.
- ***Reduced Prices.*** The cost of product is reduced since stages along the value chain are decreased.
- ***Global Marketplace.*** Consumers can shop anywhere in the world. This also provides a wide selection of products and services to consumers.
- ***Low-cost Advertsing.*** Advertising on the internet costs relatively less than advertising on print or television media.
- ***Secure Payment Systems.*** Recent advancements in payment technologies allow encrypted, secure payment online.
- ***Lower Cost of Practising Business.*** Less number of employees, purchasing costs, order processing costs associated with fax, phone calls, data entry, and eliminating physical stores results in reduced transaction costs.

Disadvantages of E-Commerce

- ***Distribution Problems.*** Distribution must be very efficient especially when catering to a global market.
- ***Hardware and Software.*** There are specific hardware and software that are essential to start an e-commerce company, which are bulky and costly.
- ***Maintenance of Website.*** Website must be maintained and updated regularly which leads to extra labour costs.
- ***Training and Maintenance.*** It is important to have well-skilled and trained workers to create and maintain e-commerce facilities of a company.

8.2 E-COMMERCE APPLICATIONS

1. Education and Training

It is very important area of E-commerce application. Many institutes and universities offer interactive classroom teaching through video conferencing and virtual classrooms.

2. Entertainment

You may select and buy audio and video disks in electronic form. It is also one of the major application of E-commerce.

3. Banking and Financial Transactions

Banking and financial transactions also may be realized using E-commerce. Home banking through credit cards, e-commerce, stock market information, bank to bank transfer, etc.

4. Essential Services

Essential services required in day-to-day life like medical, health and telephone, electricity, housing transportation etc., are the areas where E-commerce is quite useful.

8.3 E-COMMERCE CATEGORIES

E-Commerce business is expected to grow upto 300 billion dollars in 2002 as per the Forecaster research. This includes trading of goods and services involving individual consumers and large organisation. Based on the nature of business, E-Commerce may be categorized into the following three categories.

1. B to B (Business to Business) E-Com.
2. B to C (Business to Consumer) E-Com.
3. B to G (Business to Government) E-Com.

8.3.1 B to B (Business to Business) E-commerce

The most popular form of doing E-business is by establishing the website of business houses and letting the different customers interact with those websites. These websites generally present multimedia contents to provide a better image of their products and services. B to B E-commerce requires the establishment of B to B extranets which is a secure network of various houses which cooperate with each other. Thus B to B E-commerce is settlement of business transactions among large organisations.

The method of doing business in B to B E-commerce differ from traditional commerce in a number of ways as electronic commerce combines information technology telecommunications technology and business processes to make it practical to do business in ways that could not otherwise be done. The B to B extranet will help different organisations to understand their common needs and goals. Therefore, the objective of B to B E-commerce is to enable trading partners, organizations, suppliers and customers to form a tight business relationship over a secured network.

B to B E-commerce main focuses is on supply chain Magnet. A supply chain is the N/W of suppliers, manufactures and vendors within which the business works.

8.3.2 B to C (Business to Consumer) E-commerce

In B to C E-commerce the focus is on the consumers. Obtaining the feedback, from consumers and responding to their inquiries about product and design, services and price are the main functions in B to C E-commerce. This type of E-commerce binds the relationship b/w the consumers and the company. Common activities involved in B to C E-commerce include retail selling of products, marketing relationships, consumers survey forms, customizing the product and services according to the consumer needs, and providing opportunities for consumer satisfaction.

Relationship marketing is also a major activity in B to C E-commerce. It allows comperies to track the actions of consumers on the web and thereby gauge their preferences.

In conclusion, we may say that B to C E-commerce is consumer oriented and B to C websites normally offer retailing, personal investment are personal finanance. There are two technologies which are used to build any B to C E-commerce application. These are Generation, Reading and understanding of Bar codes printed on the product and implementation of Electronic Shopping Card.

8.3.3 B to G (Business to Government) E-Commerce

A new trend in E-commerce applications is the B to G E-commerce. Many government departments are setting up their websites to directly reach the common citizens. They announce various government policies, rules and regulations on their websites. A common citizen may interact with these websites to know the various details. The concept of smart city has also been introduced. One such project launched by few state governments is to bring various government departments under a single point of reace for the citizens.

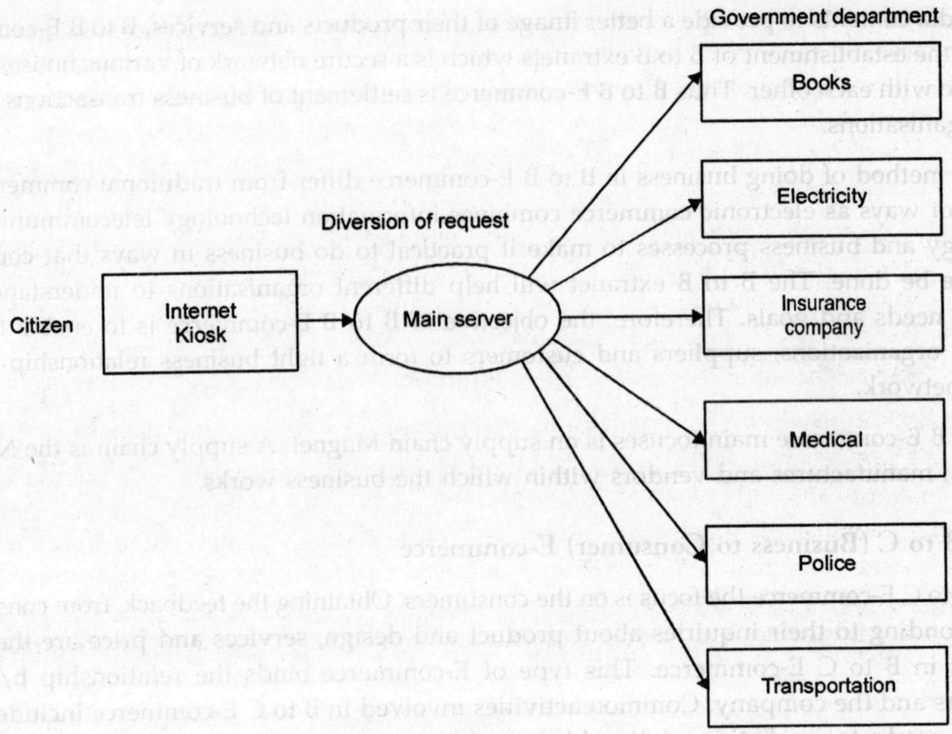

Fig. *A Model of Smart city*

8.4 ELECTRONIC TOKEN

Electronic token is similar to the various other payment instruments used by many financial institutions. Electronic token gurantees that a certain amount will be credited to the account. Electronic token may be used in following ways:

1. **Online settlement of Electronic Tokens.** Payment transactions are settled immediately on online. This type of electronic token is called electronic cash using electronic cash, the money is exchanged instantly.
2. **Prepaid Electronic Token.** In this system, the customer pays in advance to get the required item or services. The product or services are delivered to him later on. Smart cards which store the money values and Electronic Purses are good examples of prepaid electronic tokens.
3. **Post Paid Electronic Token.** In this mechanism, the purchase may be made and the accounts are settled afterwards. The company authenticates the customers by verifying that they have adequate money for the settlement of the purchase values. This is done online. After the verification, the purchase is allowed. *e.g.*, Credit and Debit cards.

8.5 ELECTRONIC PAYMENT SYSTEM (EPS)

Electronic payments are the central part of E-commerce activities as it deals with the strategies for the payment of goods and services by online customers. EPS also refers to the activity of account settlement where the prompt settlement of payments is crucial. If the debit and credit to the bank account, customer and the company are not settled immediately or suffers due to conventional processing delays, then he entire business chain may be interrupted. Payment and settlement of the business account are the bottleneck in all E-commerce activities. Various instruments which may be used to make payments on the internet are credit/Debit cards, smart Cards, Electronic cash etc.

Several protocols have been devised and deployed to provide the necessary security to payment transactions. The netseape Navigator and MS Internet Explorer have promoted their payment protocols for safe payment transaction and these have been implemented in their web browsers.

1. Secure Electronic Payment Protocol (SEPP)
2. Secure Electronic Transaction Protocol (SETP)

Smart Card—These are similar to the credit and debit cards containing a microprocessors chip with memory capable of holding more information than the traditional magnetic stripe. The chip can store significantly greater amounts of data, estimated to be 80 times more than a magnetic stripe. This card contains an encrypted key that is compared to the secret key stored on the customer's computer. Whenever a customer pays for an item from his smart card, the value is deducted from the card. Relationship based smart credit cards contain more features than a normal smart card. These cards contain the services that a financial institution delivers to its customers via a chip-based card. These new services may include access to multiple financial accounts or other information which card holders may want to store on their card.

Electronic Purses—Electronic purses are another form of Smart Cards. These are wallet-sized smart cards embedded with programmable microchips that store the money value. Every time a customer pays for an item from his card, the value is deducted from the electronic purse. Customers use this card instead of cash for buying anything from food to paying for railway or train fares. The Cash Card is an another form of electronic purse.

Electronic Cheques—Electronic cheques are another form of payment instruments popular on the Web. These cheques work on the same principle as the real world cheques.This instrument is helpful to those customers who like to pay later for the product or service they have bought. A customer, to avail the E-Cheque facility, must be registered with a bank or financial institution. The customer upon buying an item, may issue E-Cheque to the company, which will be deposited or transferred to the company's bank for the realization of money from the account of the customer. The E-Cheque are good instruments for paying small amounts on the web. The "NetCheque" is an example of electronic cheque. It was developed by the Information Science Institute and contains all the software for issuance of the Cheque, identification of signature and depositing into the account. Many organizations are using, "NetCheque" for internal applications.

8.6 SECURITY THREATS TO E-COMMERCE

Privacy, Integrity, authentication and availability of the documents are the basic objectives of a secured computer system.

Privacy. Means the isolation of the information contents. This is achieved by providing *passwords* and appropriate access control systems.

Integrity. Means that data application should not be changed or modified without the consent of the owner.

Authentication. Means that the people using computer are authorized users of the computer system or information.

Availability. Implies that the document will be available for users whenever the owner of the documents needs it.

- **Various types of Threats are:**

1. ***Information Release and Destruction.*** Any information released to an unauthorized person means the access to information on to the N/W or on the computer system. This information may be misused to provide an undue advantage to a person or conversely damage to a person. This category of security threat also includes any destruction of the information.
2. ***Information Alteration.*** This is another security threat to E-commerce. This occurs when an intruder enters into the computer system or N/W and changes the information contents. *e.g.*, Changing bank balance etc.
3. ***Denial of Service.*** Sometimes an intruder may present the authorized user from using the resources. The authorized user of a program or S/W or computer system may be denied because of any alteration in the authorization details of the user. *e.g.*, change passwords.

8.7 DIGITAL SIGNATURE

A digital signature is an electronic version of a paper signature. Once a document or transaction is digitally signed it means that it has legal stand. For this purpose, the techniques of message digest and encryption are used. The important features supported by digital signatures are message integrity and non-repudiation, *i.e.*, the sender and receiver are assured to the message contents cannot be tampered. Without getting noticed and secondly, a sender cannot refuse having sent a message. With the laws in place in various countries, this has legal implications as well. Thus, use of digital signatures usually involves two processes, one performed by the signer and the other by the receiver of the digital signature. These are:

Digital Signature Creation. Which uses a hash result derived from and unique to both the signed message and a given private key. For the hash result to be secure, there must be only a negligible possibility that the same digital signature could be created by the combination of any other message or private key.

Digital Signature Verification. The process of checking the digital signature by reference to the original message and a given publickey, thereby determining whether the digital signature was created for that some message using the private key that corresponds to the referenced public key.

8.8 NETWORK SECURITY

Computer network security refers to the protection given to computers and the information contained in them from unauthorized access. The practice of computer security also includes policies, procedure, hardware, and software tools that are necessary to protect the computer systems and the information processed, stored and transmitted by the systems. It involves the measures and controls that ensure confidentiality, integrity, and availability of the information, processed and stored by computer. These three aspects are responsible for effective computer security

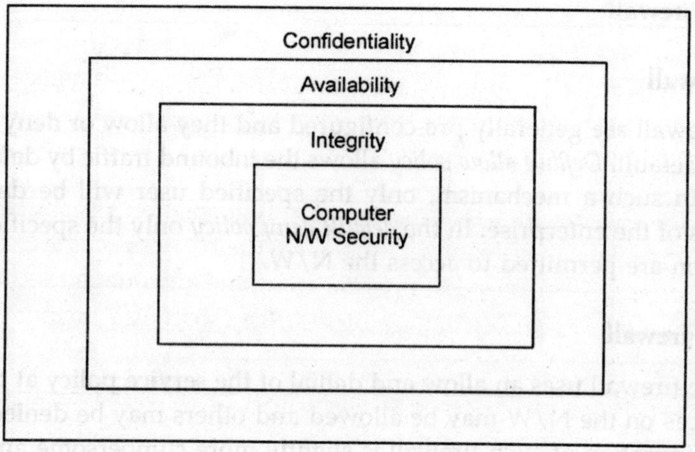

Fig. *Network Security*

8.9 FIRE WALL

The firewall have been taken from the construction industry where a protection mechanism has been deployed in buildings against fire hazards. In the computer world, the term firewall is used to protect the N/W from the outside world against any unauthorized access to network. computer hardware and S/W. Firewalls is conceived by different persons in different ways. Thus we may define firewalls as a system which is a collection of devices computer s/w, routers, host or collection of hosts. The firewall operates by screening the message packets that are passed through the gateway for the prepose of accessing the internal work.

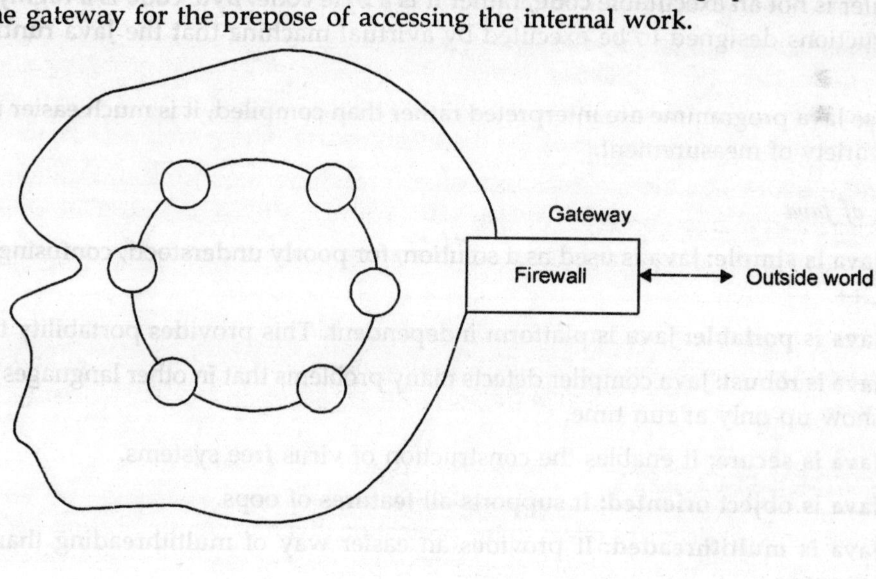

There are two types of firewall:

1. Static Firewall
2. Dynamic Firewall

8.9.1 Static Firewall

The static firewall are generally pre-configured and they allow or deny the access from the outside world by default. *Default allow policy* allows the inbound traffic by default and blocks only specified traffic. In such a mechanism, only the specified user will be derived access to the N/W or resources of the enterprise. In the *default deny policy* only the specific users, who exhibit their authentication are permitted to access the N/W.

8.9.2 Dynamic Firewall

The Dynamic firewall uses an allow and denial of the service policy at the N/W in the time basis. Some services on the N/W may be allowed and others may be denied for a specific time interval. The configuration of such firewall is slightly more cumbersome and complex.

8.10 INTRODUCTION TO WEB TECHNOLOGY

8.10.1 Java

Java is an object oriented language. It supports platform independent programming for the internet, in the form of Java applets, which are the program written in Java. Java is more interactive through the use of Java applets. Java program can be stored at the servers and be down loaded and executed by an client side, regardless of the client platform.

Why Java is platform independent? Java is platform independent because the output of a Java compiler is not an executable code, rather it is a byte code. Byte code is a highly optimized set of instructions designed to be executed by avirtual machine that the Java runtime system emulates.

Because Java programme are interpreted rather than compiled, it is much easier to run them in a wide variety of measurement.

Advantages of Java

1. **Java is simple:** Java is used as a solution, for poorly understood, confusing features of C++.
2. **Java is portable:** Java is platform independent. This provides portability to Java.
3. **Java is robust:** Java compiler detects many problems that in other languages would only show up only at run time.
4. **Java is secure:** It enables the construction of virus free systems.
5. **Java is object oriented:** It supports all features of oops.
6. **Java is multithreaded:** It provides an easier way of multithreading than any other language.

7. **Java is interpreted:** Java interpreter can execute Java byte code directly on any m/c to which the interpreter has been ported.

Java Programmer

```
Public class Sample
{
public Static void main (String orgs [   ])
{
System.out. printing (''It's easy to use JAVA'');
}
}
```

The file name of the source code is named the same as the name of the public class itself with the extension 'Java'. So the name of the above file should be sample java keep in mind that it is case-sensitive.

It is compiled an Dos Prompt.

C:/javac sample.java

For execution

C:/Java Sample

O/P—"It is easy to use Java".

8.10.2 Java Applets

Java programs that work on web pages are called applets. They are embedded in HTML files. If we want to use applets then it is necessary to have a Java enabled web browser, which interprets the byte code. It is also used to add buttons and input fields to a web pages. Applets can perform arithmetic operations, display graphics, playgrounds etc.

Life cycle of Java applets is divided into four stages:

1. Born or initialization state
2. Running state
3. Idle state
4. Dead or Destroyed state.

8.10.3 Wireless Application Protocol (WAP)

It is a new set of standards designed to extend internet services to the mobile telephony environment that includes mobile phones, pagers, and personal digital Assistants. WAP is a method of letting a wireless device, usually a mobile phone where WAP is enabled, to view very simple internet pages, through the existing wireless network.

8.10.4 Wireless Markup Language (WML)

It is a tag-based document language WML shares its heritage with the www's HTML, WML is optimized for specifying presentation and user interaction on limited capability devices such as telephone and other wireless devices.

WML requires the author to specify the presentation in very general terms and gives the user agents a great deal of freedom to determine exactly how information is to be presented to the end, WML character set is UNICODE and this allows presentation of most languages and dialects.

Salient Features of WML

1. Support for user input
2. Support for Navigation and history stack
3. Support for text and images.

8.10.5 VB Script

VB Script or the microsoft Visual Basic Scripting Edition language is a simplified version of the visual Basic Programming Language. It is a powerful and easy-to-learn tool that can be used to add interaction to the web pages. VB Script is a powerful, light weight scripting language for creating interactive, multimedia-rich and Active-x enhanced web applications. It can also be used to develop server side web application in the form of Active Server Web.

VB Script Advantages

1. VB Script is powerful
2. Light-weight, easy to use
3. Freely available
4. Cross-Platform
5. Cross Language Scripting Language for the Intsent.

8.10.6 ASP (Active Server Pages)

It is an internet framework that make our pages (Web) dyanamic. It can be used to access database like MS-Access, SQL/Oracle etc. Generally ASP is preferred to be written in VB Script ASP is written in an edition like notepad and to execute if we require an browser the code of ASP is to be placed under <% and %> symbol. ASP contain different object like response object, Request object, Application Object, etc.

8.10.7 JSP (Java Server Pages)

It allows web developers to rapidly develop and easily maintain, dynamic web pages that leverage existing business systems. JSP technology enables rapid development of web based application that are non dependent upon platform. JSP allows developers to create web-based applications that can make use of components that are developed in the Java Programming language.

8.10.8 Java Script

Java script was developed by Netscape communications corporation, the makers of the popular Netscape Navigator web browser. Java script was the *first web scripting* language to be introduced, and it is by far the most popular. Java script is almost as easy to learn as HTML, and it can be included directly in HTML documents. Java script is a kind of script which provides a set of instructions for the browser to perform. Web script provides the same type of instructions for the browser.

Java Script Program

```
<html>
<body>
<script type =  ''text/java script''>
document.write [''Hello world!'']
</script>
</body>
</html>
O/P. Hello World!
```

VB Script Program

```
<html>
<head>
</head>
<body>
<Script type = ''text/v b script'')
document. write [''Hello from VB script'']
</Script>
</body>
</html>
O/P "Hello from VB Script."
```

Features of Java Script

- Add scrolling or changing messages to the browser's status line.
- Validate the contents of a form and make calculations.
- Display message to the user, either as a part of a web page or in alert boxes.
- Animate images or creates images that change when you move the mouse over them.
- Detect the browser in use and display different content for different browser.
- Detect installed plug-ins and notify the user if a plug-in is require.

8.10.9 Enterprise Java Beans

EJB is a specification model for server side computing which is used in the distributed application environment. The EJB specification is a dramatic step forward in the standardization and simplification of distributed object computing. It is a major piece of the Java 2 enterprise edition (J2EE) platform and is receiving much support from the distributed object community.

8.10.10 Extensible Markup Language (XML)

XML is denied from SGML. SGML (Standard Generalised Markup Language) is a meta language or a language for describing mark up languages. *XML uses the features of SGML that it needs and tries to incorporate the lessons learned from HTML.* XML is a set of rules for defining the semantic tags that breaks the documents into parts. The tags in XML may be used in such a way that XML makes easy various web development tasks which were quite painful in doing with HTML.

Various Features of XML

- XML documents are easy to create.
- The design of XML is formal and concise.
- XML documents are reasonably clear to the lay person.
- It is easy to write program that process XML documents.

XML is commonly called a subset of SGML but actually it is an application profile of SGML, whereas HTML user SGML and is an application of SGML, XML is just SGML on a smaller scale.

XML Advantages

- **Modularity:** It enables you to leave out the Document type definition (DTD) altogether or combine separate DTD into one compound instance.
- **Extensibility:** XML's powerful linking mechanism allows you to link to the material without requiring the link target to be physically present in the object.
- **Distribution:** It introduces composite documents.
- **International character dealing:** Both HTML and SGML, rely heavily on ASCII which makes using foreign characters very difficult.
- **Data orientation.** XML operates on data orientation rather than readability by humans.

EXERCISES

1. What is e-commerce? Explain different types of e-commerce.
2. What is firewall? Distinguish between static and dynamic firewall.
3. What do you mean by electronic payments?
4. What is the role of firewalls in the internet? Explain various types of firewalls.
5. What is a credit card? Discuss the problem faced with credit cards.
6. What do you mean by Digital signature?
7. What are the various types of security threats? Explain.
8. Explain IWT in brief.

9

INTRODUCTORY CONCEPTS IN OPERATING SYSTEM AND DBMS

9.1 OPERATING SYSTEM

An operating system (OS) is a software program that manages the hardware and software resources of a computer. Or an operating system (OS) is a program that serves as an intermediary between a user and the computer hardware. Main tasks of an operating system as follows.

(*i*) Provide an interface for the users to work with. This interface is called as user Interface (UI).

(*ii*) When any program needs to be executed, load the program from the disk into the main memory.

(*iii*) Co-ordinate the tasks between programs, the CPU devices and other pieces of software.

(*iv*) Manage information storage and retrieval, as and when necessary.

(*v*) Manage hardware appropriately.

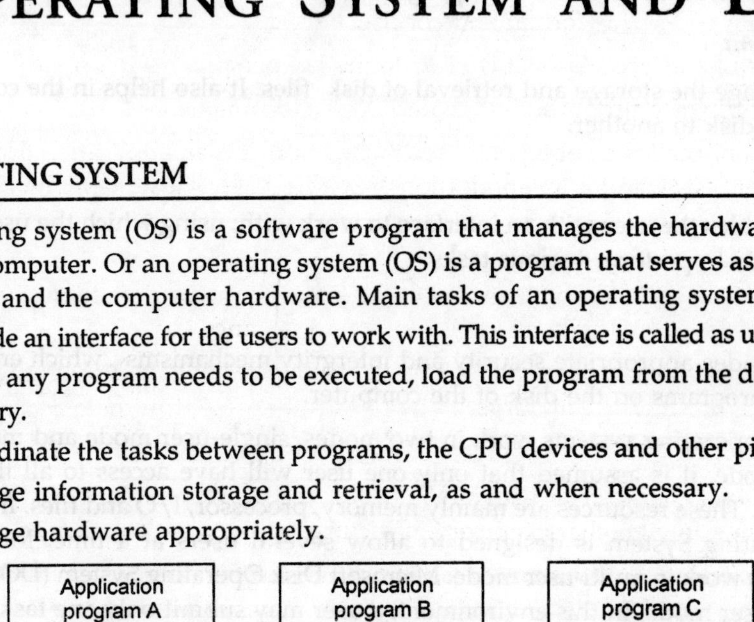

9.1.1 Main Functions of an Operating System

1. Process Management

If more than one program is executing at the same time on the computer, then it is the responsibility of the operating system to allocate CPU and other resources to these programs in turns, so that they can execute properly. At the same time, the OS has to keep a track of all these programs and ensure that the execution of one of them does not tamper with that of the other processes.

2. Memory Management

The OS has to allocate the main memory and other storage areas to the various programs appropriately.

3. I/O Management

The OS performs the co-ordination b/w the various input/output devices, such as the keyboard, mouse, screen, printer and the programs that are executing.

4. File Management

The OS manage the storage and retrieval of disk files. It also helps in the copy/movement of files from one disk to another.

5. User Interface

The OS provides the user with an interface to work with; using which the user can enter the various commands to perform various tasks.

6. Data Security

The OS provides appropriate security and intergrity mechanisms , which ensure the safety of the data and programs on the disk of the computer.

Most of the operating systems work in two modes, single-user mode and multi-user mode. In single user mode, it is assumed that only one user will have access to all the resources of computer system. These resources are mainly memory, processor, I/O and files. In the multi-user mode, the Operating System is designed to allow several users at a time. Most of the large computer systems work in multi-user mode. Microsoft Disk Operating System (DOS) is considered to be the single user mode. In this environment, a user may submit only one task at a time. If he wishes to run another application, in that case he needs to terminate the previous one. This feature excludes the DOS being multi-tasking or multi-processing Operating System. The UNIX is considered as multi-user Operating System which allows more than one user to work at a time. In the conventional UNIX-based system, the multiple users sitting at their terminal may send request to the CPU and these requests are served by the CPU one by one. The requirement and methodologies of management of resources (memory, processor, I/O devices and files) varies in single-and multi-user Operating System. Based on the resources, chiefly Operating System performs four management functions namely Memory Management, Processor Management, Device Management and File Management.

Memory Management—The memory management function finds all available free space in memory and allocates it to the processes. The process is program/ task under execution stage. The Operating System manages whole memory by dividing it into several blocks and partitions. Every job under execution stage requires memory. If there exists two or more than two processes, then Operating System allocates the memory segments as per requirement of the job. In case any job execution has to be suspended or it has been terminated, the Operating System combines the memory freed by the process and allocates the memory to other process. The Operating System therefore decides which process gets memory, when and how much and allocates the memory when that process requests it. It finally frees the allocated memory space as and when the process is executed completely. Memory Management is the important function carried out by Operation System. It is also the responsibility of the Operating System that memory be allocated in such a way that the utilization is maximum.

Processor Management—The Processor Management function of operation is related with allocation of process or job to processor. The speed of processor or CPU is much faster than peripheral devices. Every process is completed only after its processor and I/O requires. Since the speed of CPU is much faster than I/O devices, the scheduling is done in such a way that CPU remains idle for minimum amount of time. When a process waits for I/O to be completed, during that wait time, the CPU may be allocated to other process waiting for processor. There exists several scheduling techniques which maximizes CPU utilization.

Device Management—This function of Operating System deals with allocation of devices to process. Operating System schedules the I/O devices, I/O channel to process whenever it requires. For managing the different requests arising from different processes for grant of devices, scheduling of I/O devices are done according to some strategies. In I/O scheduling, after finding the status of device, channels, a schedule is prepared to which state, which process, which device is allocated to the process.

File Management—The File Management of Operating System is related with management of files stored onto secondary storage. The file is considered as collection of logically related data item which are organized in records. These files may contain set of commands, executable codes or reports. Purpose of file management is to hide the complex details of device specific aspects from the user. Users wish to rely on a uniform set of file manipulation services which are independent of details of devices from user's perspective. File Management of Operating System keeps track of all information on files. It finds and records the following for all files: location, size, usage (attribute), status etc. It also finds as to which process which file is required, checks through the protection routine, opens the file if allowed, and allocates it to the process. It essentially does the the task of mapping the request of file from process to physical disk, swapping the file contents between primary and secondary memory, keeping track of allocation and de-allocation of space and support for protection and sharing of files.

9.1.2 Give the Classification of Operating Systems

The Operating System provides software layers between user and hardware which creates an environment for user to run his application and control hardware without knowing the rigorous details of hardware. Users submit their jobs to the Operating System and Operating System schedule their jobs. The job may be handled by the Operating System serially or concurrently. The serial-processing means that the resources of the computer system are allocated to single job and remain allocated until job is finished. In concurrent processing, the resources may be dynamically allocated to the jobs as and when required. Current application requires the distributed Operating System, which co-ordinates the allocation of resources located at different sites or computer system. For the job requiring the resources located at different computer system, all of the computer system has to follow a common set of protocols. These types of requirements are being served by distributed Operating System. Based on the nature of application and functionality of Operating System, the Operating System may be classified into several categories.

One of the major deisgn issues for the Operating System is to increase the resource utilization. It also includes the reduction in CPU idle time by removing the manual or programmers intervention during the execution of program. Batch Operating Systems are based on the concepts that if several programs are batched together on input they can be executed one after another without programmer intervention. This reduces the overhead for each program, as the program need not require slower human intervention. The batch processing is suitable in programs with large computation time with no need of user interaction or involvement. For pay roll, forecasting, statistical analysis and large scientific number crunching programs, user need not wait while the job is being processed. The instructions are provided by embedding the commands in a batch stream. These commands are written in a language called *Job Control Language* (JCL). JCL commands are required to mark the beginning and end of the job, to announce their resource need and memory requirements. Batch Monitor, a part of batch operating system, reads and interprets the commands written in JCL. The total time from submission of job into the queue till, it get completed is called turn around time. The major disadvantage of batch operating system is non-interactive environment. It also imposes several drawbacks from programmer's point of view, *e.g.*, the programmer is bound to do off-line debugging. The time taken between job submission and job completion is generally very high, although the time lapsed in actual execution of program may be quite less. Since the programmer does not have any control over intermediate results of a program, batch operating systems are considered quite inflexible in software development. Offline debugging also not permit the programmer to correct the bugs whenever they occur, but has to correct them at later stage.

Multiprogramming Operating System—In Batch Operating System, the jobs are submitted in the batch and all of the resources are reserved to one job at a time. This practice improves the turn around time but shorter length jobs are suffered adversely because they have to wait for a longer time for their turn. Another disadvantage of batch operating system is that it does not maximize the resources utilization. This drawback of batch operating system is reduced in multiprogramming operating systems. The multiprogramming allows the interleaved execution of two or more than two programs. Multiprogramming operating systems are fairly sophisticated compared to batch operating systems. Multiprogramming improves both system throughput and resource utilization. The job submitted to the Operating System requires CPU for computation and I/O for their I/O needs. Multiprogramming operating system allows concurrent execution of two or more than two jobs and schedules them in such a way that whenever computation work of one job is completed and it goes for 110, this idle time of CPU may be utilized by allocating another job to the CPU who wants the services of CPU. This improves throughput of Operating System. The number of jobs active in the system is known as degree of multiprogramming. Higher degree of multiprogramming ensures higher resource utilization. Concept of multiprogramming is illustrated in the following schematic.

Multitasking Operating System—A Multitasking Operating System allows two or more than two active processes. The instance of a program execution is known as *process*. Multitasking is implemented by maintaining code and data of several processes simultaneously in the memory. Multitasking is often coupled with hardware and software support. During execution of more than two processes, it is the responsibility of the Operating System to protect the memory space reserved for one process from other process. Most of the multitasking systems out multiple processes, only process and accept the input from keyboard, mouse or other input devices. This process is known as *foreground process*. Rest of the processes are said to be running in background.

These processes are therefore called *background processes.* Those who have been extensively in the Windows 95/98 environment might have observed the concept of foreground and background process. Background processes cannot accept interactive input from a user, but they can access data stored on a disk and write the data to the video display. One may open several applications in several windows. If you have opened a word file and have given print command the computer will keep printing the document in background and Windows allows you to work at the same time in another application, e.g., Access, Word editing etc. Out of the several Windows, you have opened only one which remains active and at a time you may interact with only one application. This means that only one process will work as foreground process. This concept is called SPOOLing. (Simultaneous Peripheral Operation On Line). In addition, many communication programs are designed to run in the background. Background processes generally have a lower priority than foreground processes so that they do not interfere with interactive applications.

There exist two types of multitasking called pre-emptive multitasking and cooperative multitasking.

In pre-emptive multitasking, CPU time is shared among the different processes. In this case, fixed time slice are allocated to each process in rotation. Time slice is amount of the time allocated to each process for CPU utilization. In cooperative multitasking, each process may hold the CPU for the duration it wants. A process not utilizing the CPU may allow others to process program to use it temporarily. Windows 95, Windows NT, and UNIX Operating System are the examples of pre-emptive multitasking operating system. Windows 95/98 are considered as multitasking operating system but DOS does not qualify as multitasking operating system. Although DOS allows some of the tasks to be done in back ground like printing in the background. MS Windows 95/98, Mac OS, UNIX are the examples of Operating System which are full multitasking operating systems.

Multiprocessing Operating System—A Multiprocessing or Multiprocessor Operating System manages operations of computer system which has two or more than two (multiprocessor) processors. The multiprocessor operating systems are also multitasking operating systems because they allow multiple processes to be executed at a time on different processors. It may be noted that multitasking may not be allowed on different processors. The multiprocessor operating system provides all feautres of operating system along with the management of multiple processor. Multiprocessing can be done in two ways called symmetric and asymmetric multiprocessing. In asymmetric multiprocessing different jobs may be allocated to different processors. The disadvantage of asymmetric multiprocessing is that some processors may be overloaded while other processors remain idle. In the symmetric multiprocessing, the same job may be executed simultaneously at different processors.

Multi-user Operating System—A Multi-user OS allows two or more users to work simultaneously. It is achieved by allowing two or more users to connect to the computer system from different terminals. Multi-user Operating System does not guarantee that multi-programming or multitasking will be done. The general purpose time sharing system incorporates features of both multi-user and multiprocessing operating system.

Multithreading—Threads are used to increase the performance of operating system by reducing the context switching time. Threads are a good mechanism for achieving high degree of concurrency. Each thread represents a process and they are also called light-weight processes. Each thread corresponds to exactly one process and represents + a flow of control and have its own state. Concept of threads has been implemented in operating system Mach OS and OS/2. Threads are individual processes that execute simultaneously in multitasking operating systems. The programmer must carefully design the program in such a way that all the threads can run at the same time without interfering with each other. Programmers writing programs for multitasking operating systems can design processes that can be split up into threads. These threads may be executed simultaneously. It is always beneficial to do multitasking with threads on multiprocessor system. Even in case of single processor system, each thread is executed in turn, one after the other. A single thread does not dominate the processor, but instead is given a small amount of time to complete some or all of its tasks.

Time Sharing System—Time Sharing is extension of multi-programming where multiple jobs are executed simultaneously by the CPU. The switching between the processes occurs so frequently that its users may interact with each job in execution state. It is like a form of multi-programmed OS that operates in an interactive mode with a quick response time. The user types a request to the computer through a keyboard. The computer processes it and a response if any, is displayed on the user's terminal. A time-sharing system allows many users to simultaneously share the computer resources. Since each action or command takes a very small fraction of time, only a little CPU time is needed for each user. The CPU switches so rapidly from one user to another, that each user is given impression that he has his own computer, while actually it is one computer being shared among many users.

Real-time Systems—Real-time Systems are used in the environment where most of the input or events are accepted from the environment external to computer systems. These jobs must be processed meeting their deadlines. In real-time system meeting the deadline of job is a must. Thus, real-time systems are defined as those systems in which the correctness of the systems depend not only on the logical result of computation but also on the time in which the results are produced. Real-time Operating System intends to complete the submitted job within the time limit. The job is said to have served successfully only if the job has met the deadline. Real-time systems are deployed in mission critical application, flight control, simulation, military operation where meeting the deadline is as important as job completion. Primary objective of real-time systems are, therefore, to meet the deadline. Examples of real-time operating system are Maruti II, VRTX (Virtual Real Time Executive) and HARTOS (Hexagonal Architecture for Real Time Operating System). The deadlines in the real-time operating system are met by maintaining the calendar management. A resource-allocation chart for a job is prepared first before the execution of job. All the resources are made available to the job so that it completes the execution, meeting the deadline.

Database Operating System—Database Management System provides the set of programs for creating and processing database. Conventional database management system, *e.g.*, Oracle, Sybase etc runs on top of the Operating System. With growing demands of heavy data processing, it has been found that some of the operating systems do not yield good performance for database management system because of incompatibility in the configurations. The database management systems performance remains under-utilized as Operating System does not provide sufficient functionality to the database implementation. Database Operating Systems are those, which are designed for supporting the function needed by database management system. Development of such operating systems from the scratch is a costly affair, therefore, the existing Operating System may be modified whenever interface to the underlying database management system is changed. Conventional operating system handles the job submitted to them by following process creation, synchronization of process, memory handling for process and file management. The database systems are based on the concept of transaction. The transaction is a unit of atomicity. The atomicity of transaction means that either the transaction be executed fully and affects of its execution must not be reflected in database if the transaction has been aborted. It is required in the database system that they handle volume of data efficiently; provide concurrently control, to store the data temporarily in the storage when fetched from the secondary storage. All this has to be done without sacrificing the integrity of data. The Operating System designed by emphasizing the database systems need is called *Database Operating System*.

Network Operating System (NOS)—Computer Network refers to the collection of several computing machines, peripheral devices, storage units. The computer systems may communicate over computer network and shares the resources. These networks enable the computer to communicate a remote computer where the remote computer may be located at a distance of few meters to several thousand kilometers. The users of a computer system on network are able to share the software resources such as programs, databases, and program utilities. These computers may communicate the data to each other, participate in solving a problem collectively, share the resources available. A computer network installed in a very small area, *e.g.*, a room or building is known as *Local Area Network* (LAN). Network operating systems provide features for controlling LAN. Network Operating System is designed and developed towards the need of computer user on network *e.g.*, the users may transfer or copy files from one machine to another machine, and can log into remote machines on network. Network OS may provide a shared file system and a set of security features and controls to control user access to network resources.

Distributed Operating System—A Distributed System is defined as a collection of cooperating computer system that do not share either memory or clock. These computer systems may be geographically located. Each computer in a distributed system has its local memory and its own Operating System. Whenever the user on different computer system works, they generally realize the need of sharing the resources like data file etc. and other costly resources. The distributed system allows the users to share the resources over a communication network. Distributed operating system appears to its users like a centralized operating system but it runs on multiple-independent processors. The user views the system as virtually single processor but not as a collection of distinct machines. This is known as *transparency*.The resource located at different computer systems are so managed that users are not even aware of where their programs are being actually run or where their files are residing. These all activities are handled by distributed operating system.

Write a Short Note on:

(*i*) MS-DOS

(*ii*) Windows-95 Operating System

(*iii*) Windows NT Operating System

(*iv*) Windows-98 Operating System

(*v*) Windows-2000 Operating System

(*vi*) UNIX and Linux Operating System.

Microsoft has a family of OS products, designed to fully utilize the range of PC hardware available in the market today, while providing a consistent user interface for end users and a programming environment for developers. Windows 3.x and Windows for Workgroups 3.x on MS-DOS are designed for mainstream portable and desktop PC platforms. Windows 95 and 98 are successors of the aforementioned products running a top the same or improved hardware configuration. Windows NT 3.x and 4.0 and Windows NT 2000 (Windows NT5) are designed for the high-end business and technical workstation platforms and Windows NT Advanced Server is designed as a server platform.

(i) **MS-DOS (Microsoft Disk Operating System)**—Tim Patterson originally developed MS-DOS in 1980. From the very beginning , it was designed to be a full-fledged OS for 16-bit personal computers built around the 8086 microprocessor. Patterson originally christened it 'QDOS' for 'Quick and Dirty Operating System'. The initial versions of DOS were very simple and resembled CP/M. Work began on MS-DOS because, digital research was very slow to release a CP/M based OS to go with the new 8086 chip. Eventually they did, but by then MSDOS was well established. In 1981, IBM (International Business Machines) released its Personal Computer (PC). At the same time, it announced that MS-DOS (renamed PC-DOS) was the OS of the choice for the new machine. Practically overnight, MS-DOS became the standard OS for virtually all 16-bit microcomputers, not just the PC. Although CP/M and MS-DOS differ significantly in detail, IBM persuaded Microsoft to crreate some similarities, making easier for people familiar with CP/M to move to MS-DOS. Since IBM's selection of MS-DOS, many programs originally written for CP/M have been rewritten in 16-bit versions to run under MS-DOS or PC-DOS. A great deal of new software has been written under it as well. Subsequent versions have become increasingly sophisticated as they incorporated features of minicomputer operating systems. However, DOS is still a 16-bit Operating System and does not support multiple users or multitasking.

(ii) **Windows 95**—It was a major release of the Microsoft Windows OS in 1995, and the successor to Windows 3.x and Windows for Workgroups 3.11. Windows 95 represented a significant advancement over its precursors, Windows 3.1 and Windows for Workgroups 3.11. It is a pre-emptive, multithread, multitasking, networking 32-bit OS with advanced file systems, running on Intel-based machines. For customers, Windows 95 presented a major step forward in functionally on mainstream desktop platforms by providing a system that is easy to use, offering responsive multitasking performance, and providing a great platform for communications. Ease of use is delivered through the Plug and Play architecture and an improved, intuitive user interface. Windows 95 is a complete, integrated protect-mode OS that does not require or use a separate version of MS-DOS. In addition to wearing a new user interface, Windows 95 also included a number of important internal improvements, implementing the Win32 API (Application Programming Interface), providing pre-emptive multitasking and multiple threads of execution for 32-bit applications, which meant that applications written specifically for this OS would run much faster.

It has essentially removed DOS as the underlying platform. It included MS-DOS 7.0, but took over from DOS completely after starting. This means, removal of many of the old DOS limitations, such as 640 KB of main memory and 8-character file names. The communications capabilities of Windows are enhanced with integrated, high-performance networking, built-in messaging, and features such as Remote Network Access and File Synchronization, designed for mobile and remote computer users. Windows 95 implements new working set management technologies that optimize the use of memory on low-configuration systems. Windows 95 runs most of the current application for Windows and MSDOS. Windows 95's new shell provides a complete set of services that is tightly integrated with the OS components. It allows full access to hardware, hence it is useful for older games. Home users prefer it, as games run unobstructed.

The Windows 95 user interface offers dramatic gains in ease of learning and ease of use for the broad range of people using PCs today. Instead of mastering different kinds of tools to work with different resources on their computers, users will be able to browse for and access all resources in a consistent fashion with a single tool. This is much easier than learning separate applications such as Program Manager, File Manager, Print Manager, Control Panel, etc. as users of Windows must do windows 95's smart set-up technology uses the current system settings to present an initial configuration that is familiar for the current Windows-based user. And for corporate customers and individuals who may not want to make any user interface changes initially, Windows95 enables them to continue running their current Program Manager and File Manager configurations. A system tool bar that is always accessible makes it much easier to start and switch between full-screen tasks. The direct manipulation of data through drag-and-drop in the user interface makes working with documents easier and more intuitive. The set-up program enables customers to uninstall Windows 95, assuring customers a way to remove it if they are in any way unhappy with it, and have provided tools for system administrators to customize the configuration of Windows 95.

***(iii)* Windows NT**—It is a robust, pre-emptive, multitasking, 32-bit OS with symmetric multiprocessor support. It is intended for use in network servers, workstations and software development machines. Windows NT Workstation 4.0 version has come a long way since its coming out in 1996, so that the mainstream desktop PCs and laptops now come with Windows NT Workstation preinstalled, and has now become a great solution for all business users, not only power users but also engineers, and developers. Windows NT 4.0 comes in two versions, as Windows NT Server, designed to act as a server in networks and Windows NT Workstation for stand-alone or client workstations. Corporations prefer this version and a lot of businesses are standardizing their desktops and laptops on Windows NT workstation because it is cheaper, fast, reliable, efficient, and powerful. The Windows NT's user interface is very similar to that of Windows 3.1 and Windows 95, internally it is totally different from either of them. Windows NT ensured fully protected applications, wherein all programs are protected from each other, with virtualized hardware access. Windows NT does not allow access to hardware like UNIX. The Windows NT file system, NTFS (New Technology File System) provides lot of security are reliability.

***(iv)* Windows 98**—The successor to Windows 95 was released in 1998. Originally it was called Memphis, and then Windows 97, but Microsoft changed the name when it realized that it was going to miss its target 1997 release date. Windows 98 offers support for a number of new technologies, including AGP (Accelerated Graphics Port), MMX (Multimedia Extensions), USB (Universal Serial Bus), DVD (Digital Video Disk) etc. Its most visible feature is the Active Desktop, which integrates the Web browser Internet Explorer, with the OS. The Microsoft Windows 98 Second Edition is downloadable from the Internet. It consists of two parts: Microsoft Internet Explorer and revised core components of the OS, called Windows 98 Service Pack 1. The only new feature that is not available for download is Internet Connection Sharing (ICS), which lets networked Windows 98 systems share a single user connection. To get ICS, one needs to buy a new CD-ROM containing the complete Second Edition. Users, who already have Internet Explorer 5 installed over an existing Windows 98 setup, will see no obvious differences. The Desktop, Start Menu, and Explorer windows look the same. Window's built-in applications look and act exactly as before. The Windows 98-Second Edition, is more stable than the original, reflecting many bug fixes in the core Windows files, but performance seems identical. The most obvious change is Internet-Connection Sharing, which adds a feature previously available in Windows 98 only through third-party networking software. When ICS is installed on a home or small office network, all networked client computers can access the Internet through a single-host computer. The host can use any existing Internet connection. The Second Edition does smarter networking.

(v) **Windows 2000**—Microsoft is continually enhancing its Windows OS Product line. There is a great deal of interest in speculation about the Windows 2000 project, the technology development effort which will deliver the next major release of Windows for the mainstream desktop and portable PC. Windows 2000 is advertised as the state of the art OS that uses the latest hardware. It is supposed to be a major upgrade aimed at the OS market, which is largely dominated by the different features variants of UNIX. Windows 2000 uses a new security protocol with an encryption facility to authenticate users logging into the network. It maintains encrypted passwords in the active directory and ensures that user connections are secure. The interface of Windows 2000 is similar to that of Windows 98, with a lot of hidden features waiting to be discovered. All explorer windows have customizable toolbars. In the previous versions (both of Windows NT and Windows 98), you could view or hide various toolbars. In this, you have control over which buttons to view in the toolbar. For example, you can open My Computer, and add the Map network drive button in the toolbar, or add buttons necessary for Internet activity (like home page, refresh, stop, etc.). The display properties have also been changed in the new addition. You can view all the display modes and refresh rates for your display adapter. There is also a color management option built in.

(vi) **UNIX and Linux**—UNIX is a powerful, flexible and manageable as with good utilities, communication abilities and GUIs. The UNIX project was justified to the management, as a vehicle for document preparation-the first users of UNIX were in Bell patent department, which used the system's document preparation software. Dennis Ritchie wrote a C complier under UNIX, and in 1973, Thompson and Ritchie rewrote the UNIX kernel in C.

Linux is a free, powerful, UNIX-like as. It is a 32-bit as that runs on a variety of platforms, including Intel, SPARC, Power PC, and DEC Alpha processors as well as multiprocessing systems. A young computer science student, Linus Torvalds, at the University of Helsinki in Finland initially created it as a hobby. He developed the original as a college project. When he realized that the lack of UNIX programming facilities was hampering its work, he decided to rectify it, by writing his own UNIX-like micro-kernel on a 386 machine. Linus had an interest in Minix, a small UNIX system, and decided to develop a system that exceeded the Minix standards. He began his work in 1991 when he released version 0.02, including all the source code of the software. Source code is the exact specifications by which a computer makes an executable program. With the help of literally thousands of volunteers, Linux grew dramatically. Linux is a 'user-developed' product, meaning that users around the world who ran the as for their own use have developed many of its components and drivers. Linus worked steadily with the assistance of developers around the world, and in 1994, version 1.0 of the Linux Kernel was released. Torvalds remained the co-ordinator of the project, and determined which of several competing designs for feature implementations would make the next distribution, often combining the best of several implementations to make a tool far better than any of the original designer's intentions. The current full-featured version is 2.2, released on 25th January 1999, and the development continues. Linux is now well-supported and gaining ground as a respectable as despite its homegrown roots. Linux also has an official mascot, the Linux Penguin, which was selected by Linus Torvalds to represent the image he associates with the Operating System he created.

The Linux as is available at free of cost. Its source code is freely available to everyone. This however, does not mean that Linux and its various distributions are free; companies and developers may charge money as long as the source code remains available. Thereby, a number of companies have developed their own 'distribution' of Linux, so there are many different Linux distributions, or versions available in the market. A 'distributioin' is the compiled Linux source code, usually combined with extra features and software, and some are equipped towards specific types of computer systems. You can download Linux from the Web. Some distributions are available for download at no charge while others are available at affordable prices on CD-ROM from Linux retailers world-wide, the top commercial Linux vendors today being Caldera and Red Hat. Other options include purchasing Linux pre-installed on a computer, or purchasing a book or magazine containing a complimentary CD-ROM. You can purchase a book that includes a CD-ROM with the entire OS. In India, PC-Quest magazine has recently issued several versions of LINUX Red Hat distributions in its CD-ROMs. Each distribtuion has its own purpose, and a number of factors should go into deciding which distribution is best for each user. Some distributions are better suited to home users, others are excellent for commercial settings. Some are better suited for Intel or Machintosh PCs, other are excellent for use on high-performance computers. The only problem with this approach is that drivers and fixes are only available if some user decides to develop them. Support is another issue since you cannot call any particular vendor. Anyone that plans to use this OS for production use should first make sure those applications runs on the OS and that appropriate drivers are available to support hardware and software.

9.2 TEXTUAL VERSUS GRAPHICAL INTERFACE

Windows is said to have a Graphical user Interface. To perform task such as to open a file, delete it, select a file, in windows, the user can click/double click/right click/drags the mouse and perform the operation visually.

In windows, GUI, two items are of special importance, they are start button, and the taskbar, other buttons are radio button allows the selection of only one among several choices. The check box allows either selecting or deselecting something completely. The most striking benefit of the GUI approval his that it is not only quite intutitive and easy to use but also that it is uniform across applications.

Microsoft borrowed the concept of a GUI based operating system from Apple's Macintosh Operating system, whereas in Textual interface the user has to give the commands, without giving proper command the user cannot perform any operation e.g., of operating system of GUI are all windows version i.e., windows 95, 98, 2000, XP etc., whereas e.g., of operating system of TUI are DOS, UNIX etc.

9.3 INTRODUCTION TO DOS COMMANDS

9.3.1 Disk Operating System (DOS)

- DOS was developed by Microsoft primarily as a single user operating system working on PC (in 1981)
- It is essential for the operating system *programs* to be resident in the memory of the computer. The process of loading these programs into the memory is termed as Booting the computer. In DOS these programs are:

- MS DOS.SYS,
- I0.SYS and
- COMMAND.COM

- However MSDO.SYS and I0.SYS are hidden programs and cannot be seen in the Directory listing.
- In order to load DOS files from floppy to Harddisk the following command is used

  A:> SYS A: C:
- If one needs to make a system floppy from the HDD the DOS command used is

  C:> SYS C: A:
- **Directories:** Each disk is organised into directories. Each Directory holds files. The default directory is the Root. Directory and contains the minimum DOS files. Root Directory cannot show more than 132 files in its Directory listing.
- **Commands to create a Directory (internal)**

  C:\>MD\PRAMOD

  or type

  C:\>MKDIR\PRAMOD
- **Changing your working Directory (Internal)**

  Internal to work with files in the directory PRAMOD type.

  C:\> CD \ PRAMOD.
- **Removing a Directory (Internal)**

  To remove a directory, please ensure that the directory is empty and enter the command

  C:\>RD\PRAMOD.

  +s: Mark file as DOS system file.

  –S: Removes DOS system file setting
- **Renaming a file (Internal)**

  C:\> RENAME PROMOD PRAKASH

  (renames the file named PROMOD to PRAKASH)
- **Deleting a file (Internal)**

  C:\> DEL PROMOD.
- **The DELTREE Command (External)**

  C:\> DELTREE C:\PROMOD

  (To remove unwanted directories and their contents (files and subdirectories).
- **Printing on Screen (Internal)**

  C:\> TYPE PRAMOD

  (This command will output the contents of the file PRAMOD on the screen)

- **Piping (Internal)**

  C:\> Type PRAMOD\MORE (Internal)

  More forces DOS to display output one screen at a time.

- **Format Command (External)**

  C:\> FORMAT A: (Formats the floppy in drive A).

  C:\> FORMAT A:/S (formats the floppy and also transfers the systems files to the floppy).

- **The Scandisk Command (External)**

  C:\> SCANDISK / ALL (repairs logical and physical disk errors). V 6.2 ↑

  or

  C:\> CHKDISK / F (V .6.2 ↓)

- **Config.Sys file**

  Commands in DOS

  DOS commands can be divided into two categories.

  1. **Internal Commands:** Are those commands that can be entered once the Dos prompt is available i.e., they do not need any special files for their execution.
  2. **External Commands:** Are those commands that need separate files, containing their source codes, to involve them. The external commands basically are accessories to the operating system that in case its extensibility.

- **BREAK. (Internal)**

  C:\> BREAK on or OFF. (Stop the execution of the current DOS command).

  DOS will present a screen. You can then enter your program or text in the box and exit out of the editor by using the ALT +F Key and then press X.

- **Commands to Copy files (internal)**

  C:\>COPY PRAMOD A: (This command will copy the file named PRAMOD in the foot Directory to a Floppy).

  C:\> COPY PRAMOD\ PRABHAT (This command will copy the file PRAMOD from the root Directory to the PRABHAT directory).

- **The ATTRIB Command (external)**

  C:\> ATTRIB - R PRAMOD: (This command is used for making your file PRAMOD as read and write) other notations are!

  +R : Makes the file read only

  +H: Suppresses the file in the directory listing, i.e., makes it hidden.

  –H: Unhides the previously hidden file.

  +A: Changes file settings to Archived.

  A: Change's file settings to Not Archived.

- **The DIR Command Internal**

  This command enables onto view the contents of a directory.

  C:\> DIR—This gives a complete listing of files and directories.

  C:\>DIR/P—This command pauses the directory listing at every screen.

  C:\>DIR/W—This command shows the listing width wise on the screen.

- **Files:** The most common requirement of a computer users are commands to manage his files.

  Files can have names upto 8 characters. This can be followed by a (.) dot and an extension of upto 3 characters. However, special characters like commas, slashes, blanks etc., are not allowed in a file name. e.g.,:

  MYFILE

  MYFILE.BAK
- **Eveating a file Using Editor**

  In order to create a file named PRAMOD enter the command.

  C:\DOS> EDIT PRAMOD (external)

  CD. (Int.) (Internal)

  C:\> CD drive:\ path. (Change the directory).
- **CHKDSK (Ext)**

  C:\>CHKDSK drive: \path\file\switches (diagousses for errors).
- **CLS (I)**

  C:\> CLS. (Clears the screen).
- **COPY (I)**

  C:\> COPY source drive:\path\files target drive:\path\file.
- **DATE (I)**

  C:\> DATE (displays current system data)
- **DIR**

9.3.2 62 Internal Commands Contained within the COMMAND.COM.

Break	Buffers	Call	Cd
Chicp	Chdir	Choice	Cls
Copy	Country	Ctty	data
Del	Device	Device high	dir
Dos	drivparm	echo	erase
Errerlevel	exist	exit	febs
Files	For	goto	if
Include	Install	Last drive	lh
Loadfix	Loadhigh	md	menu color
Menudefault	Menu item	Mkdir	Move
Not	Numlock	Path	Pause
Prompt	Rd	rem	ren
Rename	rmdir	set	shell
shift	stacks	submenu	switches
time	true name	type	ver.
verify	vol		

9.3.3 61 External Commands Contained within COMMAND.COM.

append	assign	attrib	backup
chkdsk	command	comp	dblspace
debug	defrag	deloldos	deltree
diskcomp	diskcopy	doskey	dosshell
edit	emm386	exe2bin	expand
fasthelp	fastopen	fc	fdisk
find	format	graftabl	graphics
help	himem	interlnk	intersvr
join	keyb	label	mem
memmaker	mirror	mode	more
msav	msbackup	mscdex	msd
nlsfune	power	print	replace
restore	scandisk	select	server
share	sort	subst	sys
tree	undelete	unformat	vsafe
xcopy			

9.4 MS-OFFICE APPLICATIONS

1. **Microsoft Word:** Used for word processing MS-word is a very powerful and popular tool for word processing. It facilitates creating of documents, mamos, newsletters and web pages.
2. **Microsoft Excel:** Used for creating workbooks. MS-Excel is an electronic spreadsheet, that provides features for data analysis and charts/graphs we can manage payroll, accounting, tables etc.
3. **Microsoft Power Point:** Used for creating presentation. MS-power point is an application for making presentation on a slide/overhead projector or by using <CD devices.
4. **Microsoft Access:** Used for creating databases and database applications. It is DBMS. It provides features for query, reporting and mailing list. e.g., library management.
5. **Microsoft Outlook:** Used for e-mails. Primarily used for e-mails, MS-outlook also take care of document management. Calender scheduling, meeting planning and resource management. We can use MS outlook for composing an e-mails etc.
6. **Microsoft Publisher:** Used for creating newsletters, brochures, visiting cards, etc., we can create publications, such as letter heads, brochures, etc.
7. **Microsoft Front Page :** Used for creating web pages.
8. **Microsoft Photo Draw:** Use for creating artwork and illustrations.
9. **Microsoft Business Tools:** Package of applications such as bookshelf, financial manager etc.

10. **Mail Merge:** The mail merge feature is a very important in MS-word, like all other word processing s/w applications. This is useful in carrying out the activities of mass mailing using this feature, we can first store the information about the addresses (such as their names and addresses) in one file. We can then create another file which contains the actual contents of the letter. In this file, we substitute the recipient names and addresses with special identifiers.

9.4.1 List out Some Important Functions and Their Functionality

In this section, the tips for doing some important functions in the windows are given.

To Open a File or Folder :

1. Double-click My Computer on the desktop.
2. Double-click the drive that contains the file.
3. Double-click the file or folder you want to open.

It will then open the file for you.

To Open a File You have Used Recently :

1. Click Start, and then point to Documents.
2. Click the document you want to open.

To Copy a File or Folder from One Disk/Folder to Another :

1. In My Computer or Windows Explorer, click the file or folder you want to copy.
2. On the Edit menu, click Copy.
3. Open the folder or disk where you want to put the copy.
4. On the Edit menu, click Paste.

To Change the Name of a File or Folder :

1. In My Computer or Windows Explorer, click the file or folder you want to rename.
2. On the File menu, click Rename.
3. Type the new name, and then press ENTER.

To Delete a File or Folder :

1. In My Computer or Windows Explorer, click the file or folder you want to delete.
2. On the File menu, click Delete.
3. You can also drag file or folder icons into the Recycle Bin. If you press SHIFT key while dragging, the item will be deleted from your computer without being stored in the Recycle Bin.

To Find a File or Folder :

1. Click Start, point to find, and then click files or folders.
2. In Named, type all or part of the file name.

   Enter a word or phrase in dialogue box if you do not know the name of a file but know a distinctive word or phrase it contains.

   If you want to specify the location to start the search, click Browse.
3. Click on Find Now.

***To See What's on Your Computer* :**

1. Double-click My Computer.
2. Double-click the icon of the drive you want to see.

   Windows displays the files and folders on the drive. Folders can contain files, programs, and other folders.
3. To open a file or folder, or to start a program, double-click it.

***To Change the Background of the Desktop* :**

1. Go to start-setting control panel and double click on display icon.
2. Alternatively you may right click the mouse and select properties.
3. In Wallpaper, click the background you want to use or click Patern to choose or modify the background.
4. Click Apply to see the changes before you close the dialog box, or click OK to accept the changes and close the dialog box.

***To Set up a Screen Saver* :**

1. Go to start-setting-control panel and double click on display icon.
2. Alternatively you may right click the mouse and select properties.
3. To open the Display Properties dialog box at the Screen Saver tab.
4. In Screen saver, click the screen saver your want to use.
5. To customize the screen saver, click Settings.

   Display properties are shown in Figure.

***To Adjust the Rate at which the Cursor Blinks* :**

1. Go to start-setting control panel and double click on keyboard icon.
2. On the Speed tab, drag the Cursor blink rate slider.

   The test cursor to the left of the slider area blinks at the new rate.

***To Send a File or Folder to a Disk* :**

1. If you are copying a file or folder to a floppy disk, insert disk in the disk drive.
2. In My Computer or Windows Explorer, click the file or folder you want to copy.
3. On the File menu, point to Send To, and then click the drive you want to copy the file or folder to.
4. After selecting a file or folder to copy, right click the mouse and select Send to Floppy Disk.

***To Move a File or Folder* :**

1. In My Computer or Windows Explorer, click the file or folder you want to move.
2. On the Edit menu, click Cut or Copy.
3. Open the folder where you want to put the file or folder.
4. On the Edit menu, click Paste.

Creating a Shortcut :

1. A shortcut is a quick way to start a program or open a file or folder without going to its permanent location in Windows Explorer. Shortcuts are especially useful for programs, files and folders you use frequently. There are three ways you can create a shortcut.

To Put a Shortcut on the Desktop :

1. In My Computer or Windows Explorer, click the item, such as a file, program, folder, printer, or computer, for which you want to create a shortcut.
2. On the File menu, click Create Shortcut.
3. Drag the shortcut icon onto the desktop.

To Create a Folder :

1. Click the drive in windows Explorer where you want to create the new folder.
2. On the File menu, point to New, and then click Folder.

   The new folder appears with a temporary name.
3. Type a name for the new folder, and then press ENTER.

List the basic working of each of following:

(*i*) MS-Word

(*ii*) MS-Excel

(*iii*) MS-Power Point

Microsoft office package consists of several software which are frequently used by MS Windows users. The MS Windows provides the platform for office tools. These are given the name office tools because they are very useful in disposing various day-to-day office works. The office tool is a bunch of several other tools like Word, Access, Excel, Power Point etc. The office tools are tightly integrated with the MS Windows and gives best performance with MS Windows platform. The documents created in one of the office tools may be used in another office tool.

For example—The MS Excel may use the MS Word files. These tools use graphical user interface and are quite easy to learn. Most of the tasks in these tools may be accomplished by few clicks of the mouse. These packages may also be utilized at other places also for specialized work. This package is a bunch of following important software or tools:

(*i*) **MS-Word:** used for word processing.

(*ii*) **MS-Excel:** used for calculation and analysis of data.

(*iii*) **MS-Power Point:** used for business and technical presentations.

(*iv*) **MS Access:** used for database applications.

MS-Word—The MS Word package is one of most important and widely used tools for word processing applications. This package allows you to type the text, format the text and helps generating documents. The documents, once entered, may be saved for longer time and whenever the documents need to be reproduced with modification, it can be done with little effort. MS Word allows you to do the following:

- Creat, open, save and print the documents.
- Typing, editing, copy, paste and justifying the text.

- Search for spelling and grammatical errors.
- Formatting the paragraphs.
- Create and manipulate the tables.
- Page setup, paper size, margin, header, footer, page numbering etc.

MS Excel—MS Excel is widely used software which is a part of MS Office package. It is used mainly for simple calculation and tabular management of data. Various analyses of data may also be performed by MS Excel. MS Excel is considered to be a good tool for organizing numerical data. It not only helps to organize and manage the data but queries may also be performed on the data. MS Excel application may be started by clicking MS Excel on *'Program'* option of *'Start'* button.

The major operations done by MS Excel are given below:

1. Create, Open, save, edit work book.
2. Page Setup, Menu Commands, Alignment.
3. Calculation in the worksheet, Entering & Editing a formula.
4. Working with Charts.

MS-Power Point—The MS Power Point is a widely used tool for business and academic presentations. This allows including images, Graphics, Audio, and Video in the presentation. One may prepare a multimedia presentation using this tool. In the current days presentations are being prepared to present the profile of an organization, strategies, policies, lectures. These presentations are prepared to address the mass gathering by putting the different ideas and plans in a systematic way. It helps audience to understand the ideas and views narrated in the presentations. To prepare a good presentation, it is not only necessary to be aware of the audience level and contents of matter but also it is equally important to include the contents in the presentation in simplified manner.

A Power Point presentation is basically a collection of various slides which contain images and audio visual components also. Each slide may be tuned with animation and other settings. Power Point allows you to create presentation in three ways given below:

1. Auto Contents Wizard.
2. Templates.
3. Blank Presentation.

You can start by working with the Auto Content wizard, in which you begin with a presentation that contains suggested content and design or with design templates which determines design of the presentation but doesn't include content or by using blank presentation which does not suggest either.

9.5 BASICS OF DBMS

9.5.1 Introduction

An Overview of database Management System: "A database Management System (DBMS) is a collection of interrelated data and a set of programs to access those data." The collection of data, usually referred to as the database, contains information relevant to an enterprise. The primary goal of a DBMS is to provide a way to store and retrieve database information that is both convenient and efficient.

Database is the combination of two words

Database + Management System = DBMS

A Database is a collection of related information stored, So that it is available to many users for different purposes.

On the other hand Management system is a collection of programs that enables users to create and maintain the database.

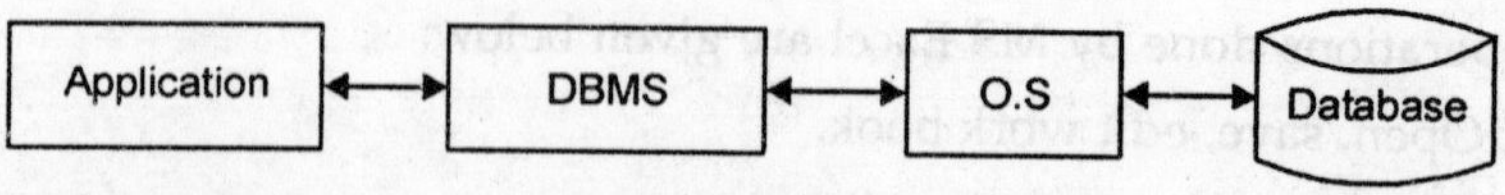

DBMS can also be defined as an interface between the application program and the operating system to access or manipulate that database.

A DBMS is a software system that allows access to data contained in the database. It's objective is to provide a convenient and effective method of defining, storing and retreving the information contained in the database. The DBMS interfaces with application programs so that the data contained in the database can be used by multiple applications and users.

9.5.2 Applications of DBMS

Some of the important application fields of DBMS are:

1. **Banking:** For maintaining customer information, accounts loans and banking transactions.
2. **Universities:** For maintaining student records, course registration and grades.
3. **Railway Reservation:** For checking the availability of reservation in different trains, tickets, etc.
4. **Airlines:** For reserva'ion and schedule information.
5. **Telecommunication:** For keeping records of calls made, generating monthly bills etc.
6. **Finance:** For storing information about holdings, sales and purchase of financial instruments.
7. **Sales:** For customer, product and purchase information.

9.5.3 Advantages and Disadvantages of DBMS

Advantages

1. **Less Redundancy and Inconsistency:** DBA has the centralized control of the data, so it will avoid the inconsistency because now we have to make the changes at one place only.
2. **Data Independence:** Application programs should be as independent as possible from details of data representation and storage. The DBMS can provide an abstract view of the data to insulate application code from such details.

3. **Reduced Application Development Time:** Clearly, the DBMS supports many important functions that are common to many applications accessing data stored in the DBMS.
4. **Efficient Data Accessing:** A DBMS utilizes a variety of sophisticated techniques to store and retrieve data efficiently. This feature is especially important if the data is stored on external storage devices.
5. **Data Integrity and Security:** A DBMS provides the integrity constraints on the data. It also provides the access control to the data. Not every user of the database system should be allowed to access all the data.
6. **Data Administration:** When several users share the data. Centralizing the administration of data can offer significant improvements.
7. **Concurrent Access and Crash Recovery:** A DBMS schedules concurrent accesses to the data in such a manner that users can think of the data as being accessed by anyone user at a time. Further it also protect users from the effects of the system failure.

Disadvantages

1. **Problems Associated with Centralization:** Centralization increases the security problems and disruption due to the downtimes and failures.
2. **Cost of Software:** Today's there are several software which are very costly. Hence from economic point of view it is the drawback.
3. **Cost of Hardware:** It incurred in the application of DBMS is its major disadvantage. Cost of the H/W is also one of the major drawback.
4. **Complexity of Backup and Recovery:** DBMS provides the centralization of the data, which requires the adequate backups of the data so that in case of failure, the data can be recovered. Hence backup problem is also the drawback.

9.5.4 Database System Versus/File Systems

Database systems are designed to manage large bodies of information. Management of data involves both defining structures for storage of information and providing mechanisms for the manipulation of information.

On the other hand File Processing System is supported by a convential operating system. The system stores permanent records in various Files and it needs different application programs to extract records from, and add records to the appropriate files. Before DBMS came along, organizations usually stored information in such systems.

DBMS	*File Processing System*
1. Date Redundancy problem is not found.	Here Redundancy problem exist.
2. Data Inconsistency does not exist.	It also exist in this.
3. Accessing database is easier	Accessing database is comparatively difficult.
4. The problem of data Isolation is not found in it.	Data are scattered in various Files in different formats. Writing new program to retrieve appropriate data is difficult.
5. Atomicity and Integrating problems are not found.	Atomicity and Integrating problems are found.
6. Security of data is in DBMS.	Here it is not good.

9.5.5 Database System Concepts and Architecture

■ *View of Data*

Data Abstraction. System hides some of the details how the data is stored or maintained.

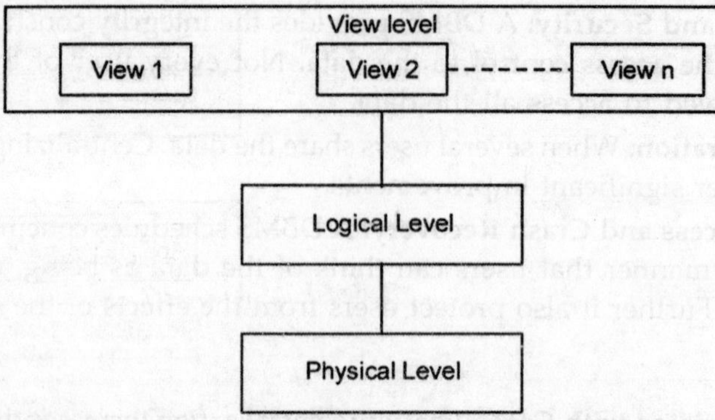

There are three levels of data abstraction:

1. **Physical Level.** This is the lowest level of abstraction and describes how the data are actually stored. The physical level describes complex low-level data structures in details.
2. **Logical Level.** This is the next-higher level of abstraction and it describes what data are stored in the database, and which relationship exist among those data. The logical level thus describes the entire database in terms of a small number of relatively simple structures. This is used by Database Administrator.
3. **View Level.** This is the highest level of abstraction describes only part of the entire database. Even though the logical level uses simpler structures, complexity remains because of the variety of information stored in a large database. The view level of abstraction exists to simplify their interaction with the system. The system may provide many views for the same database.

9.5.6 Application Architecture of DBMS

Basically there are two types of architecture of DBMS:

1. Two-tier architecture.
2. Three-tier architecture.

In a two-tier architecture, the application is partitioned into a component that resides at the client machine, which invokes database system functionary at the server machine through query language statements. Application program interface standards like ODBC (Open Database Connectivity) and JDBC (Java Database Connectivity) are used for interaction between the client and the server.

In a three-tier architecture, the client machine acts as merely a front end and does not contain any direct database calls. Instead, the client end communicates with an application server, usually through a forms interface. The application server in turn communicates with a database system to access data. Three-tier applications are more appropriate for large applications, and for applications that run on the world wide web.

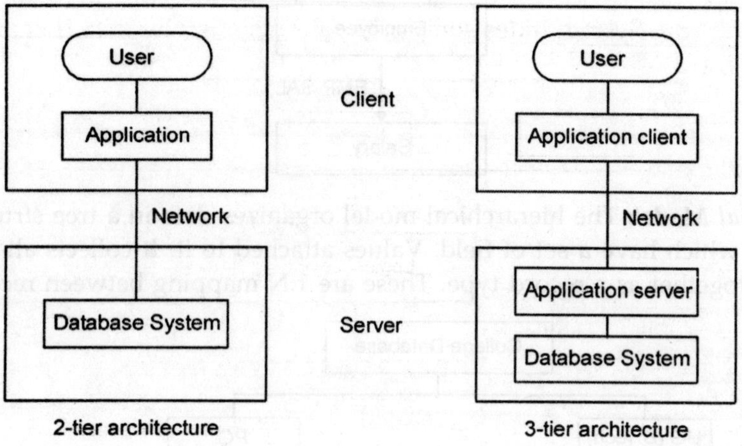

9.5.7 Data Models

Data Model is a collection of conceptual tools for describing data, data relationships, data semantics and consistency constraints. A Data Model can also be define as the collection of high level data description constructs that hide many low-level storage details.

1. Object Based Local Models.
2. Record Based Local Models.
3. Physical Model.

There are five types of Data Models:

1. Relational Data Model.
2. Object-oriented Data Model.
3. Network Data Model.
4. Hierarchical Data Model.
5. Object Relational Data Model.

1. *Relational Data Model*: The Relational Model uses a collection of tables to represent both data and the relationship among those data. Each table has multiple columns, and each column has a unique name. This model uses the certain Mathematical operations from relational Algebra and relational calculus on the relation, such as Projection, Union and joins etc.

Roll No.	Name	Class	Address	Contact No.
1001	RAM	3rd Year	Noida	094261846

2. *Object-oriented Data Model*: The object-oriented mode can be seen as extending the E-R model with notions of encapsulation, methods (functions), and object identity. The object-oriented provides higher performance management of objects, and it enables better management of the inter-relationships between objects.

3. ***Network Model*****:** The network model permit the modeling of many to many relationships in data. The basic data model construct in the network model is the set construct.

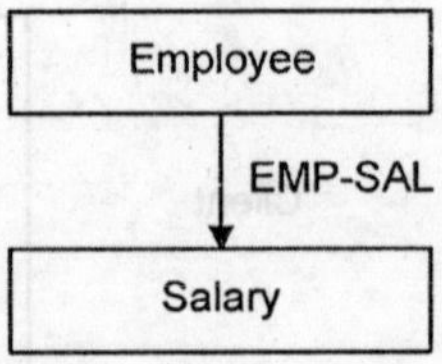

4. ***Hierarchical Model*****:** The hierarchical model organizes data in a tree structure. Data in a series of records, which have a set of field. Values attached to it. It collects all the instances of a specific record together as a record type. These are 1:N mapping between record types.

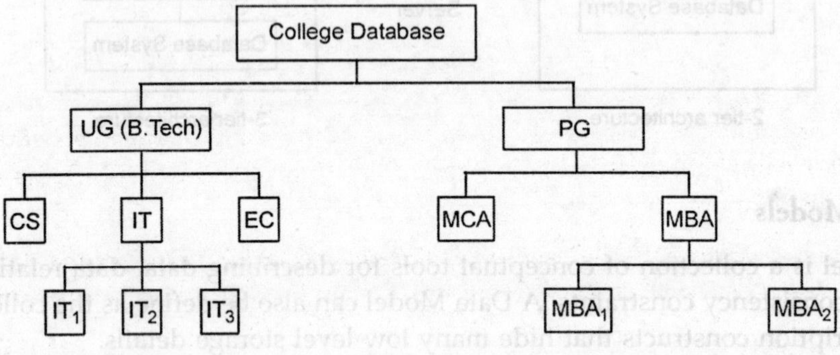

5. ***Object-relational Data Model*****:** Object-relational database management system (ORDBMSs) add new object storage capability to the relational system at the core of modern information system. By encapsulating methods with data structures and ORDBMS, server can execute complex analytical and data manipulation operation to search and transform multimedia and other complex objects.

9.5.8 Schema and Instances

The collection of information stored in the database at a particular moments is called an **"instance of the database"**. The over all design of the database is called the **"database schema"**.

The concept of database schema and instance can be understood by analogy to a program written in a programming language. A database schema corresponds to the variable declaration in a program. Each variable has a particular value at a given instant. The values of the variables in a program at a point in time corresponds to an instance of a database schema.

There are three types of schema:

1. Physical Schema.
2. Conceptual Schema.
3. External Schema.

1. ***Physical Schema*****:** Physical schema describes the database design at the physical level. It specifies additional storage details. Essentially, the physical schema summarizes how the relations described in the conceptual scheme are actually stored on secondary storage devices such as disks and tapes.

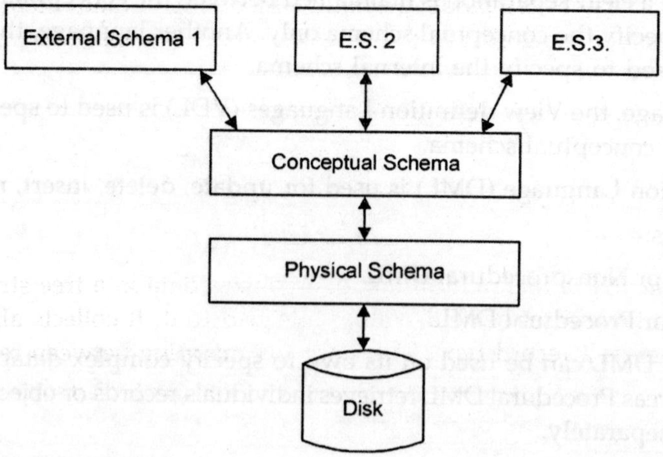

2. *Conceptual Schema*: The conceptual schema (Sometimes called Logical Schema) describes the stored data interms of the data model of the DBMS. In a relational DBMS, the conceptual. Schema describes all relations that are stored in the database.

3. *External Schema*: External schemas, which usually are also interms of the data Model of the DBMS allow data access to be customized at the level of individual users or groups of users.

9.5.9 Data Independence

The ability to modify a schema defination in one level without affecting a schema definition in the next higher level is called Data Independence.

Data Independence is one of the main advantage of the DBMS

It is of two types:

1. Physical Data Independence.
2. Logical Data Independence.

1. *Physical Data Independence*: It is the ability to modify the physical schema without causing application programs to be rewritten. In other words, old programs do not have to be rewritten, when changes are made to physical storage structure or the physical devices on which data are stored.

2. *Logical Data Independence*: It is the ability to modify the conceptual schema without causing application program to be rewritten. Logical data independence is more difficult to achieve than physical data independence, since program are having dependence on the logical structure of the database.

9.5.10 Database Language and Interfaces

In many DBMSs where no strict separation of levels is maintained, one language called the data definition Language (DDL), is used by the DBA and by database designers to define both schemas.

In DBMSs where a clear separation is maintained between the conceptual and internal levels, the DDL is used to specify the conceptual schema only. Another language, the storage definition Language (SDL) is used to specify the internal schema.

The third Language, the View definition Languages (VDL) is used to specify user views and their mapping to the conceptual schema.

Data Manipulation Language (DML) is used for update, delete, insert, retrieve.

It is of two types:

1. High-level or Non-procedural DML.
2. Low-level or Procedural DML.

Non-procedural DML can be used on its own to specify complex database operations in a concise manner. Whereas Procedural DML retrieves individuals records or objects from the database and processes each separately.

9.5.11 DBMS Interfaces

There are six types of Interface provided by a DBMS:

1. Menu-Based Interfaces for Browsing.
2. Forms-Based Interfaces.
3. Graphical-user Interfaces.
4. Natural Language Interfaces.
5. Interface for parametric users.
6. Interfaces for the DBA.

1. *Menu-Based Interfaces for Browsing*: These interfaces present the user with lists of options, called menus, that lead the user through the formulation of a request. Pull-down menus are becoming a very popular technique in window-based user interfaces. They are often used in browsing interfaces, which allow a user to look through the contents of a database in an exploratory and unstructured manner.

2. *Forms-Based Interfaces*: A form-based interfaces displays a form to each user. Users can fill out all of the form entries to insert new data, or they fill out only certain entries, in which case the DBMS will retrieve matching data for the remaining entries. Many DBMSs have forms specification languages, special languages that help programmers specify such forms.

3. *Graphical User Interfaces*: A Graphical user Interface (GUI) typically displays a schema to the user in diagrammatic form. The user can then specify a query by manipulating the diagram. In many Cases, GUI utilize both menus and forms. Most GUI use a pointing devices such as a mouse, to pick certain parts of the displayed schema diagram.

4. *Natural Language Interface*: These interfaces accept requests written in English or some other language and attempt to "understand" them. A natural language interface usually has its own "Schema" which is similar to the database conceptual schema.

5. *Interfaces for Parametric users.* Parametric users, such as bank tellers, often have a small set of operation that they must perform repeatedly. System analyst and programmers design and implement a special interface for a known class of naive users.

6. *Interfaces for the DBA*: Most database system contain privileged commands that can be used only by the DBA's staff. These includes commands for creating accounts, setting system parameters etc.

9.5.12 Data Definition Language (DDL)

It is a set of SQL commands used to create, modify and delete database structures but not data. These commands are normally not used by a general user, who should be accessing the database via an application. They are normally used by the DBA to a limited extent, a database designer or application developer. These statements are immediate *i.e.,* they are to susceptible to Roll Back Commands.

DDL also updates a special set of tables called the data dictionary or data directory.

A data dictionary contains Metadata-*i.e,* data about data. The schema of a table is an example of metadata. A database system consults the data dictionary before reading or modifying actual data.

9.5.13 Data Manipulation Language (DML)

It is the area of SQL that allows changing data within the database.

A DML is a language that enables users to access or manipulate data or organized by the appropriate data model.

Through DML, we can.

1. **Insert the new data in the database:** For example if a person joins the company then we have to insert the information of that employee in our employee database.
2. **Modify the data, already stored in the database:** For example in employee database, if an employee gets hike (increament) in his salary than we have to modify the record of that employee.
3. **Deletion of the data:** For example if an employee resigns from the company than we have to delete that record from the database.
4. **Retrieve the information:** For example if we want to display the address of an employee then we have to write the query statement for that information.

It is of two types:

1. Procedural DML
2. Non-Procedural DML.

1. *Procedural DML*: It requires a user to specify what data are needed and how to get those data. It also requires writing the procedures/methods to specify what data is needed. Procedural DML Language has all the features of any other high-level language including control constructs, error handling and other features.

2. *Non-Procedural DML:* It is also called as declarative DML and it require a user to specify what data are needed without specifying how to get those data. Non-procedural DML is the collection of commands for data manipulation including insert, update, delete and query the data.

3. *DCL (Data Control Language)*: It is the component of SQL statement that control access to data and to the database. Occasionally DCL Statements are grouped the DML statements.

Through DCL, we can:

1. Commit— Save work done.
2. Roll back— Restore database to original since the last commit.

Data Query Language (DQL) : It is the component of SQL statement that allows getting data from the database and imposing ordering upon it. It includes the SELECT statement. This command is the heart of SQL. *"A query is a statement requesting the retrieval of information."*

Through DQL, we can.

1. SELECT–Retrieve data from the database.

9.5.14 Architecture of DBMS

■ ***Overall Database Structure***

The major component of a DBMS Architecture are:

1. **DDL Compiler :** The DDL statements are sent to DDL compiler, which converts these statements to a set of tables. These tables contain the metadata. Concerning the database and are in a form that can be used by other components of the DBMS.
2. **DML Pre-compiler and Query Processor :** The DML pre-compiler converts the DML statements embedded in an application program to normal procedure calls in the host. language. If the DML statements include the queries then it goes to query processor, which interprets the query and converts it into an efficient series of operations.

   The Query processor components include:

   (*i*) **DDL Interpreter**—Which iterprets DDL statements and records the definitions in the data dictionary.

   (*ii*) **DML Compiler**—Which translates DML statements in a query language into an evaluation plan consisting of low-level instructions that the query evaluation engine understands. The DML compiler also performs query optimization, *i.e.*, it picks the lowest cost evaluation plan from among the alternatives.

   (*iii*) **Query Evaluation Engine**—Which executes low-level instructions generated by the DML compiler.

3. **Data Manager :** Data Manager controls the database. It provides the interface between the database and the application programs. Data Manager converts the user's requests coming directly via the query processor or via applications programs to a physical file system. The data manager is responsible for interactions with the file manager, integrity and security enforcement and concurrency control.
4. **File Manager :** File manager is responsible for allocation of space on disk storage and the data structures used to represent information stored on physical media.
5. **Data files :** These are the files, which contain the data.
6. **Data Dictionary :** Which is used to store the metadata about the structure of the database. It also keeps track of relationships that exist between various data structures.
7. **Indices :** Which provide fast access to data items that hold particular values.

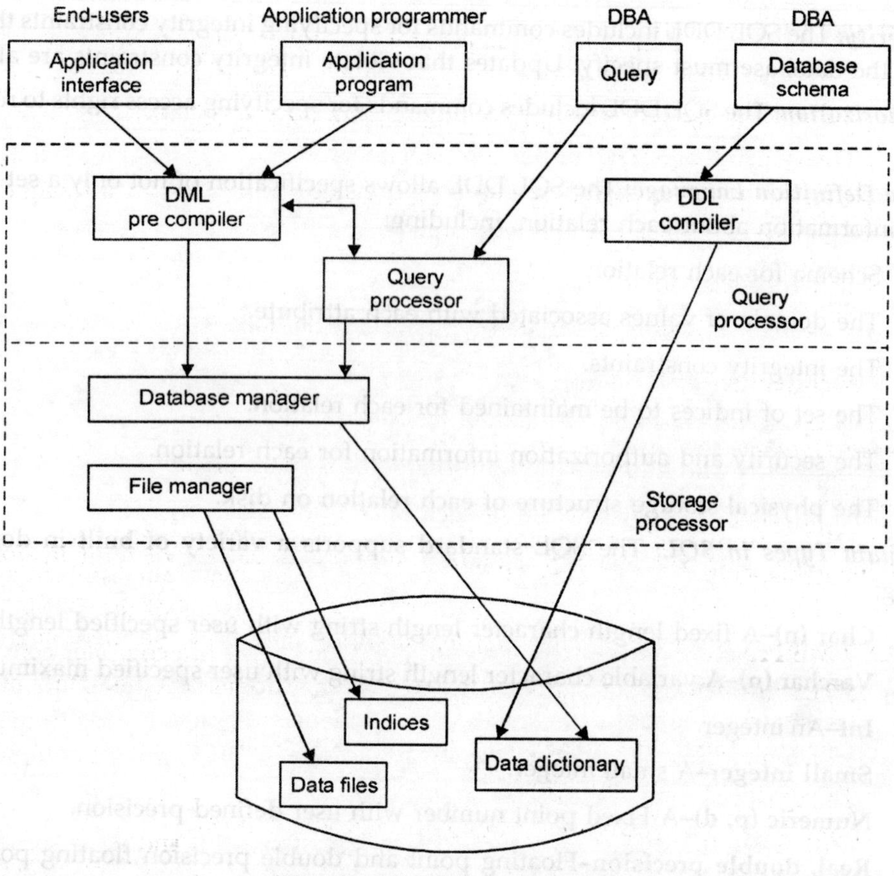

Fig. *Overall Database Structure*

9.6 INTRODUCTION TO BASIC COMMANDS OF SQL

Objective 1: Create tables and specify the Questionries in SQL.

9.6.1 Theory and Concepts

Introduction about SQL: SQL (Structured Questionry Language) is a nonprocedural language, you specify what you want, not how to get it. A block structured format of English key words is used in this Questionry language. It has the following components.

DDL (Data Definition Language): The SQL DDL provides command for defining relation schemas, deleting relations and modifying relation schema.

DML (Data Manipulation Language): It includes commands to insert tuples into, delete tuples from and modify tuples in the database.

View Definition: The SQL DDL includes commands for defining views.

Transaction Control-SQL includes for specifying the beginning and ending of transactions.

Embedded SQL and Dynamic SQL: Embedded and Dynamic SQL define how SQL statements can be embedded with in general purpose programming languages, such as C, C++, JAVA, COBOL, Pascal and Fortran.

Integrity: The SQL DDL includes commands for specifying integrity constraints that the data stored in the database must specify. Updates that violate integrity constraints are allowed.

Authorization: The SQL DDL includes commands for specifying access rights to relations and views.

Data Definition Language: The SQL DDL allows specification of not only a set of relations but also information about each relation, including:

- Schema for each relation.
- The domain of values associated with each attribute.
- The integrity constraints.
- The set of indices to be maintained for each relation.
- The security and authorization information for each relation.
- The physical storage structure of each relation on disk.

Domain Types in SQL: The SQL standard supports a variety of built in domain types, including:

- **Char (n)**–A fixed length character length string with user specified length.
- **Varchar (n)**–A variable character length string with user specified maximum length n.
- **Int**–An integer.
- **Small integer**–A small integer.
- **Numeric (p, d)**–A Fixed point number with user defined precision.
- **Real, double precision**–Floating point and double precision floating point numbers with machine dependent precision.
- **Float (n)**–A floating point number, with precision of at least n digits.
- **Date**–A calender date containing a (four digit) year, month and day of the month.
- **Time**–The time of day, in hours, minutes and seconds Eg. Time '09:30:00'.
- **Number**–Number is used to store numbers (fixed or floating point).

9.6.2 DDL Statement for Creating a Table

Syntax

Create table tablename

(columnname datatype(size), columnname datatype(size));

Creating a table from a table:

Syntax

CREATE TABLE TABLENAME

[(columnname, columnname,.......)]

AS SELECT columnname, columnname.......From Tablename'

Insertion of data into tables:

Syntax

INSERT INTO tablename

[(columnname, columnname,..............)]

Values (expression, expression);

Inserting data into a table from another table:

Syntax

INSERT INTO tablename

SELECT columnname, columnname,..........

FROM tablename;

Insertion of selected data into a table from another table:

Syntax

INSERT INTO tablename

SELECT columnname, columnname...........

FROM tablename;

WHERE Columnname = expression;

Retrieving of data from the tables:

Syntax

SELECT * FROM tablename;

The retrieving of specific columns from a table:

Syntax

SELECT columnname, columnname, ...

FROM tablename;

Elimination of duplicates from the select statement:

Syntax

SELECT DISTINCT columnname, columnname

FROM tablename;

Selecting a data set from table data:

Syntax

SELECT columnname, columnname

FROM tablename

WHERE searchcondition;

Q.1. Create the following tables:

(*i*) Client_master

Columnname	*Datatype*	*Size*
client_no	varchar2	6
name	varchar2	20
address1	varchar2	30
address2	varchar2	30
city	varchar2	15
state	varchar2	15
pincode	number	6
bal_due	number	10,2

(*ii*) Product_master

Columnname	*Datatype*	*Size*
Product_no	varchar2	
Description	varchar2	
Profit_percent	number	
Unit_measure	varchar2	
Qty_on_hand	number	
Reoder_lvlnumber		
Sell_price	number	
Cost_price number		

Q.2. Insert the following data into their respective tables:

Clientno	*Name*	*City*	*Pincode*	*State*	*Bal.due*
0001	Ivan	Bombay	400054	Maharashtra	15000
0002	Vandana	Madras	780001	Tamilnadu	0
0003	Pramada	Bombay	400057	Maharashtra	5000
0004	Basu	Bombay	400056	Maharashtra	0
0005	Ravi	Delhi	100001		2000
0006	Rukmini	Bombay	400050	Maharashtra	0

***(i)* Data for Product Master :**

Product No.	*Desciption*	*Profit % Percent*	*Unit measured*	*Qty on hand*	*Recorder lvl*	*Sell price*	*Cost price*
P00001	1.44 floppies	5	piece	100	20	525	500
P03453	Monitors	6	piece	10	3	12000	11200
P06734	Mouse	5	piece	20	5	1050	500
P07865	1.22 floppies	5	piece	100	20	525	500
P07868	Keyboards	2	piece	10	3	3150	3050
P07885	CD Drive	2.5	piece	10	3	5250	5100
P07965	540 HDD	4	piece	10	3	8400	8000
P07975	1.44 Drive	5	piece	10	3	1050	1000
P08865	1.22 Drive	5	piece	2	3	1050	1000

Q.3. On the basis of above two tables answer the following Questions:

(i) Find out the names of all the clients.

(ii) Retrieve the list of names and cities of all the clients.

(iii) List the various products available from the product_master table.

(iv) List all the clients who are located in Bombay.

(v) Display the information for client no 0001 and 0002.

(vi) Find the products with description as '1.44 drive' and '1.22 Drive'.

(vii) Find all the products whose sell price is greater than 5000.

(viii) Find the list of all clients who stay in city 'Bombay' or city 'Delhi' or 'Madras'.

(ix) Find the product whose selling price is greater than 2000 and less than or equal to 5000.

(x) List the name, city and state of clients not in the state of 'Maharashtra'.

Objective 2: To Manipulate the Operations on the table.

DML (Data Manipulation Language) Data manipulation is:

- The retrieval of information stored in the database.
- The insertion of new information into the database.
- The deletion of information from the database.
- The modification of information stored by the appropriate data model. There are basically two types.

  (i) **Procedural DML:** Require a user to specify what data are needed and how to get those data.

  (ii) **Non Procedural DML:** Require a user to specify what data are needed without specifying how to get those data.

Updating the Content of a Table

In creation situation we may wish to change a value in table without changing all values in the tuple. For this purpose the updata statement can be used.

Update table name

Set columnname = experision, columnname = expression......

Where columnname = expression;

Deletion Operation: A delete requestionst is expressed in much the same way as Questionry. We can delete whole tuple (rows) we can delete values on only particulars attributes.

Deletion of all rows

Syntax

Delete from tablename:

Deletion of specified number of rows

Syntax

Delete from table name

Where search condition;

Computation in expression lists used to select data

+	Addition	– subtraction
*	multiplication	** exponentiation
/	Division	() Enclosed operation

Renaming columns used with Expression Lists: The default output column names can be renamed by the user if required.

Syntax

Select columnname result_columnname,

Columnname result_columnname,

From table name;

Logical Operators

The logical operators that can be used in SQL sentenced are:

AND all of must be included

OR any of may be included

NOT none of could be included.

Range Searching: Between operation is used for range searching.

Pattern Searching: The most commonly used operation on string is pattern matching using the operation 'like' we describe patterns by using two special characters.

- Percent (%); the % character matches any substring we consider the following examples.

- '% idege % matches any string containing' idge as substring.
- '------' matches any string exactly three characters.
- '----%' matches any string of at least of three characters.

Oracle functions: Functions are used to manipulate data items and return result. Function follow the format of function_name (argument1, argument2...). An arrangement is user defined variable or constant. The structure of function is such that it accepts zero or more arguments.

Examples

Avg return average value of *n*.

Syntax:

Avg ([distinct/all]n)

Min return minimum value of expr.

Syntax:

MIN ((distict/all) expr)

Count Returns the no of rows where expr is not null

Syntax:

Count ([distinct/all)expr]

Count (*) Returns the no rows in the table, including duplicates and those with nulls.

Max Return max value of expr

Syntax:

Max ([distinct/all]expr)

Sum Returns sum of values of *n*

Syntax:

Sum ([distinct/all]n)

Sorting of data in table

Syntax:

Select columnname, columnname

From table

Order by columnname;

Q.4. Using the table client master and product master answer the following **Questionries.**

(*i*) Change the selling price of '1.44 floppy drive to Rs. 1150.00.

(*ii*) Delete the record with client 0001 from the client master table.

(*iii*) Change the city of client_no '0005' to Bombay.

(*iv*) Change the bal_due of client_no '0001, to 1000.

(*v*) Find the products whose selling price is more that 1500 and also find the new selling price as original selling price * 15.

(*vi*) Find out the clients who stay in a city whose second letter is a.

(*vii*) Find out the name of all clients having 'a' as the second letter in their names.

(*viii*) List the products in sorted order of their description.

(*ix*) Count the total number of orders.

(*x*) Calculate the average price of all the products.

(*xi*) Calculate the minimum price of products.

(*xii*) Determine the maximum and minimum prices. Rename the tittle as 'max_price' and min_price respectively.

(*xiii*) Count the number of products having price greater than or equal to 1500.

Objective 3: To Implement the restrictions on the table.

Data constraints: Besides the cell name, cell length and cell data type there are other parameters i.e., other data constrains that can be passed to the DBA at check creation time. The constraints can either be placed at column level or at the table level.

(*i*) **Column Level Constraints:** If the constraints are defined along with the column definition, it is called a column level constraint.

(*ii*) **Table Level Constraints:** If the data constraint attached to a specify cell in a table reference the contents of another cell in the table then the user will have to use table level constraints.

Null Value Concepts: While creating tables if a row locks a data value for particular column that value is said to be null. Column of any data types may contain null values unless the column was defined as not null when the table was created.

Syntax:

Create table tablename

(columnname data type (size) not null .....)

Primary Key: Primary key is one or more columns is a table used to uniquickly identity each row in the table. Primary key values must not be null and must be uniQuestion across the column. A multicolumn primary key is called composite primary key.

Syntax: primary key as a column constraint

Create table tablename

(columnname datatype (size) primary key,....)

Primary key as a table constraint

Create table tablename

(columnname datatype (size), columnname datatype (size)...

Primary key (columnname, columnname));

UniQuestion key concept: A uniQuestion is similar to a primary key except that the purpose of a uniQuestion key is to ensure that information in the column for each record is uniQuestion as with telephone or devices license numbers. A table may have many uniQuestion keys.

Syntax: UniQuestion as a column constraint.

Create table name

(columnname datatype (size) uniQuestion);

UniQuestion as table constraint

Create table tablename

(columnname datatype (size), columnname datatype (size...uniQuestion (columnname, columnname));

Default Value Concept: At the line of cell creation a default value can be assigned to it. When the user is loading a record with values and leaves this cell empty, the DBA will automatically load this cell with the default value specified. The data type of the default value should match the data type of the column.

Syntax:

Create table tablename

(columnname datatype (size) default value,....);

Foreign Key Concept: Foreign key represents relationship between tables. A foreign key is column whose values are derived from the primary key of the same of some other table. The existence of foreign key implies that the table with foreign key is related to the primary key table from which the foreign key is derived. A foreign key must have corresponding primary key value in the primary key table to have meaning. Foreign key as a column constraint.

Syntax:

Create table tablename

(Columnname datatype (size) references another table name);

Foreign key as a table constraint

Syntax:

Create table name

(columnname datatype (size)...

Primary key (columnname);

Foreign key (columnname) references table name);

Check Integrity Constraints

Use the check constraints when you need to enforce intergrity rules that can be evaluated based on a logical expression following are a few examples of appropriate check constraints.

- A check constraints name column of the coient_master so that the name is entered in upper case.
- A check constraint on the client_no column of the client_master so that no client_no value starts with 'c'.

Syntax:

Create table tablename

(columnname datatype (size) CONSTRAINT constraintname)

Check (expression));

Q.5. Create the following tables:

(*i*) Sales_master

Columnname	*Datatype*	*Size*	*Attributes*
Salesman_no	varchar2	6	Primary key/first letter must start with 's'
Sal_name	varchar2	20	Not null
Address	varchar2		Not null
City	varchar2	20	
State	varchar2	20	
Pincode	Number	6	
Sal_amt	Number	8,2	Not null, cannot be 0
Tgt_to-get	Number	6,2	Not null, cannot be 0
Ytd_sales	Number	6,2	Not null, cannot be 0
Remarks	Varchar2	30	

(*ii*) Sales_order

Columnname	*Datatype*	*Size*	*Attributes*
S_order_no	varchar2	6	Primary/first letter must be 0
S_order_date	Data	6	Primary key reference clientno of client_master table
Client_no	Varchar2	25	
Dely_add	Varchar2	6	
Salesman_no	Varchar2	6	Foreign key references salesman_no of salesman_master table
Dely_type	Char	1	Delivery part (p)/full (f), default f
Billed_yn	Char	1	
Dely_data	Data		Can not be less than s_order_data
Order_status	Varchar2	10	Values ('in process';' fulfilled'; back order';' canceled.

(iii) Sales_order_details

Column	*Datatype*	*Size*	*Attributes*
S_order_no	Varchar2	6	Primary key/foreign key references s_order_no of sales_order
Product_no	Varchar2	6	Primary key/foreign key references product_no of product_master.
Qty_order	Number	8	
Qty_disp	Number	8	
Product_rate	Number	10,2	

Insert the following data into their respective tables using insert statement:

(iv) Data for sales_man master table

Salesman_ no	*Salesman name*	*Address*	*City*	*Pin code*	*State*	*Sal amt*	*Tgt_ to_tet*	*Ytd Sales*	*Remark*
500001	Kiran	A/14 worli	Bom bay	400002	Mah	3000	100	50	Good
500002	Manish	65, narim an	Bom bay	400001	Mah	3000	200	100	Good
500003	Ravi	P-7 Bandra	Bom bay	400032	Mah	3000	200	100	Good
500004	Ashish	A/5 Juhu	Bom bay	400044	Mah	3500	200	150	Good

(v) Data for salesorder table:

S_orderno	*S_orderdata*	*Client no*	*Dely type*	*Bill yn*	*Salesman no*	*Delay date*	*Order status*
019001	12-jan-96	0001	F	N	50001	20-jan-96	Ip
019002	25-jan-96	0002	P	N	50002	27-jan-96	C
016865	18-feb-96	0003	F	Y	500003	20-feb-96	F
019003	03-apr-96	0001	F	Y	500001	07-apr-96	F
046866	20-may-96	0004	P	N	500002	22may-96	C
010008	24-may-96	0005	F	N	500004	26-may-96	Ip

(vi) Data for sales_order_details table:

S_order no	*Product no*	*Qty ordered*	*Qty disp*	*Product_rate*
019001	P00001	4	4	525
019001	P07965	2	1	8400
019001	P07885	2	1	5250
019002	P00001	10	0	525
046865	P07868	3	3	3150
046865	P07885	10	10	5250
019003	P00001	4	4	1050
019003	P03453	2	2	1050
046866	P06734	1	1	12000
046866	P07965	1	0	8400
010008	P07975	1	0	1050
010008	P00001	10	5	525

Objective 4: To Implement the structure of the table.

9.6.3 Modifying the Structure of Tables

After table command is used to changing the structure of a table. Using the alter table clause you cannot perform the following tasks:

(*i*) change the name of table
(*ii*) change the name of column
(*iii*) drop a column
(*iv*) decrease the size of a table if table data exists.

The following tasks you can perform through alter table command.

(*i*) Adding new columns:

Syntax:

```
ALTER TABLE tablename
ADD (newcolumnname newdatatype (size));
```

(*ii*) Modifying existing table

Syntax:

```
ALTER TABLE tablename
MODIFY (Newcolumnname newdatatype (size));
```

Note: Oracle not allow constraints defined using the alter table, if the data in the table, violates such constraints.

9.6.4 Removing/Deleting Tables

Following command is used for removing or deleting a table.

Syntax:

DROP TABLE tablename:

Defining Integrity constraints in the ALTER TABLE command.

You can also define integrity constraints using the constraint clause in the ALTER TABLE command. The following examples show the definitions of several integrity constraints.

1. **Add Primary Key:**

   Syntax:

   ALTER TABLE tablename

   ADD PRIMARY KEY (columnname);

2. **Add Foreign KEY:**

   Syntax:

   ALTER TABLE tablename

   ADD CONSTRAINT constraintname

   FOREIGN KEY (columnname) REFERENCES tablename;

Droping integrity constraints in the ALTER TABLE command:

You can drop an integrity constraint if the rule that if enforces is no longer true or if the constraint is no longer needed. Drop the constraint using the ALTER TABLE command with the DROP clause. The following examples illustrate the droping of integrity constraints.

1. **DROP the PRIMARY KEY:**

   Syntax:

   ALTER TABLE tablename

   DROP PRIMARY KEY

2. **DROP FOREIGN KEY:**

   Syntax:

   ALTER TABLE tablename

   DROP CONSTRAINT constraintname.

EXERCISES

1. "Operating system is a resource manager," justify this statement by giving suitable reasons.
2. Differentiate between internal and external commands of DOS. Give three examples for each category.
3. Why is windows called GUI based system? How does recycle bin help to present-undertrial deletions?
4. Define SQL. What are advantages of using it? Given the classification of SQL statements.
5. Discuss the general Architecture of Database Management System. Explain the role of transaction manager.
6. Discuss the different levels of Data Abstraction.
7. Name three models of database management system and explain any one in detail.
8. Write down five advantages of using MS Excel for accounting purpose.
9. Write syntax for creating table and SELECT command and illustrate it with an example.
10. Briefly explain the different components of DBMS.

10

INDUSTRY TRENDS OF IT AND ITS APPLICATIONS IN INDIA

10.1 SCIENTIFIC, BUSINESS AND EDUCATION APPLICATIONS OF IT

Scientists use computers to develop theories, gather data and test results and exchange information with colleagues. Scientists also use computers for simulating complicated events, such as predicting rainfalls or change in weather patterns.

Computers help tremendously in exploring the outer space. Satellites have beamed back to earth a great amount of information about the solar system and the cosmos.

Nowadays, computers are such flexible tools that most people use them everyday. Some examples of this are:

- Multimedia Applications
- Multimedia Entertainment
- Multimedia Training
- Multimedia Business.

Computers have truly revolutionized the area of education. Computer's can be found everywhere from classrooms to museums and from libraries to laboratories. In fact computers are now as relevant as notes, books, paper and pens. Students can make use of computers to create science projects. They can also prepare project reports, and gather information from the internet. In the library, they can read articles and other material of interest from magazines and journals hosted on a computer.

Computers can be used for distance education programs as well. Called as visual classrooms, here the teacher and the students can be far away from each other. They can be in different cities, countries, or even continents. Yet, the technology of computers and communications enables them to interact with each other as if they are setting in the same room.

10.2 INDUSTRY AUTOMATION

Industry Automation updates the industries by using digital computers to solve the most intricate scientific and industrial problems. Design of electrical appliance, transformers, simulations of power generation and distributions, mechanical and nuclear reactor designs, civilstructures, beams, building and bridge design need complex computations. Several S/W for handling these complex and specialized applications are available. Computer Aided Design (CAD) tools are examples of this. Computers are also being used intensively for the process control in an automated plant. Microprocessor based controllers in the process plant are programmable, and once programmed they perform specialized tasks effectively and accurately. On several occasions, the humans are not employed in hazardous working conditions such as gas chambers, working under high temperature or in high current zones etc. In these areas, computers are being deployed. The computer are also playing a very important role in military communications.

10.3 WEATHER FORECASTING

Weather forecasting is one of the important areas of application of information technology. Traditional weather forecasting methods were based upon the analysis and prediction through experiences. It was a combination of both science and art. In modern days after utilizing the enormous processing capabilities of digital computers, several scientific methods for weather forecasting have been developed. These methods employ numerous factors such as availability of data, previous experiences and the level of difficulty that the forecast situation presents. In the modern and scientific techniques, it is possible to read the weather maps in digital medium and these maps may be processed in such a way, that a pattern for the next few days is obtained.

10.4 E-GOVERNANCE

E-Governance or electronic governance may be defined as delivery of govt. services and information to the public using electronic means. Such means of delivering information is often referred to as IT. Use of it in govt facilitates an efficient, speedy and transparent process for disseminating information to the public and other agencies, and for performing govt. administration activities.

E-Governance advantages:

- Effective and efficient communication among the employees of the department.
- Provides online training to the employees on new issues and policies.
- Provide the facility for video conferencing.
- It stores the records electronically.
- The minimum efforts are required to process the information stored in digital form.

10.5 NICNET (NATIONAL INFORMATICS CENTER N/W)

NIC is a government organisation set up in 1980s. Its purpose is to provide support in terms of IT to govt. and public sector organisations. (NICNET) is a very important n/w that links govt. departments and organisations across the country. NICNET is set up to facilitate storage and fast communication of information between the various department and organisations of the govt. It also acts as a backbone to the development planning and administrative checking for the Govt.

NICNET uses satellite technology. It connects govt. agencies at the central, state and district levels. NIC also develops S/W for govt projects and activities. NIC also undertakes projects to be developed using third party S/W products.

NICNET provides VSAT and dial up internet access to govt. departments and S/W exports divisions.

ERNET and NICNET are considered as India's first ISPs that have provided internet access. However, several other government agencies like DOT (Deptt. of Telecom) and VSNL (Videsh Sanchar Nigam Limited) are offering Internet services to a variety of subscribers on commercial basis.

10.5.1 CMC Ltd

Computer Maintenance Corporation, a government company has established it's own network called INDONET for the computer users community in the country. The N/W provides distributed data processing facilities on all -India basis to large organisations using CMC's computer for their data processing operations. CMC has also taken up large software projects for the automation of Railways and other government departments. Other important N/W already under operation under the aegis of the govt are SIRNET (Scientific and Industrial N/W), BTISNET (Biotechnology Information System N/W) and SOFTNET by software Technology Park. All these N/W are self sufficient and are being used for file transfers, E-mail, Video telephony and other internet services.

10.6 ERNET (EDUCATIONAL AND RESEARCH NETWORK)

The Department of Electronics (DOE) initiated the ERNET in 1987. The aim behind setting up ERNET was to help the academic and research community of India. One of the aims of ERNET was to enable communication b/w these community participants. DOE, the Govt. of India, and the United Nation Development Program (UNDP) jointly developed ERNET.

ERNET is actually, a computer N/W. As such, it is India's first TCP/IP N/W for facilitating educational and research institutions in India's premier institutions and research laboratories. ERNET provides internet access to researchers, students, professors and academicians.

ERNET Connected Eight Institutions in India:

- IIT (Mumbai, Kharagpur, Kanpur, Chennai and New Delhi)
- IIS, Bangalore
- National Center for S/W Technology, Mumbai.
- DOE, New Delhi.

■ Following were the Primary Motives Behind the Creation of ERNET:

- Establish a computer N/W of the premier educational and research Institutions around the country to facilitate education and research.
- Develop India's Infrastructure.
- Develop HR By means of education and training to enhance the awareness of information available on the internet.
- Make available information about India to the outside world.

10.7 MULTIMEDIA ENTERTAINMENT

The word 'multimedia' is made up of two separate words, multi meaning many, and media meaning materials through which information may be transmitted. Therefore, multimedia can be described as an integration of multiple media elements together to influence the given information so that it can be presented in an attractive and interactive manner. In simple words, the word multimedia simply means being able to communicate in more than one way.

Multimedia is mainly concerned with the computer-controlled integration of text, graphics, drawings, video, animation and audio where every type of information can be represented stored, transmitted and processed digitally.

Drawing line between education and entertainment in multimedia is almost impossible. Hence a new term has been coined 'edutainment which means using multimedia to make learning entertaining. How ever, multimedia also has a purely entertainment side. Anything that is possible in sound and images is possible on a multimedia CD. Multimedia means interaction, and to many interactive entertainment means games. A game is one of those multimedia domains where all the elements of multimedia play an equally important role in making it realistic and interactive.

EXERCISES

1. Explain the salient features of NICNET. List other specialized and dedicated network existing in the country.
2. Discuss the application of information technology in various areas.
3. Explain the role of I. T in weather forecasting. What is the impact of I.T use in this on common people in India?
4. Write a short Note on any two:
   (*i*) NICNET
   (*ii*) ERNET
   (*iii*) CMC Limited.
5. What do you mean by electronic governance?

Computer Programming LAB

LIST OF PRACTICALS

1. Practice of all internal and External DOS Commands.
2. Write simple batch program.
3. Giving exposure to Windows environment.
4. File and program management in windows.
5. Practice of all UNIX commands.
6. Write simple shell script.
7. Introduction to text editing and word processing.
8. Exposure to advance feature supported by some editors.
9. Net Surfing.
10. Creation and usage of E-mail account.
11. Write small program using C language.
12. Handling of data structure in C.
13. Familarizing mail account using PINE, deleting, creating folder/ mail-messages, adding signature, creating directory of addresses.

ASSIGNMENT–1

Objective

To give the knowledge of basic DOS commands to the students and use of DOS editor.

Theory and Concepts

Basically the purpose of the operating system is to interact with user and control the various operation of the devices. Operating system is a software which gives control to the user to do the **desired.**

In operating system category first you will **microsoft disk** operating system. It is single user and single tasking operating system.

DOS is command based operating system. You just type the command and press the enter key then the command will execute, e.g., in **question** 1 some commands are given. For executing the command type the command on the command prompt and by pressing the enter key the command will execute.

In question 1 for executing the DATE command, first type the date and press enter key, and the current date will be shown on screen.

By DIR command user can see the directories present in the hard disk.

In question 2 to form the following tree first make the directory by MD command.

C:> MD SRMS (press Enter)

Then by CD command change current directory to SRMS and again by MD command form new directory like this. Given tree can be seen by TREE command. In question 3 first make file by using Copy Con command.

C:> Copy con abc.txt (press Enter)

SRMSCET

Bareilly

Ctrl+Z (press Enter)

To make the modification in the file by using editor.

C:> Edit abc.txt (press Enter)

And then in editor change can be made.

1. Explain following commands dir, date, time, version, cls, type, edit, rd and commands.
2. Create the following tree with the help of md, cd, cd\, cd.. and tree commands.

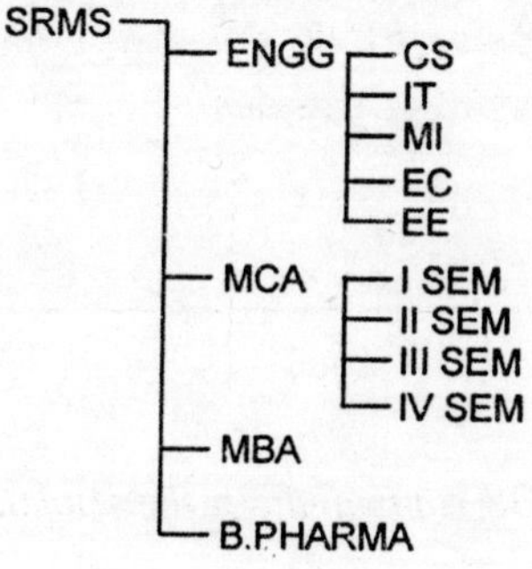

3. Create a file "abc.txt" using copy con command and then make modifications in file using MS-DOS Editor.

ASSIGNMENT – 2

Objective

To explain the difference between internal and external DOS commands and make simple batch programs.

Theory and Concepts

Internal commands are defined in the file command.com. As the system is boot the file is reside in main memory and these commands are the basic commands which are necessary to run DOS.

e.g., DIR, TYPE, MD, CLS, TIME

External commands not require certain special DOS file for being executed.

e.g., FORMAT, CHKDSK, XCOPY, ATTRIB, etc.

In question 2 mention the type of command syntax and options like if we want to see the directories page wise use the switch p like that options should be shown.

Batch file is just the collection of two or more DOS commands. Batch file is created as follows:

1. Open MS DOS prompt.
2. Move the specified directory at which you want to create batch file.
3. Write two or more DOS commands, save and exit.
4. Now for executing the batch file just type the name of file and by pressing enter key file will be executing.
5. Bring out the difference between external and internal commands.
6. Explain the use of following DOS commands, mentioning whether they are internal or external commands, syntax and available options.
   - MD
   - CD
   - RD
   - CLS
   - DIR
   - DATE
   - TIME
   - COPY CON
   - TYPE
   - TREE
   - COPY
   - DOSKEY

- PATH
- REM
- DEL
- CHKDSK
- FORMAT
- DISKCOPY
- MORE
- FDISK
- PROMPT
- SORT
- FIND
- ATTRIB
- XCOPY
- MEM

7. What is batch file? How the batch file is created?
8. Create a batch file that clears the screen and show the date and time.
9. Create a batch file that

   (*i*) Show the directories

   (*ii*) Clear the screen

   (*iii*) Make the directory named SRMS

   (*iv*) Delete the directory SRMS

Without showing the commands to user.

ASSIGNMENT – 3

Objective

To give the basic knowledge of windows operating system to the student.

Theory and Concepts

Windows is multiuser and multitasking operating system. It is the most popular operating system. It is the most popular operating system of the world. It based on GUI (Graphical User Interface). User can interact and work on this operating system easily. There are different versions of windows operating system is present like win 98, win 2000, win Xp etc.

In second question different terms are given which is easily visualize to the user. In third question display properties like resolution, background, screensaver, colors of bars etc., are adjusted. In fourth question basic operations like delete of directory or file. Deleting can be done by keyboard also by mouse.

1. Explain the features of windows operating system.

2. Define the terms:
   (*a*) Desktop
   (*b*) Taskbar
   (*c*) Toolbar
   (*d*) Windows Explorer
   (*e*) Icons
   (*f*) Buttons
   (g) Scrollbar
   (*h*) Menubar
3. Define display properties. How it can be changed?
4. Define the term Drag And Drop.
5. How to perform these operations:
   (*a*) Copy
   (*b*) Delete
   (*c*) Make new file and directory
   (*d*) Restore?

ASSIGNMENT – 4

Objective

To give the basic knowledge of notepad, wordpad, powerpoint and internet.

Theory and Concept

As we know the OS is an system software. In which we can interact with hardware and do desired tasks but as the need arises, we need different software to meet our objects. To fullfill different other software are used to perform particular thing are called application software. In this assignment we interact with software like Ms-word, Ms-paint, Ms-powerpoint, these are the application softwares used for the formatting of text, for making paintings, designings a seminar report etc.

These software can be easily opened by just clicking by the mouse.

Question no. 4,5 and 6 is related to the internet. Basically internet is the vast network of the computers linked by cables and telephone lines. By internet user can see the different websites. Search on a particular topic and also by using webcam users can see to each other. For doing such type of thing we need a software microsoft internet explorer by which we can open the sites. Many other browsing software is also available.

1. In MS-Word, Note Pad, Word Pad.

   Write application to principal for one day leave.

   Write application to administrator for bonafide student certificate.

2. In Paint.

   Draw the map of India with state distribution (color).

   Map of UP with district distribution (color).

3. In Ms-Powerpoint.

   Make a presentation on the topic role of computer in village.

   Make a presentation on any topic of your choice.

4. Define the topic Internet.

   Internet browser Search engine.

5. Using google.com search engine, search jobs sites of India.

6. Make a E-mail account in rediffmail.com.

ASSIGNMENT – 5

Objective

To implementation of Unix commands.

Theory and Concepts

Unix is a multiuser and multitasking operating system. In this assignment some commands are given are used to do some basic operations.

For example to show the files and directories we use the **ls** command. For execution of commands simply type the command and press enter key.

Explain the following UNIX commands.

1. To show current path and directory.
2. To create a file by CAT command.
3. To show the content of a file by CAT command.
4. To copy one file in another file by CP command
5. To show the directory by LS command.
6. To move one file to another file by MV command.
7. To rename a file by MV command.
8. To make a new directory by MKDIR command.
9. To change the directory by CD command.
10. To show the calendar of current year by CAL command.
11. To show system date by DATE command.
12. To check how many users are working in network by WHO command.

13. To check our identity by WHO AM I command.
14. To remove file by RM command.
15. To remove directory by RMDIR command.
16. To clear the screen by CLEAR command.
17. To show the content of file as page wise by MORE command.
18. Sort the content of a file by SORT command.
19. To calculate and solve some problems by BC.

ASSIGNMENT – 6

Objective

Implementation of 'C' program using the output and input functions.

Theory and Concepts

C is a general purpose programming language. C is invented by Dennis Ritchie. C is also called system programming language because it is useful for writing compilers and operating systems. It has been used equally well to write the major programs in many different domains.

C provides a variety of data types. The fundamental types are character and floating point of different size. In addition there is a hierarchy of derived data types created with the points, arrays, structure and union.

In this assignment user just declare the data type and by using input function (scanf) and output function (printf) can make the program.

E.g., To add two numbers.

```
#include<stdio.h>
main()
{
Int a, b, sum;
scanf("%d %d ", &a, &b);
sum= a+b;
printf("%d", sum);
  }
Input a=3, b=4
```

Like this first header file stdio.h is included. Then by further program is written.

Q.l. WAP to print the statement:

SRMS IS THE BEST INSTITUTE.

Q.2. WAP to print the ODD, 12.00, 12.43, 12, *c*, *a* using the constants.

Q.3. WAP to calculate to sum, division and multiplication of the two numbers.

Q.4. WAP to swapping of the two numbers.

Q.5. WAP to calculate the simple interest the values of rate of interest, time and amount is input by the user.

Q.6. WAP to change the temperature into Fahrenheit to Celsius.

ASSIGNMENT–7

Objective

To implementation of c program using control and switch statement.

Concepts and Theory

If-else (Control statement)

The if else statement is used to express decisions. The syntax of if-else is

If (expression)

```
                Statement 1
else
                statement 2
```

In this else part is optional

e.g., if we want to give condition that print the statement 'Yes' by input 1 and 'No' by input 0 then program will like that

```
#include<stdio.h>
main()
{
int a;
scanf("%d",&a);
if(a=1)
printf("Yes");
else
printf("No");
}
```

Switch

Switch statement is a multiway decisions that tests whethere an expression matches of a number of constant integer values and branches accordingly.

e.g.,

```
switch (expression)
{
case const expr : statement
case const expr : statement
        default : statements
}
```

loops

Loops are used to execute a particular statement, instruction more than one time then loops are used. Loops are for, while , do while loop.

For loop

```
for(initialize counter; test counter; increment counter)
{
   do this;
   and this;
   and this;
}
```

e.g., to print any statement five times then loop will be like that

```
for (i=0; i<=4; i++)
{
printf("SRMS");
}
```

Programs In C using Control Instructions, Loop Switch and Goto Statements

1. A grocery shop decides to give its customers a discount on the total purchases if it exceeds Rs. 1000. The quantity purchased and price per item is entered through the keyboard. WAP to calculate the final sales bill.
2. The current year and the year of joining of any employee are taken as input from the keyboard. If the number of years of service is more than 3 then a bonus of Rs. 2500 is given else nothing else is done. The pay of an employee is calculated as under: If basic salary is less than Rs. 1500 then HRA-10% and DA-90% of basic. If basic salary is greater than or equal to Rs. 1500 then HRA = Rs.500 and DA = 98% of basic salary.
3. WAP to find the greatest of three numbers using if-else and conditional operators.
4. WAP to determine whether a given year is a leap year or not using operators.

5. Marks of 5 subjects are entered through the keyboard and division is allotted according to the following criteria:

Greater than or equal to 60%	I Division
Between 50% and 59%	II Division
Between 40% and 49%	III Division
Less than 40%	Fail

6. A character is entered through the keyboard; find whether it is a capital letter, small letter or special symbol. The ASCII values are given below for reference

A-Z	65-90
a-z	97-122
0-9	48-57
Special symbols	0-47, 58-64, 91-96, 123-127

ASSIGNMENT– 8

Objective

To implementation of various gates using 'C' language.

Theory and Concept

In this assignment we will show the output of the gates using C programs. Gates can be easily implement by the control structure If-else and logical operator (AND) and ||(OR).

e.g., For AND gate

```
if(a=0  b==0)
    printf("Output  is=  0"");
else
    if  (a>1  ||  b>1)
        printf(''Wrong no.'');
else
        printf("Output  is=  1");
getch();
}
```

1. Write a program to get the output of AND gate.
2. Write a program to get the output of OR gate.
3. Write a program to get the output of NOR gate.
4. Write a program to get the output of X-OR gate.

5. Write a program to get the output of X-NOR gate.
6. Write a program to get the output of NAND gate.
7. Write a program to get the output of NOT gate.

ASSIGNMENT–9

Objective

To implement the loops and the arithmetic operator using 'C'.

Theory and Concepts

Simply in this assignment nesting of loops is done. How the loops are run to get the desired pattern or series?

e.g., In 1 program we want to print number between 1 to 100 than number is divisible by 2 or not. If divisible by 2 than number is even else it is odd. So program will be like as follows:

```
#include<stdio.h>
main()
{
int i;
for(i=1;i<=100;i++)
{
if(i%2==0)
printf("number is even");
else
printf("number is odd");
}
```

Q.1. WAP to print the seven number between 1 to 100 and also print how many numbers are even.

Q.2. WAP to find the factorial of the given number.

Q.3. WAP to check whether the given number is prime or composite.

Q.4. WAP to find the sum of the digits of a number.

Q.5. WAP to check whether the given number is palindrome or not.

Q.6. WAP to print fibonacci series.

Q.7. WAP to print given pattern-

(a)
```
*
*   *
*   *   *
*   *   *   *
```

(b)
```
1
1   2
1   2   3
1   2   3   4
```

ASSIGNMENT –10

Objective

To implement of arrays, matrices and strings in 'C' language.

Theory and Concepts

This assignment is based on Arrays. An array is a collection of similar types of data items. Previously, we declared variable for taking and value but it can hold only one value at a time. Problem arises when we want to store the age of 80 employees or elements of any matrix. The concept array useful in this situation. The elements of array share the same variable name. The elements of arrays are indicated by specifying the array name followed by subscript in bracket. For example arr[10] declaration of array:

Int a[10];

For multidimensional array declaration is like that

Int a[3][3];

It means 3 rows and 3 columns, 9 values can be stored in array a[3][3].

To store 5 values in arrays

```
#include<stdio.h>
main()
{
Int a[5],I;
for (i=0 ; i<=4 ; i++)
scanf("%d",&a[i]);
}
for (i=0 ; i<=4 ; i++)
{
printf("%d",a[i]);
}
For
e.g. #include<stdio.h>
```

```
main()
{
char name[ ]="RAM";
int i=0;
while (i<=3)
{
printf(%c",name[i]);
i++;
}
}
```

It prints RAM.

1. WAP to store 10 numbers in array and then print them.
2. WAP to find out sum of all elements of an array.
3. WAP to find the largest and second largest in the given array.
4. WAP to transpose of the given matrix.
5. WAP to multiply of two matrices and print the result.
6. WAP to input a string and print it.
7. WAP to count the length of the string. String is input by the user.
8. WAP to count the numbers of vowels, consonants and spaces.
9. WAP to sort the string alphabetically.
10. WAP to check whether given string is palindrome or not.

NOTES ON C

ALGORITHMS

An algorithm represents the method of solving a given problem as a sequence of well defined steps. In case of a computer algorithm, the steps must be such that they can be easily implemented in a computer program. The sequence has to be rigorously followed. Otherwise, the solution will not be correct.

Once you know the algorithm you have to code it in a computer programming language. The important features of algorithm are :

Definiteness. An algorithm must have a single output for a particular input.

Specified Input. The input to the algorithm must be clearly specified.

Specified output. The output to the algorithm must be clearly specified.

Finiteness. The algorithm must terminate in a finite time.

Correctness. The algorithm must provide the correct answer for the problem for which it is designed.

FLOWCHARTS

Flowcharts are a convenient way of expressing the algorithm for the solution of a given problem. They are a pictorial representation and, hence are easy to understand. Thus, they serve the purpose of documentation as well as aid understanding of the algorithm.

In developing application software, a general chart to reveal the overall purpose and structure of the application is created. This is usually called the **system flowchart** or the **application flowchart.**

FLOWCHART SYMBOLS

Terminal. The terminal symbol, as the name implies is used to indicate the starting (BEGIN), stopping (END), and pause (HALT) in the program logic flow. It is the first symbol and also the last symbol in the program logic. In addition, if the program logic calls for a pause in the program, that is also indicated with a terminal symbol.

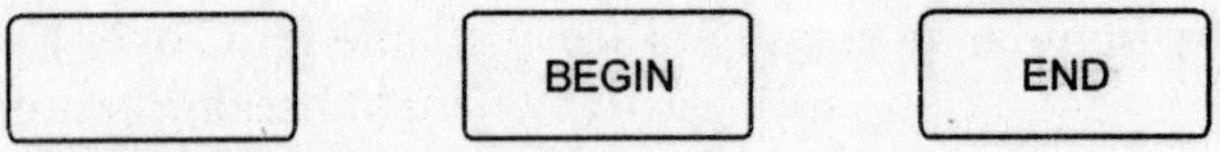

TERMINAL

Input /Output. The input/output symbol is used to denote any function of an input/output device in the program.

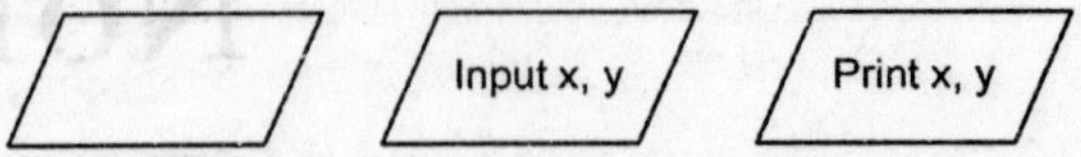

Input/Output

Processing. A processing symbol is used in a flowchart to represent arithmetic and data movement instructions.

Processing

Flowlines. Flowlines with arrowheads are normally used to indicate the flow of operations, that is, the exact sequence in which the instructions are to be executed.

Flowlines

Decision. The decision symbol is used in a flow chart to indicate the points at which a decision is to be made and a branch to one or more alternative points is possible.

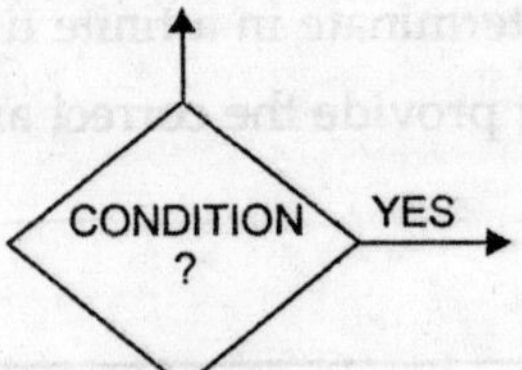

Connector. If a flowchart becomes very long, the flowlines begin to crisscross each other then connectors are used in a flowchart.

SPECIAL FEATURES OF C

A Middle Level Language

It combines the elements of High Level Languages (HLL) with the functionality of an assembly language. The incorporation of the elements of the HLL's helps the programmers to code their logic in a simple way thus increases the programmer's efficiency. C code may approach the speed of the assembly language because of its efficient generation of machine code.

The C code is very popular as compilers are available for C over a wide range of machines. C performs no run time error checking such as array bounds checking or argument type compatibility checking. These checks are the responsibility of the programmer.

A Structured Language

C is called a structured language because of structural similarities to ALGOL, Pascal and Modula 2.

Several software tools have been produced to aid the programmers in this task. These are:

Editors, Assemblers, Compilers, Interpreters, Loaders and Linkers, Debuggers, Profilers, Integrated Development Environments (IDE).

Editor is a program that helps you key in the program and save it in the disk so that it may be retrieved later as per requirement.

Assemblers are programs that convert a program in assembly language into its equivalent machine language program.

Compilers are programs that convert an HLL program into its equivalent machine language program (executable program). In the context" of C Programming, a C compiler reads the statements written in C language and translates these statements into machine code that the processor on which the program is to be run understands. This process is called compilation. After compilation, the program runs as an independent application from an operating system like DOS or Windows.

Interpreters are programs that do not produce any executable files of the HLL program. Instead, they decode the HLL program line by line and provide the necessary instructions to the processor for executing it. They are useful at the program development stage as it is possible to verify the veracity of individual instruction. However, interpreted programs are slower than the programs that are executed from the executable file. Therefore, once the program development is over, the executable file is typically prepared and run.

Loaders and Linkers are programs that help in putting the program into the appropriate place in the RAM so that it can be executed. Further, the linker also establishes the connection between the modules prepared separately.

Debuggers are programs that help in finding the errors in the code that is being executed. Running the program step by step with the help of the debugger does this.

How is a C program Compiled and Executed ?

C compilation is a multi-pass process. To create a program, a C compiler system performs the following steps.

- It runs the source file text through a "C preprocessor". All this does is perform various text manipulations on the source file, such as macro expansion, constant expansion, file inclusion, and conditional compilation. The output of the preprocessor is a second - level source for actual compilation.

- Next, it runs the second-level source file through the compiler proper, which actually converts the source code statements into their binary equivalents. That is, it creates an "object file" form the source file.
- The object file still cannot be executed, however, if it makes use of C library functions such as "printf()" above, the binary code for the library functions has to be merged , or linked, with the program object file. Furthermore, some addressing information needs to be linked to the object file so that it can actually be loaded and run on the target system.
- These linking tasks are performed by a "linker" that takes one or more object files and links them to binary library files to create an "executable" file that can be run. Note that you can create programs from multiple object files using the linker. Note also that C has a large number of libraries and library functions. C by itself has a very few statements; so much of its functionality is implemented as library calls.
- After all this executable program has to be loaded into the memory and then executed.

C Character Set

The set of allowable symbols in the language that have some well-defined meaning form its character set. The character set used in C consists of the following characters belonging to the set of ASCII characters :

- **Alphabets.** The 26 upper case and lower case alphabets of English language *i.e.*, A-Z, a-z. C is a case sensitive language i.e. if two words are spelt same but have different case for one or more characters, they are treated as different.
- **Digits.** The numerals from 0–9.
- **Special Characters.** ~ # % & * () – + = | '{} [] ; , \ / " ? < >
- **White Space characters.** Space, Tab, carriage return, formfeed and newline.

KEYWORDS IN C (AS DEFINED BY ANSI STANDARD)

The keywords of a language are those that have a well-defined meaning in the language and are always used in the same sense.

Keywords in C

asm	Auto	break	case	char	const	continue	define
Do	double	else	if	enum	extern	far	float
For	Goto	if	include	int	long	near	register
Return	Short	signed	static	struct	switch	typedef	union
unsigned	Void	while					

Identifiers

Identifiers are used to specify the different quantities that are needed in a C program. You use different names for specifying the quantities that are encountered in your numerical problems. Similarly, identifiers are names that are used for specifying the quantities of interest in computer programs. In C, an identifier can be a combination of alphanumeric characters subject to the following restrictions:

(*a*) The first letter must be an alphabet or an underscore (_).

(*b*) The subsequent letters can be either alphabets or digits.

(*c*) The first 32 characters are typically significant in distinguishing between two identifier names. This number may, however differ from compiler to compiler.

(*d*) Two consecutive underscore are not permitted.

(*e*) The keywords have their meaning pre-defined and cannot be used as an identifier to denote some other meaning.

(*f*) No other special character is permitted.

However, different compilers might offer subtly different facilities for defining the identifiers.

Constant and Variables

Data processed by a program is stored either as a variable or a constant. Variables are memory locations in the computer's memory that hold data. Variables hold different kind of data, and the same variable might hold different values during the execution of a program.

Constants are numbers, characters, or words /strings that you put in your program. Constants are useful for defining minimum or maximum values, program titles- any data that does not change while the program is being executed.

A literal constant is a value that is used directly in your program statement or expression. The number 1234 is a literal constant.

A symbolic constant is a user specified constant. You may realize that 9.806 is the value of 'g' but a value like 100 may mean anything. So it is better that you give it a name that you easily comprehend. This is defined by using a preprocessor directive called the # define directive. As mentioned earlier, a preprocessor directive is the first thing that is written in the program. You can write,

```
#defme g 9.806
#define MAX 100
```

The third variety, called the object constants, is a hybrid of a variable and a literal constant.

DATA TYPES

C supports a rich variety of data types. You can deal with integer numbers, real numbers, and characters. At the bit level, the computer may deal with all these only as sequences of 1s and 0's. T herefore, it is up to the compiler to make sure that the computer handles bits and bytes in a way that is consistent with their data type. A data type is just an interpretation applied to a string of bits. A data type is also defined as a finite set of values along with the set of rules for permissible operations.

1. Simple Data Type.
2. Structured Data Type.
3. Enumerated Data Type.
4. Pointer Data Type.
5. The void Data Type.

Simple Data Types

Under simple data types you have integer numbers, real numbers, and characters. The various kinds of data types supported by C under this category below along with description and their memory requirements.

Name	*Description*	*Bytes*
Integers		
Short integers (short int or short)	Very small whole numbers	2
Normal integers (int)	Small whole numbers	2
Long integers (long int or long)	Large whole numbers	4
Floating point		
Single precision (float)	Small real numbers	4
Double precision (double or long float)	Large real numbers	8
Character	A single character	1

signed long int	32	–2147483648 to 2147483647
float	32	3.4E–38 to 3.4 E+ 38
Double	64	1.7E–308 to 1.7 E + 308
long double	80	3.4E–4932 to 1.1 E + 4932

Local Variables and Global Variables

Variables that are declared inside a function are called local variables. These variables can be referenced only by statements that are written in the function in which they are declared. Declaring them outside of any function creates global variables. These are known throughout entire program. A common practice is to declare global variable at the top of the program although this is not mandatory.

Storage Class Specifiers

There are 4 storage class specifiers in C. These are used to tell the compiler how the variable that follows should be stored. These classes are:

Extern. Tells the compiler that the following variable types and names have been, declared elsewhere(may be in other file), e.g., extern int x,y;

Static. Static variables are permanent variables within their own function or file. They are not known outside their function or file but they maintain their values between calls to their function.

Register. This type of variable is stored in a manner that allows the fastest access time possible. Register can't be applied to global variables.

Auto. A local variable is created a new each time a procedure is called in Pascal. If C programmer takes no action the same is true for C. So whether a variable is declared as auto or default mode is taken the variable is created anew every time the function is called.

The printf ( ) and scanf () functions

You shall learn the details of the I/O capabilities that C provides later. But. for now it is necessary to get familiar with the two most often used functions:

printf () : for writing on the screen

scanf () : for reading input from the keyboard

printf()

printf ( ) is a function that C provides to enable you to print the values of the variables you desire on the screen e.g., for getting to know the output of the program, printf ( ) requires you to specify the variable that you want to print and also the format in which you want to print.

```
//include  <stdio.h>
main  ()
{
int  count;
char  letter;
printf  (  "Count  =  %d  \n"  ,  count);
printf  (  "Letter  =  %c  \n"  ,  letter);
}
```

scanf ()

This is a function in C that allows you to accept input from a keyboard. The following program illustrates the use of this function.

```
//include  <stdio.h>
main  ()  /*  program  which  introduces  keyboard  input*/
{
int  num;
printf  (  "Type  in  a  number  \n"  );
scanf("%d",&num);
printf  (  "The  number  you  typed  was  %d\n"  ,  num);
}
```

Formatters for scanf ( ) and printf ()

The following characters, after the % character, in a scanf argument, have the effect given in the table below:

Modifier	*Meaning*
d	Read a decimal integer
0	Read an octal value
X	Read a hexadecimal value
h	Read a short integer
1	Read a long integer
f	Read a float value
e	Read a double value
c	Read a single character
S	Read a sequence of character

Integer Data Type

The integer data type consists of a subset of integers. An integer value is an exact representation of the corresponding integer. An integer constant consists of a sequence of digits preceded by an optional sign, plus (+) or minus (–).

Type	*Bytes*	*Range*
int/short	2	–32768 to 32767
long int	4	–2147483648–21474813647
unsigned int	2	0–65535
unsigned long int	4	0–4294967295

We can declare integer data type as follows int *x* ; or int a,b,c ; or int c=9,d,r;

Single Precision Real Data Type

A single precision real value is an approximation of the desired real number and occupies 4 bytes of memory. The range of single precision real values is from 3.4×10^{-38} to $3.4 \times 10^{+38}$. The precision of this data type is six decimal digits.

We can declare integer data type as follows:

float x ; or float a, b, c ; or float c = 9.0, d, r;

Double Precision Real Data Type

This subset is larger than the subset of the single precision real data type. A double precision value occupies 8 bytes of memory. The range of real values is from 1.7×10^{-308} to $1.7 \times 10^{+308}$. The precision is ten decimal digits.

We can declare integer data type as follows

double *x* ; or double a, b, c ; or double c = 9.0, d, r;

CHARACTER

These are single characters. The keyword used to define character variables is,

```
char
```

An example of a character value is the letter A. An example of declaring a character variable called **letter** is,

```
char letter;
letter = 'A';
```

Note the assignment of the character to the variable *letter* is done by enclosing the value in **single quotes.** Remember the golden rule: Single character - Use single quotes. It takes 1 byte.

Sample Program Illustrating Each Data Type

```
#include < stdio.h >
main ()
{
        int sum;
        float money;
        char letter;
        double pi;
        sum = 10;            /* assign integer value */
        money = 2.21;        /* assign float value */
        letter = 'A';        /* assign character value */
        pi = 2.01E6;         /* assign a double value */
        print f ("value of sum = %d\n", sum );
        print f ("value of money = %f\n", money);
        print f ("value of letter = %c\n", Letter);
        print f ("value of pi = %e\n", pi ) ;
}
```

Sample program output

```
value of sum = 10
value of money = 2.210000
value of letter = A
value of pi = 2.010000e + 06
```

Data Types with Type Modifiers

Type	*Bit Width*	*Range*
Char	8	-128 to 127
unsigned char	8	0 to 255
signed char	8	-128 to 127
Int	16	-32768 to 32767
unsigned int	16	0 to 65535
signed int	16	-32768 to 32767
short int	16	-32768 to 32767
unsigned short int	16	0 to 65535
long int	32	-2147483648 to 2147483647

>=	Greater Than or Equal to
<	Less Than
<=	Less Than or Equal to
= =	Equal to
! =	Not Equal to
&&	Logical AND
||	Logical OR

Bit-Wise Operators

The Bit-wise operators operate on individual bits. These are

Operator	*Meaning*
&	AND
|	OR
^	XOR
~	Ones complement
>>	Shift right
<<	Shift left

Miscellaneous Operators

There are a variety of other operators that can be classified in the class of miscellaneous operators. You shall now look at some of them. x++, ++x, x--, --x.

x++ and ++x are increment operators operating on the variable x. Similarly –x and x--are the decrement operators operating on the variable x. when the increment or decrement operator precedes its operand, C performs the increment or decrement operation prior to using the operands value. This form is called the prefix form. If the operator follows its operand C uses the operands value before incrementing or decrementing it.

The & and * Operator

A pointer is essentially a the address of another variable. Pointers have two main functions in C.

- They can provide a very fast means of referencing of array elements.
- They allow C functions to modify their calling parameters.

The Size of Compile Time Operator

[...]	Read character string. The characters inside the brackets indicate the characters that are to be contained in the string. If any other character is typed, the string is terminated. If the first character is a ^. The remaining characters inside the brackets indicate that typing them will terminate the string.
*	This is used to skip input fields.

Operators

C provides a wide selection of operators. The operators provided by C can be classified into several different classes for convenience in understanding them. These are as follows:

- Arithmetic operators
- Relational and logical operators
- Bitwise operators
- Miscellaneous operators

Arithmetic Operators

The arithmetic operators include those mentioned in the table below. The purpose of the operators is clear from the symbol used for them.

Operator	*What it does*
–	Subtraction, also unary minus
+	Addition
*	Multiplication
/	Division
%	Modulus division
--	Decrement
++	Increment

You are advised to go through the following example carefully to understand an important concept about working of the arithmetic operator.

Relational and Logical Operators

The relational and logical operators include:

Operator	*Meaning*
!	Not
>	Greater Than

size of is a unary compile time operator that returns the length in bytes of the variable or paranthesised type specifier it precedes.

For example,

```
float a;
printf("%f, sizeof a);
printf ("%f", sizeof (int));
```

The . and ->operator

The .(dot) operator and the -> operator are used to reference individual elements of structures and unions. The dot operator is used when operating on the actual structure or union to refer to a particular field in it.

Expressions

An expression is a formula consisting of one or more operands and zero or more operators linked together to compute a value. An operand may be a function reference, a variable or a constant. For example, in the expression.

a + b ; a and b are operands and '+' is the operator.

The operators in C can be used in a variety of expressions. There are four types of expressions in C as given below:

- Arithmetic expressions
- Relational expressions
- Logical expressions
- Conditional expressions

A SIMPLE C PROGRAM

The following program is written in the C programming language.

```
#include <stdio.h>
main ()
{
```

```
    printf("Programming in C is easy.\n");
}
```

Sample Program Output

```
Programming in C is easy.
_
```

A NOTE ABOUT C PROGRAMS

In C, lowercase and uppercase characters are very important! All commands in C must be lowercase. The C programs starting point is identified by the word

```
main ()
```

This informs the computer as to where the program actually starts. The brackets that follow the keyword *main* indicate that there are no arguments supplied to this program. The two braces, { and }, signify the begin and end segments of the program. The purpose of the statement

```
#include <stdio.h>
```

is to allow the *use of the printf statement* to provide program output. Text to be displayed *by printf ()* must be enclosed in double quotes. The program has only one statement

```
printf ("Programming in C is easy./n");
```

printf () is actually a function (procedure) in C that is used for printing variables and text. Where text appears in double quotes "", it is printed without modification. There are some exceptions however. This has to do with the \ and % characters. These characters are *modifier's*, and for the present the\followed by the n character represents a newline character. Thus the program prints Programming in C is easy.©

And the cursor is set to the beginning of the next line. As we shall see later on, what follows the\character will determine what is printed, *i.e.*, a tab, clear screen, clear line etc. Another important thing to remember is that all C statements are terminated by a semicolon.

PREPROCESSOR STATEMENTS

The **define** statement is used to make programs more readable. Consider the following examples,

```
#define TRUE, 1 /*Don't use a semi-colon, # must be first character on line */
#define FALSE   0
#define NULL    0
#define AND     &
#define OR      |
#define EQUALS  ==
game_over = TRUE;
while (list_pointer != NULL )
      ................................
```

Note that preprocessor statements begin with a # symbol, and are NOT terminated by a semicolon. Traditionally, preprocessor statements are listed at the beginning of the source file.

Preprocessor statements are handled by the compiler (or preprocessor) before the program is actually compiled. All # statements are processed first, and the symbols (like TRUE) which occur in the C program are replaced by their value (like 1). Once this substitution has taken place by the preprocessor, the program is then compiled.

In general, preprocessor constants are written in **UPPERCASE.**

LITERAL SUBSTITUTION OF SYMBOLIC CONSTANTS USING #define

Lets now examine a few examples of using these symbolic constants in our programs. Consider the following program which defines a constant called TAX_RATE.

```
#include <stdio.h>
#define TAX_RATE 0.10
main ()
{
      float balance;
      float tax;

      balance = 72.10;
      tax = balance * TAX_RATE;
      printf (''The tax on %.2f is %.2f/n'', balance, tax );
}
```

The pre-processor first replaces all symbolic constants before the program is compiled, so after preprocessing the file (and before its compiled), it now looks like,

```
#include <stdio.h>
#define TaX_RATE 0.10
main ()
{
    float balance;
    float tax;

    balance = 72.10;
    tax = balance * 0.10;
    printf (''The tax on %.2f is %.2f/n'', balance, tax);
}
```

YOU CANNOT ASSIGN VALUES TO THE SYMBOLIC CONSTANTS

Considering the above program as an example, look at the changes we have made below. We have added a statement which tries to change the TAX_RATE: to a new value.

```
#include <stdio.h>
#define TAX_RATE 0.10
main ()
{
    float balance;
    float tax;
    balance = 72.10;
    TAX_TATE = 0.15;
    tax = balance * TAX_TATE;
    printf (''The tax on %.2f is %.2f/n'', balance, tax);
}
```

This is **illegal.** You cannot re-assign a new value to a symbolic constant.

ITS LITERAL SUBSTITUTION, SO BEWARE OF ERRORS

As shown above, the preprocessor performs literal substitution of symbolic constants. Lets modify the previous program slightly, and introduce an error to highlight a problem.

```
#include <stdio.h>
#define TAX_RATE 0.10;
main ()
{
    float balance;
    float tax;
    balance = 72.10;
    tax = (balance * TAX_RATE_ + 10.02;
    printf (''The tax on %.2f is %.2f/n'', balance, tax);
}
```

In this case, the error that has been introduced is that the *#define* is terminated with a semi-colon. The preprocessor performs the substitution and the offending line (which is flagged as an error by the compiler) looks like

```
tax = (balance * 0.10; )+ 10.02;
```

However, you do not see the output of the preprocessor. If you are using TURBO C, you will only see

```
tax = (balance * TAX_RATE ) + 10.02;
```

flagged as an error, and this actually looks okay (but its not! after substitution takes place).

MAKING PROGRAMS EASY TO MAINTAIN BY USING #define

The whole point of using *#defme* in your programs is to make them easier to read and modify. Considering the above programs as examples, what changes would you need to make if the TAX_RATE was changed to 20%.

Obviously, the answer is once, where the # *define* statement which declares the symbolic constant and its value occurs. You would change it to read

```
# define TAX_RATE = 0.20
```

Without the use of symbolic constants, you would hard code the value 0.20 in your program, and this might occur several times (or tens of times).

This would make changes difficult, because you would need to search and replace every occurrence in the program. However, as the programs get larger, **what would happen if you actually used the value 0.20 in a calculation that had nothing to do with the TAX_RATE!**

SUMMARY OF #define

- allow the use of symbolic constants in programs.
- in general, symbols are written in uppercase.
- are not terminated with a semi-colon.
- generally occur at the beginning of the file.
- each occurrence of the symbol is replaced by its value.

ARITHMETIC OPERATORS

The symbols of the arithmetic operators are:

Operation	*Operator*	*Comment*	*Value of Sum before*	*Value of sum after*
Multiply	*	sum = sum * 2;	4	8
Divide	/	sum = sum / 2;	4	2
Addition	+	sum = sum + 2;	4	6
Subtraction	–	sum = sum -2;	4	2
Increment	++	++sum;	4	5
Decrement	--	- sum;	4	3
Modulus	%	sum = sum % 3;	4	1

The following code fragment adds the variables *loop* and *count* together, leaving the result in the variable *sum*

```
sum = loop + count;
```

Note: If the modulus % sign is needed to be displayed as part of a text string, use two, i.e., %%

```
#include <stdio.h>
main ()
{
      int sum = 50;
      float modulus;
      modulus = sum % 10;
      printf (''The %% of %d by 10 is %f\n'', sum, modulus);
}
```

Sample Program Output

```
The % of 50 by 10 is 0.000000
```

- ms readable and easy to maintain

GOOD FORM

Perhaps we should *say programming style* or *readability.* The most common complaints we would have about beginning C programmers can be summarised as.

- they have poor layout
- their programs are hard to read

Your programs will be quicker to write and easier to debug if you get into the habit of actually formatting the layout correctly as you write it.

For instance, look at the program below

```
#include<stdio.h>
main ()
  {
      int sum,loop,kettle,job;
      char Whoknows;

          sum = 9;
      loop = 7;
      whoknows = 'A';
      printf (''Whoknows = %c, kettle = %d\n'', whoknows, kettle);
  }
```

It is our contention that the program is hard to read, and because of this, will be difficult to debug for errors by an inexperienced programmer. It also contains a few deliberate mistakes!

Okay then, lets rewrite the program using good form.

```
#Include <stdio.h>

main ()
    {
        int sum, loop, kettle = 0, job;
        char whoknows;

            sum = 9;
          loop = 7;
        whoknows = 'A';
        printf (''Whoknows = %c, kettle = %d\n'', whoknows, kettle);
    }
```

We have also corrected the mistakes. The major differences are:

- the { and } braces directly line up underneath each other

  This allows us to check indent levels and ensure that statements belong to the correct block of code. This becomes vital as programs become more complex
- spaces are inserted for readability

  We as humans write sentences using spaces between words. This helps our comprehension of what we read, (if you don't believe me, try reading the following sentence, wishihadadollarforeverytimeimadcamistake. The insertion of spaces will also help us identify mistakes quicker.
- good indentation

  Indent levels (tab stops) are clearly used to block statements, here we clearly see and identify functions, and the statements which belong to each { } program body.
- initialization of variables

  The first example prints out the value *of kettle, a* variable that has no initial value. This is corrected in the second example.

KEYBOARD INPUT

There is a function in C which allows the programmer to accept input from a keyboard. The following program illustrates the use of this function.

```
#include <stdio.h>
main()        / * program which introduces keyboard input */
{
          int number;
          printf ("Type in a number \n");
          scanf("%d", & number);
```

```
        printf("The number you typed was %d\n", number);
}
```

Sample Program output

```
Type in a number
23
The number you typed was 23
```

An integer called *number* is defined. A prompt to enter in a number is then printed using the statement

```
printf ("Type in a number \n:");
```

The scanf routine, which accepts the response, has two arguments. The first ("%d") specifies what type of data type is expected (i.e., char, int. or float). The second argument (&number) specifies the variable into which the typed response will be placed. In this case the response will be placed into the memory location associated with the variable *number*.

This explains the special significance of the & character (which means the address of).

Sample program illustrating use of scanf() to read integers, characters and floats

```
#include < stdio.h >
main ()
{
int sum;
char letter;
float money;
printf (''Please enter an integer value'');
scanf (''%d'', &sum);
printf("Please enter a character ");
/* the leading space before the %c ignores space characters in the
input */
scanf(" %c", &letter ) ;

printf("Please enter a float variable'');
scanf ("%f", &money );

printf (''\nThe variables you entered were\n'');
printf (''value of sum = %\n'', sum);
printf (''value of tetter = %c\n'', letter);
printf (''value of money = %f\n'', money);
}
```

```
Sample Program Output
Please enter an integer value
34
Please enter a character
W
Please enter a float variable
32. 3
The variables you entered were
value of sum = 34
value of letter = W
value of money = 32.300000
```

This program illustrates several important points.

- **the c language provides no error checking for user input. The user is expected to enter the correct data type. For instance, if a user entered a character when an integer value was expected, the program may enter an infinite loop or abort abnormally.**

ITERATION, FOR LOOPS

The basic format of the for statement is.

```
for( start condition; continue condition; re-evaulation)
{
   program statement;
}
/* sample program using a for statement */
#include <stdio.h>
main ()  /* Program introduces the for statement, counts to ten */
{
      int count;
      for (count = 1; count <= 10; count = count + 1)
      printf (''%d'', count);
      printf (''\n'');
}
Sample Program (Output
1 2 3 4 5 6 7 8 9 10
```

The program declares an integer variable *count*. The first part of the for statement

```
for( count = 1;
```

initialises the value *of count to* 1. The *for* loop continues whilst the condition

```
count  <=  10;
```

evaluates as TRUE. As the variable *count* has just been initialised to 1, this condition is TRUE and so the program statement

```
printf("  %d  ",  count );
```

is executed, which prints the value *of count* to the screen, followed by a space character. Next, the remaining statement of the *for* is executed

```
count  =  count  +  1  );
```

which adds one to the current value *of count*. Control now passes back to the conditional test,

```
count  <=  10;
```

which evaluates as true, so the program statement

```
printf  ("%d",  count);
```

is executed. *Count* is incremented again, the condition re-evaluated etc., until count reaches a value of 11.

When this occurs, the conditional test

```
count  <=  10;
```

evaluates as FALSE, and the *for* loop terminates, and program control passes to the statement

```
printf  ("  \n  "}  ;
```

which prints a newline, and then the program terminates, as there are no more statements left to execute.

```
/*  sample  program  using  a  for  statement  */
#include  <stdio.h>

main  ()
{
     int  n,  t  number;
     t_number  =  0;
     for  (n  =  1;  n  <=  200;  n  =  n  +  1)
          t_number  =  t_number  +  n;
     printf  ("The  200th  triangular_number  is  %d\n",  t_number);
}
```

Sample Program Output

```
The  200th  triangular_number  is  20100
```

The above program uses *a for* loop to calculate the sum of the numbers from 1 to 200 inclusive (said to be the *triangular number).*

An example of using a for loop to print out characters

```
#include  <stdio.h>
```

```
main ()
{
        char letter;
        for (letter = 'A'; letter <= 'E'; letter = letter + 1)
        {
                printf("%c ", letter);
        }
}
```

Sample Program Output

A B C D E

An example of using a for loop to count numbers, using two initialisations

```
#include <stdio.h>
main ()
{
        int total, loop;
        for(total = 0, loop = 1; loop <= 10; Loop = loop + 1 )
{
        total = total + loop;
        }
        printf ("Total = %d\n", total );
}
```

Sample Program Output

Total = 55

In the above example, the variable *total* is initialised to 0 as the first part of the for loop. The two statements,

`for( total = 0, loop = 1;`

are part of the initialisation. This illustrates that more than one statement is allowed, as long as they are separated by **commas**.

SELECTION (IF STATEMENTS)

The if statements allows branching (decision making) depending upon the value or state of variables. This allows statements to be executed or skipped, depending upon decisions. The basic format is,

```
if( expression )
    program statement,
```

Example;

```
if (students < 65 )
        ++student_count,
```

In the above example, the variable *student_count* is incremented by one only if the value of the integer variable *students* is less than 65.

The following program uses an if statement to validate the users input to be in the range 1–10.

```
#include <stdio.h>
main ()
{
        int number;
        int valid = 0;
        while ( valid = = 0 )
    {
            printf ("Enter a number between 1 and 10 -->");
            scanf("%d", & number);
            /* assume number is valid */
            valid = 1;
            if ( number < 1 )
    {
            printf ( "Number is below 1. Please reenter\n");
            valid = 0;
            }
            if ( number > 10)
            {
            printf ("Number is above 10. Please reenter\n");
            valid = 0;
            }
    }
    printf ("The number is %d\n", number);
}
```

Sample Program Output

```
Enter a number between 1 and 10 --> -78
Number is below 1. Please re-enter
Enter a number between 1 and 10 --> 4
The number is 4
```

Consider the following program which determines whether a character entered from keyboard is within the range A to Z.

```
#include <stdio.h>
main ()
{
        char letter;
        print f ( "Enter a character -->");
```

```
            scanf(" %c", &letter );
            if( letter >= 'A' )
            {
                    if( letter <= 'Z' )
                    printf ("The character is within A to Z\n");
            }
    }
```

Sample Program Output

```
Enter a character --> C
The character is within A to Z
```

The program does not print any output if the character entered is not within the range A to Z. This can be addressed on the following pages with the *if else* construct.

Please note use of the leading space in the statement (before %c)

```
scanf(" %c", &letter );
```

This enables the skipping of leading TABS, Spaces, (collectively called whitespaces) and the ENTER KEY. If the leading space was not used, then the first entered character would be used, and *scanf* would not ignore the whitespace characters.

Switch() Case

The switch case statement is a better way of writing a program when a series of if elase occurs. The general format for this is,

```
switch ( expression )
{
    case valuel:
        program statement;
        program statement;
        ......
        break;
    case valuen:
        program statement;
        ......
        break,
default:
        ......
        ......
}
```

The keyword *break* must be included at the end of each case statement. The default clause is optional, and is executed if the cases are not met. The right brace at the end signifies the end of the case selections.

Rules for Switch Statements

```
values for 'case' must be integer or character constants
the order of the 'case' statements is unimportant
the default clause may occur first (convention places it last)
you cannot use expressions or ranges
```

```
#include <stdio.h>
main ()
{
        int menu, numb1, numb2, total;
        printf("enter in two numbers -->");
        scant("%d %d", &numb1, &numb2);
        printf("enter in choice\n");
        printf ("1=addition \n ") ;
        printf ("2=subtraction\n") ;
        scanf("%d", &menu ) ;
        switch( menu )
         {
                case 1: total= numb1 + num2 ; break;
                case 2: total = numb1- numb2; break;
                default: printf ("Invalid option selected\n");
        }
        if( menu == 1 )
        printf("%d plus %d is %d\n", numb1, numb2, total);
        else if (menu == 2)
        printf("%d minus %d is %d\n", numb1, numb2, total);
}
```

Sample Program Output

```
enter in two numbers --> 37 23
enter in choice
1=addition
2=subtraction
2
37 minus 23 is 14
```

The above program uses a *switch* statement to validate and select upon the users input choice, simulating a simple menu of chACCEPTINC SINGLE CHARACTERS FROM THE KEYBOARD

getchar

The following program illustrates this,

```
#include <stdio.h>
main ()
{
        int i ;
        int ch;
        for( i = 1; i<= 5; ++i )
       {
                ch = getchar() ;
               putchar(ch) ;
       }
}
```

Sample Program Output

```
AACCddEEtt
```

The program reads five characters (one for each iteration of the for loop) from the keyboard. Note that *getchar()* gets a single character from the keyboard, and *putchar()* writes a single character (in this case, *ch)* to the console screen.

The file ctype.h provides routines for manipulating characters.

THE CONDITIONAL EXPRESSION OPERATOR

This conditional expression operator takes THREE operators. The two symbols used to denote this operator are the ? and the ∴. The first operand is placed before the'.'. the second operand between the ? and the :, and the third after the :. The general formal is.

```
condition? expression1:expression2
```

If the result of condition is TRUE (non-zero), expression 1 is evaluated and the result of the evaluation becomes the result of the operation. If the condition is FALSE (zero), then expression2 is evaluated and its result becomes the result of the operation. An example will help,

```
s = ( x < 0 ) ? -1 : x * x;
If x is less than zero then s = -1
If x is greater than zero then s = x * x
```

Example program illustrating conditional expression operator

```
#include <stdio.h>
main ()
    {
    int input;
```

```
    printf("I will tell you if the number is positive, negative
or zero!"\n");
    printf ( "please enter your number now - -->");
    scanf ("%d", & input );
    (input < 0) ? printf ("negative\n") : ((input > 0) ?
    printf ("positive\n") : printf ("zero\n"));
}
```

Sample Program Output

```
I will tell you if the number is positive, negative or zero!
please enter your number now ---> 32.
positive
```

ARRAYS

Arrays are a data structure which hold multiple variables of the same data type.

Consider the case where a programmer needs to keep track of a number of people within an organisation. So far, our initial attempt will be to create a specific variable for each user. This might look like,

```
int name1 = 101;
int name2 = 232;
int name3 = 231;
```

It becomes increasingly more difficult to keep track of this as the number of variables increase. Arrays offer a solution to this problem.

An array is a multi-element box, a bit like a filing cabinet, and uses an indexing system to find each variable stored within it. In C, indexing starts at **zero.**

Arrays, like other variables in C, must be declared before they can be used. The replacement of the above example using arrays looks like.

```
int names [4];
names[0] = 101;
names[1] = 232;
names[2] = 231;
names[3] = 0;
```

We created an array called *names*, which has space for four integer variables. You may also see that we stored 0 in the last space of the array. This is a common technique used by C programmers to signify the end of an array.

Arrays have the following syntax, using square brackets to access each indexed value (called an **element).**

```
x[i]
```

so that *x[5]* refers to the sixth element in an array called *x*. In C, array elements start with 0. Assigning values to array elements is done by,

```
x[10]  = g;
```

and assigning array elements to a variable is done by,

```
g= x [10];
```

In the following example, a character based array named *word* is declared, and each element is assigned a character. The last element is filled with a zero value, to signify the end of the character string (in C, there is no string type, so character based arrays are used to hold strings). A printf statement is then used to print out all elements of the array.

```
/* Introducing array's, 2 */
#include <stdio.h>
main ()
{
        char word[20];
        word[0]  =  'H';
        word[1]  =  'e';
        word[2]  -  '1';
        word[3]  -  '1';
        word[47  "  '0';
        word/"57 - 0;
        printf ("The contents of word[ ] is --> %s\n", word);
}
```

Sample Program Output

```
The contents of word[] is Hello
```

TWO-DIMENSIONAL ARRAYS

- One-dimensional arrays represent lists of homogeneous items.
- Two-dimensional arrays are collections of components, all of the same type, structured in two dimensions. Each component is accessed by a pair of indices that represent the component's position in each dimension.

	[0]	[1]	[2]
[0]			
[1]			
[2]			
[3]			

- The above table represents a two-dimensional array with 4 rows and 3 columns. This is referred to as a 4 × 3 array.

- To declare a multidimensional array, specify the size of each of the dimensions enclosed in square brackets:

```
const int NUM_ROWS = 4;
const int NUM_COLS = 3;
float alpha [NUM_ROWS] [NUM_COLS] ;
```

- References to individual members of the array are made just like one-dimensional array references, except that two index values are used:

```
alpha [1] [2] = 12.8;
```

Processing Two-Dimensional Arrays

- Most two-dimensional array processing consists of accessing the data either by rows or by columns.
- Example—Sum the rows and columns of an array:

```
const int NUM_ROWS = 40;
const int NUM_COLS = 35;
int table [NUM_ROWS][NUM_COLS];
long rowSum[NUM_ROWS];
long colSum[NUM_COLS];
int row;
int col;
// sum the rows
for (row = 0; row < NUM_ROWS; row++)
{
rowSum[row] = 0;
for (col = 0; col < NUM_COLS; col++)
rowSum[row] += table(row) [col];
}
// sum the columns
for (col = 0; col < NUM_COLS; col++)
{
colSum[col] = 0;
for (row = 0; row < NUM_ROWS; row++)
colSumfcol] += table [row] [col];
}
```

- To initialize a two-dimensional table, use a declaration similar to the following:

```
int  table  [2]   [3]
{
(14,  3,  -5},
(0,  46,  65}
};
```

Passing Two-Dimensional Arrays as Parameters

- When a one-dimensional array is defined as a formal parameter, the side of the arra may be omitted.

```
void Fun(float  list[],  int  size]
{
. . .
}
```

- With two-dimensional arrays, the first dimension (number of rows) may be omitted, b not the second dimension (number of columns).

```
void Fun(float  table  []  [5],  int  'rows,  int.  cols)
{
. . .
}
```

You can specify both dimensions if you choose to.

```
void Fun(float  table[2][5],  int  rows,  int  cols
{
. . .
}
```

- When a function is called with an array as an argument, the base address (memo location of the first element) is passed to the function. C++ computes the actual addre of each element from this base address plus the number of elements in each colum

```
int  table[4][2]
table[0][0]  1
table[0][1]  2
table[1][0]  7
table[1][1]  3
table[2][0]  56
table[2][1]  -6
table[3][0]  99
table[3][1]  -54
```

FUNCTIONS

A function in C can perform a particular task, and supports the concept of modular programming design techniques.

We have already been exposed to functions. The main body of a C program, identified by the keyword *main,* and enclosed by the left and right braces is a function. It is called by the operating system when the program is loaded, and when terminated, returns to the operating system.

Functions have a basic structure. Their format is

```
return_data_type  function_name  ( arguments,  arguments  )
data_type__declarations_of_arguments;
{
function_body
}
```

It is worth noting that a return_data_type is assumed to be type *int* unless otherwise specified, thus the programs we have seen so far imply that *main()* returns an integer to the operating system.

ANSI C varies slightly in the way that functions are declared. Its format is

```
return_data_type  function_name  data_type  variable_name,  data_type
variable_name.  ..)
{
function  body
}
```

This permits type checking by utilizing function prototypes to inform the compiler of the type and number of parameters a function accepts. When calling a function, this information is used to perform type and parameter checking.

ANSI C also requires that the return_data_type for a function which does not return data must be type *void.* The default return_data_type is assumed to be integer unless otherwise specified, but must match that which the function declaration specifies.

A simple function is,

```
void  print_message  (  void  )
{
printf("This  is  a  module  called  print_message.\n");
}
```

Note the function name *is print_message.* No arguments are accepted by the function, this is indicated by the keyword *void in* the accepted parameter section of the function declaration. The return_data_type is void, thus data is not returned by the function.

An ANSI C **function prototype** *for print_message()* is.

```
void  print_message  (  void  );
```

Function prototypes are listed at the beginning of the source file. Often, they might be placed in a users .h (*header*) file.

Parameter passing in function:

The parameters can be passed by two ways.

1. Call By value : copy of the parameter is passed.
2. Call by reference: address of parameter is passed.

```
int main ()
{
      int a, b;
      a = 5;
      change (a);
      printf ("%d", a);
}
void change (int x)
{
      x = 7;
}
```

The change(a); statement in the main function is in fact a function call to the change function a is the **actual parameter** in this function call, and it corresponds with the x (**formal Parameter**) which is found in the declaration of the change function.

Of course, the question we are interested in here is what will the statement printf("%d", a) print out? There are only 2 obvious choices. It's either 5 or 7. (Now we are assuming that we don' know anything about parameter passing in C.) Does C pass parameters (arguments) by value or by reference?

According to usual definitions, if it is pass-by-reference. That means that a is going to be changed. Thus it will print out 7. If it is pass-by-value, that means that a is not passed over to change, only the value of a is passed over to change (note the distinction that I make between a and the value of hus 'a' doesn't change and it will print out 5.

C only passes parameters by value. That means, given a function call, it passes values over to the other function.

```
int main()
{
      int a,b;
      a=5;
      b = 7;
      change(&a, &b);
      printf("%d %d\n", a,b);
}
      void change(int *x, int *y)
```

```
{
*x = 6;
*y = 8;
}
```

You see the first question to ask .. is what values are passed over from the function call to change? It is & *a* and & *b*, which are addresses of *a* and *b* respectively. Thus x contains the address of variable *a*. And *y* contains the address of variable *b*. (if we are lost, we can try to find our way by reading on pointers in the notes or in the other FAQ question).

Since **x* is the deference operator, we can say that instead of referring to x, *x is referring to a, thus effectively assigning 6 to a and the same for *y = 8. C is still passing by value, but now it is simulating pass-by-reference. Because these pointers variables being passed in as arguments into change helps change to indirectly refer to a and b which are local variables in another function.

Recursion

We can write functions in C that call other functions to perform a part of a problem. Just as this is possible in C, procedures or functions in C can also call themselves under certain conditions. These are recursive functions, and are defined using two basic components:

The Basis Cases. The conditions under which the function does not call itself recursively, and

The Recursive Cases. The conditions under which the function does call itself recursively.

In general, the recursive cases are met and executed with subsequently smaller (or larger) values until the basis cases are met, at which point the function no longer calls itself recursively, and the recursive returns are executed.

In general, we find that for certain problems, a recursive solution is more elegant than an iterative solution.

Example 1: Factorials

For example, consider the problem of calculating factorials. The **nth factorial** n! is the series of multiplications from I to *n; i.e.,*

$$n! = n * n\text{-}1 * n\text{-}2 * .... * 2 * 1$$

Notice that the (n-1) st factorial (n-1)! is:

$$(n\text{-}1)! = n\text{-}1 * n\text{-}2 * ... * 2 * 1$$

Then, we can calculate the nth factorial using the (n-l)st factorial as:

$$n! = n * (n\text{-}1)!$$

We can continue to calculate the factorial values in a similar way; *i.e.,*

$$(n\text{-}1)! = (n\text{-}1) * (n\text{-}2)!$$

$$(n\text{-}2)! = (n\text{-}2) * (n\text{-}3)!$$

$$(n\text{-}3)! = (n\text{-}3) * (n\text{-}4)!$$

We can continue to calculate the subsequent factorial values as follows:

$$4! = 4 * 3!$$

$$3! = 3 * 2!$$

$$2! = 2 * 1!$$

$$1! = 1 * 0!$$

At this point, we can stop calculating, as the original problem statement defined the nth factorial as the series of multiplications from 1 to n. Therefore, we can define the 0th factorial as 0! = 1.

Here, then, we see the basis cases and the recursive cases of our recursion:

For the 1st through nth factorials, we use the calculation $i! = i * (i - 1)!$; this is the **recursive** case. For the 0th factorial, we define 0! = 1; this is the **basis** case. In other words, we can define the factorials as:

$$n! = \begin{cases} 1 \text{ for } n = 0 \text{ (basis case)} \\ n * (n-1) \text{ for } n > 0 \text{ (recursive case)} \end{cases}$$

The following recursive function solves the problem of the factorial:

```
int n_fact  (int n)
{
    int result;
    if ( n == 0 )  /* Base case */
        result = 1;
    else
        result = n * n_fact ( n-1 ); /* General
          (recursive) case */
    return( result);
}/*Endofn_fact*/
```

Example 2: Power Function

As a second example, we implement the power function recursively and non-recursively.

To implement the power function, we note that the power $base^{exp}$ can be calculated as:

$$base^{exp} = base * base^{exp-1}$$

This gives us the recursive case for the recursion; the basis case is when exp = 0, since $x^0 = 1$ for any x.

Then, we can define the power function as:

$$base^{exp} = \begin{cases} 1 & \text{for exp} = 0 \\ base * base^{exp-1} & \text{for exp} > 0 \end{cases}$$

The recursive version is as follows.

```
int power (int base, int exp )
{
    int result;
    if ( exp == 0 )   /* Base case */
        result = 1;
    else
    result = base * power ( base, exp - 1 ); /*
    Recursive case */
    return( result);
} /* End of power */
```

The non-recursive version of the power function is then as follows:

```
int power it ( int base, int exp )
{
    int product, count;
    product = base;
    for ( count = exp-1, count >= 1; count - -)
            product = product * base;
    return( product);
} /* End of power_it */
```

DDITIONAL ASSIGNMENT OPERATOR

Consider the following statement,

```
numbers[loop] + = 7;
```

This assignment += is equivalent to add equals. It takes the value of *numbers[loop]*, adds it 7, then assigns the value to *numbers [loop]*. In other words it is the same as,

```
numbers[loop] = numbers[loop] + 7;
```

ntrolling the Cursor Position

The following characters, placed after the \character in *a printf ()* statement, have the following ect.

Modifier	*Meaning*
\b	Backspace
\f	form feed
\n	new line
\r	carriage return
\t	horizontal tab

\v	vertical tab
\\	Backslash
\"	double quote
\'	single quote
\<enter>	line continuation
\nnn	nnn = octal character value
\0xnn	nn = hexadecimal value (some compilers only)

STRUCTURES

A Structure is a data type suitable for grouping data elements together. Lets create a new data structure suitable for storing the date. The elements or fields which make up the structure use the four *basic data types*. As the storage requirements for a structure cannot be known by the compiler, a definition for the structure is first required. This allows the compiler to determine the storage allocation needed, and also identities the various sub-fields of the structure.

```
struct date
{
    int month;
    char day[10];
    int year;
};
```

This declares a NEW data type called *date*. This date structure consists of three basic data elements, integer, array of characters. Other data structures may be defined as consisting of the same composition as the *date* structure,

```
struct data todays_date;
```

defines a variable called *todays_date* to be of the same data type as that of the newly defined data type struct *date. Total* memory taken by this structure will be 2 + (10*l) + 2 = 14 byte since month will take 2 byte as it is integer, array day will take 10 byte since there are 10 element in array of type character and year will take 2 byte as it is integer.

UNIONS

This is a special data type which looks similar to a structure, it is also the collection of different data type, but is very different, declaration is,

```
union mixed
{
    char letter;
    float radian;
```

```
        int number;
    };
    union mixed all;
```

The first declaration consists of a union of type mixed, which consists of a char, float, or int variable. NOTE that it can be ONLY ONE of the variable types, they cannot coexist.

This is due to the provision of a single memory address which is used to store the largest variable, unlike the arrangement used for structures.

Thus the variable *all* can only be a character, a float or an integer at any one time. The C language keeps track of what *all* actually is at any given moment, but does not provide a check to prevent the programmer accessing it incorrectly.

ENUMERATED DATA TYPES

Enumerated data type variables can only assume values which have been previously declared.

```
    enum month { jan = 1, feb, mar, apr, may, jun, jul, aug, sep, oct,
nov, dec };
    enum month this_month;
    this_month = feb;
```

In the above declaration, *month* is declared as an enumerated data type. It consists of a set of values, jan to dec. Numerically, jan is given the value 1, feb the value 2, and so on. The variable *this_month* is declared to be of the same type as month, then is assigned the value associated with feb. This_month cannot be assigned any values outside those specified in the initialization list for the declaration of month.

```
    #include <stdio.h>
    main ()
    {
        char *pwest = "west", *pnorth = "nort h ", *peast = "east",
*psouth = "south";
        enum location { east = 1, west =2, south=3, north = 4};
        enum location direction;

        direction = east;

        if (direction = = east)
            printf ("Cannot go %s\n", peast);
    }
```

The variables defined in the enumerated variable *location* should be assigned initial values.

POINTERS

Pointers enable us to effectively represent complex data structures, to change values as arguments to functions, to work with memory which has been dynamically allocated, and to more concisely and efficiently deal with arrays. A pointer provides an indirect means of accessing the value of a particular data item. Lets see how pointers actually work with a simple example,

```
int count = 10, *int_pointer;
```

declares an integer *count* with a value of 10, and also an integer pointer called *int_pointer.* Note that the prefix * defines the variable to be of type pointer. To set up an indirect reference between *int_pointer* and *count,* the & prefix is used, i.e.,

```
int_pointer = &count
```

This assigns the memory address *of count* to int_pointer, not the actual value *of count* stored at that address.

POINTERS CONTAIN MEMORY ADDRESSES, NOT VALUES!

To reference the value *of count* using *int_pointer,* the * is used in an assignment, e.g.,

```
x = *int_pointer;
```

Since *int_pointer* is set to the memory address of *count,* this operation has the effect of assigning the contents of the memory address pointed to by *int_pointer* to the variable *x,* so that after the operation variable *x* has a value of 10.

```
#include <stdio.h>
main ()
{
        int count = 10, x, *int_pointer;
        /* this assigns the memory address of count to int_pointer*1
        int_pointer = &count;
        /* assigns the value stored at the address specified by
int_pointer to x */
        x = *int_pointer;
        printf("count = %d, x = %d\n", count, x);
}
```

This however, does not illustrate a good use for pointers.

The following program illustrates another way to use pointers, this time with characters.

```
#include <stdio.h>
main ()
{
     char c = ' Q ';
     char *char_pointer = &c;
     printf("%c %c\n", c, *char_pointer) ;
```

```
        c = 'Z';
        printf("%c %c\n", c, *char_pointer) ;
        * char_pointer = 'Y';
        /* assigns Y as the contents of the memory address specified
by char__pointer */
        printf("%c %c\n", c, *char_pointer) ;
    }
```

COMMAND LINE ARGUMENTS

It is possible to pass arguments to C programs when they are executed. The brackets which follow main are used for this purpose, *argc* refers to the number of arguments passed, and *argv[]* is a pointer array which points to each argument which is passed to main. A simple example follows, which checks to see if a single argument is supplied on the command line when the program is invoked.

```
# include <stdio.h>
main ( int argc, char *argv[ ] )
{
        if ( argc = 2 )
                printf("The argument supplied is %s \n", argv [1]);
        else if (argc > 2 )
                printf ('"Too many argument's supplied.\n");
        else
                printf ( "One argument expected.\n");
}
```

Note that **argv[0]* is the name of the program invoked, which means that **argv [1]* is a pointer to the first argument supplied, and **argv[n]* is the last argument. If no arguments are supplied, *argc* will be one. Thus for n arguments, *argc* will be equal to n + 1. The program is called by the command line,

```
myprog argument1
```

SOLVED PROGRAM ON C

PROGRAM NO. 1

WAP to print hello

```
# include <stdio.h>
# include <conio.h>
void main ()
{
clrscr ();
printf ("hello");
getch ();
}
```

PROGRAM NO. 2

WAP for addition of two numbers

```
# include <stdio.h>
# include <conio.h>
void main ()
{
clrscr ();
int x, y, z;
printf ("enter the two number");
scanf ("%d%d", & x, & y);
z = x + y;
printf ("the sum of two number is = % d,"z);
getch ();
}
```

PROGRAM NO. 3

WAP to print hello 5 times

```
# include <stdio.h>
# include <conio.h>
void main ()
{
int x = 0 ;
clrscr ();
while  (x < 5)
{
printf ("In hello");
x++;
}
getch ();
}
```

PROGRAM NO. 4

WAP to print table of any number

```
# include <stdio.h>
# include <conio.h>
void main ()
{
int x, y, z;
x = 1;
clrscr ();
printf ("enter the number");
scanf ("%d", & y);
while (x < = 10)
{
z = x × y;
printf ("%d\n,"z);
x + +;
}
getch ();
}
```

PROGRAM NO. 5

WAP for SI

```
# include <stdio.h>
```

```
# include <conio.h>
void main
{
int p, n, r;
float Si;
clrscr ();
printf ("enter the value of p, n, r");
scanf ("%d%d%d", & p, & n, & r);
si = P * n * r/100;
printf ("the value of Si = %f," Si);
getch ();
}
```

PROGRAM NO. 6

```
//WAP to find binary sum of odd & even no. from 1 to 100
# include <stdio.h>
# include <conio.h>
void main ()
{
int num, i, j;
int even_sum = 0, sum_odd = 0;
clrscr ();
printf ("\n the sum of odd no. is \n");
printf ("0");
for (i = 1; i < = 99; i = i + 2)
{
sum odd = sum_odd + i;
printf ("+%d", i);
}
printf ("%d\n\n\n", Sum_odd);
printf ("The sum of even no. \n\n");
printf ("0");
for (i = 2; i < = 100; i = i + 2)
{
even_sum = even_sum + i;
printf ("+%d", i);
```

```
}
printf ("= %d", even_sum);
getch ();
}
```

PROGRAM NO. 7

```
//WAP to find greatest of three number
# include <stdio.h>
# include <conio.h>
void main ()
{
int P, a, r;
printf("Enter the three no.")
scanf ("%d%d%d", &P, &a, &r);
if (P>a&&a> r)
printf ("P is greatest no.");
else if (a > r)
printf ("a is greatest no.");
else
printf ("r is greatest no.");
getch ()
}
```

PROGRAM NO. 8

```
//WAP to find fib series
# include <stdio.h>
# include <conio.h>
# include <math.h>
void f (int to, int f1, int n)
{
if (n = 0)
return:
n - -;
printf ("%d\n", to + f1);
f (t1, to + f1, n);
```

```
}
main ()
{
in to = 0, f1 = 1, n;
clrscr ();
scanf ("%d", & n);
printf ("%d\n%d\n", to, f1);
f (to, t1, n);
return (0);
}
```

PROGRAM NO. 9

```
//WAP to find out whether the given string is palindrome or not
# include <stdio.h>
# include <conio.h>
# include <math.h>
void main ()
{
clrscr ();
int i, j, l;
char a [20];
printf ("Enter the string");
scanf ("%S", a) ; 1
l = strlen (a);
for (i = 0, j = l - 1; i < j; i ++, j - - )
{
if (a[i]! = a[j])
break;
}
if (i > = j)
printf ("The string is palindroem");
else
printf ("The string is not palindrome");
getch ();
}
```

PROGRAM NO. 10

```
//WAP reverse print sum of digit
# include <stdio.h>
# include <conio.h>
void main ()
{
int S = 0 , n, K;
clrscr ();
printf ("Enter the no.");
scanf ("%d", & n);
While (n! = 0)
{
   K = n% 10;
   S = S + K;
   n = n/10;
   }
printf ("%d", S);
getch ();
}
```

Note : For process of working on Email refer article 8.9.

PROGRAM NO. 11

```
/* Program to convert upper case letters to lower case letters */
# include <stdio.h>
main ()
{
char Ucase, Lcase; printf
("Type a letter in upper case");
scanf ("%c", & Ucase);
Lcase = Ucase + 32;
printf ("Letter in Lower case is % c", Lcase);
}
```

PROGRAM NO. 12

```
/* Program to arrange 10 numbers in ascending order through
pointers */
```

```
# include <stdio.h>
int swap (int [], int[]);
void main ()
{
int num, *a, j = 0, i, item [50];
printf ("Enter the limit");
scanf ("%d", & num);
printf ["Enter the numbers"];
for (i = 0, j < = num; i++)
Scanf("%d", & item Ii);
for (i = 0; i < num - 1; i++)
{
j = j + 1;
if (item [i] > item [j])
{
swap (item *[i], item *[j]);
}
}
printf ("the elements are");
for (i = 0; i< = num-1; i++)
{
printf ("%d", item [i]);
}
getch ();
}
int swap (int * a, int * b)
{
int temp = *a;
   *a = *b;
   *b = temp;
   return (*a, *b);
}
```

PROGRAM NO. 13

```
/* Program to swap two numbers without using third variable */
# include <stdio.h>
main ()
{
```

```
int n1, n2;
printf ("Enter the two number")
scanf ("%d%d", &n1, &n2);
printf ("n1 = %d, n2 = %d", n1, n2);
n1 = n1 + n2;
n2 = n1 - n2;
n1 = n1 - n2;
printf ("After swapping the numbers are");
printf ("n1 = %d, n2 = %d", n1, n2);
}
```

PROGRAM NO. 14

```
/* Program to print the sum of diagonal elements of a matrix */
# include <stdio.h>
main ()
{
int m[10] [10], i, j, r, c, sum = 0;
printf ("Enter the number of rows and columns in the matrix");
scanf ("%d%d", &r &c);
printf ("Enter the elements of matrix");
for (i = 0; i < = r - 1; i++)
  {
  for (j = 0; j < = c - 1; j++)
    {
    scanf ("%d", &m [i][j]);
    }
  }
  for (i = 0; i < = r - 1; i++)
    {
    for (j = 0; j < = c - 1; j++)
{
    if (i = j)
    Sum = Sum + m [i][j];
    }
}
```

```
printf ("sum of diagonal elements of the given matrix is= %d,
sum");
}
```

PROGRAM NO. 15

```
/* Program to print the mirror image of matrix */
# include <stdio.h>
main ()
{
int m[10][10], i, j, r, c;
print ("Enter the number of row & column in matrix");
scanf ("%d%d", &r, &c);
printf ("Enter the elements of the matrix");
for (i = 0; i< = r -1; i++)
    {
    for (j = 0; j < = c - 1; j++)
    {
    scanf ("%d", & m[i][j]);
    }
    printf ("\n");
    }
    printf ("Mirror image of given matrix is");
    for (i = 0; i < = r -1; i++)
    {
    for (j< = c - 1; J = 0; j- -)
    {
    printf ("%d", m [i][j]);
    }
    printf ("\n");
    }
}
```

PROGRAM NO. 16

```
/* Program to count the number of words in a statement */
# include <stdio.h>
```

```
main ()
{
    char*s, ch;
    int c = 0 ;
    printf ("Enter the string");
    fflush (stdin);
    gets (s);
    do
    {
    ch = getch (stdin);
    if (ch = = ' ')
    c = c + 1;
    } while (ch ! = '\n');
    c = c + 1;
    printf ("Number of words in the given string are %d", c);
    getch ();
}
```

PROGRAM NO. 17

/* Program to find number of integers & sum of integer greater than 99 and less than 150 that are divisible by 5*/

```
# include <stdio.h>
main ()
{
int n [20], sum = 0, c = 0; i;
for (i = 100; i < 150; i++)
{
if (i%5 = = 0)
{
n[c] = i;
c = c + i;
sum = sum + i;
}
}
printf ("The number of integers are");
for (i = 0; i < c; i++)
```

```
{
printf ("%d", n[i]);
}
printf ("Total number is %d the sum of these numbers are %d", c,
sum);
getch ();
}
```

PROGRAM NO. 18

```
/* Program to calculate sine values for angle 0 to 90 */
# include <stdio.h>
# include <math.h>
main ()
{
    int i, Pl;
    float angle;
printf ("The sine value of angle between 0 and 90");
for (i = 0; i < = 90; i = i + 10)
{
    angle = (float) (Pl/180)* i;
printf ("\n %3d \t %7.5f", i, sin (angle));
}
getch ();
}
```

PROGRAM NO. 19

```
/* Program to convert meters into centimeters */
# include <stdio.h>
main ()
{
float m, cm;
printf ("Enter the value in meters");
scanf ("%f", & m);
cm = m * 100;
printf ("Value in centimeter is");
```

```
print ("%f", cm);
}
```

PROGRAM NO. 20

```
/* Program to calculate the simple interest for a given principal */
# include <stdio.h>
main ()
{
int P;
float r, t, Sl
printf ("Enter the principal, rate & time");
scanf ("%d%f%f", &P, &r, &t);
Sl = (P * r * t)/100;
printf ("Simple interest is "%f", Sl);
}
```

PROGRAM NO. 21

```
/* Program to calculate the compound interest for a given principal */
# include <stdio.h>
main ()
{
float P, O, r;
int i, t;
float Sl, Cl;
printf ("Enter the principal");
scanf ("%f", &P);
O = P;
printf ("Enter the rate & time");
scanf ("%f%d", &r, &t);
Sl = (P * r * t)/100;
for (i = 1; i < = t; i++)
{
Sl = (P * r * i)/100;
P = P + Sl;
}
```

```
Cl = P - O;
printf ("Compound Interest is = %f", Cl);
getch ();
}
```

PROGRAM NO. 22

```
/* Program to calculate the difference between two matrix */
# include <stdio.h>
main ()
{
int a [5][5], b[5][5], c[5][5], i, j;
int r1, c1, r2, c2;
printf ("Enter the number of row & column of 1st matrix");
scanf ("%d%d", &r1, &c1);
printf ("Enter the number of row & column of IInd matrix");
scanf ("%d%d", &r2, &c2);
if (r1 = = r2 && c1 = = c2)
{
printf ("Enter the element of 1st matrix");
for (i = 0, i < r1; i++)
{
for (j = 0, j < c1; j++)
{
scanf ("%d", & a[i][j]);
}
}
printf ("Enter the elements of IInd matrix");
for (i = 0; i < r2; i++)
    {
for (j = 0; j < c 2; j ++)
    {
    scanf ("%d", & b[i][j]);
    }
}
printf ("Difference of two matrix is");
for (i = 0; i < r1; i++)
    {
```

```
for (j = 0; j < c1; j++)
  {
  c[i][j] = a [i][j] - b[i][j];
  printf ("%d", c[i][j]);
     }
  }
} /+ End of if */
else
  {
  printf ("Calculation of difference is not possible");
  }
} /* End of main */
```

QUESTION SET OF C

Fundamentals

1. Display "Hello World" by using Printf().
2. WRITE A PROGRAM to calculate the roots of quadratic equation.
3. Write a program to find the simple interest by using the formula.
4. Two find the GCD of two number.
5. Write a program to convert Fahrenheit temperature to Celsius temperature C/5 = (f–32)/9.
6. Find Out the percentage of marks of five subjects.
7. WRITE A PROGRAM to sWrite a program the value of two variables.
   * by using third variable.
   * without using third variable.

IF, IF-ELSE, IF ELSEIF and Nested IF

8. Write a program to check given character is vowel or not.
9. Write a program to check entered character is digit, alphabet or symbol.
10. Write a program to check given no is even or odd.
11. Write a program to check entered year is leap year or not.
12. Write a program to display the age group:
    (*a*) 0.12 Infant.
    (*b*) 13.19 Teenage.
    (*c*) 20.30 Youth.
    (*d*) 31.50 Middle age.
    (*e*) 51.64 Old Age.
    (*f*) 65 and Above Senior Citizen.

LOOPING

13. Write a program to display the table of 4.
14. Write a program to calculate ^nCr.
15. Write a program to calculate the SIN(X) series.
16. Write a program to calculate the COS(X) series.
17. Write a program to calculate the LOG(1+X) series.
18. Write a program to calculate the e^x series.
19. Write a program to display the sum of digits of entered number.
20. Write a program to display the number in reverse order.
21. Write a program to check given no is Armstrong or not.
22. Write a program to check the given no is prime number or not.
23. Write a program to display the fibonaci series.
24. Write a program to display prime no from 1 to 100.
25. Write a program to display the first 100 primes no.

ARRAY

26. Write a program to find the sum of elements in the array.
27. Write a program to find the maximum value among the elements of array.
28. Write a program to sort the array in ascending and descending order.
29. Write a program to multiply two matrices.
30. Write a program to addition two matrices.
31. Write a program to transpose matrix.

STRINGS

32. Write a program to check the given string is palindrome or not.
33. Write a program to count the total no of vowels in given string.

FUNCTIONS

34. Write a program by using function to calculate the factorial.
35. Write a program by using function to display the sum of two no.
36. Write a program by using function to calculate the power of any no.
37. Write a program by using function to calculate NCR and NPR.
38. Write a program by using recursion to calculate factorial.

STRUCTURE/UNION

39. Write a program by using Structure to handle the information of single student.
40. Write a program by using Structure to handle the information of multiple students.

Previous Year Papers

INFORMATION TECHNOLOGY

B.Tech.

FIRST SEMESTER EXAMINATION, 2004–2005

Time: 3 Hours *Total Marks : 100*

Note: *Attempt* **all** *questions*

1. Attempt any two parts of the following : **10 × 2 = 20**

(*a*) What is data compression ? Why is it needed ? Differentiate between lossy and lossless data compression techniques with suitable examples.

(*b*) A text string contains total seven distinct symbols. The symbols and their frequencies are given below :

Symbol	*Frequency*
B	35
N	25
F	15
Q	10
E	5
M	5
R	5

Compute the following :

(*i*) Information bits for each symbol

(*ii*) Construct Shannon-Fano tree and generate Shannon-Fano codes.

(*iii*) Construct Huffman tree and generate Huffman codes.

(*iv*) Show the code for string "B F N Q B B M F R" using Huffman technique.

(c) What is dictionary based compression ? Differentiate between LZ78 and LZW compression schemes. Code and decode the string "EJSEJESESEJEJSEJEJTEJEJ" using LZW compression scheme.

2. Attempt any **two** parts of the following : **10 × 2 = 20**

(a) What are software development life cycle models ? Why is it important to consider software development life cycle model for developing a large software project ? Explain various phases of waterfall model.

(b) Differentiate between :

(i) Static and Dynamic RAM

(ii) Compiler and Interpreter

(iii) High level language and Fourth generation language

(iv) System software and Application software

(v) Alpha testing and Beta testing.

(c) Draw the block diagram of digital computer and explain functioning of its various blocks. How can the computers be classified ?

3. Attempt any **four** parts of the following : **5 x 4 = 20**

(a) Convert the following decimal numbers to Binary, Octal, Hexadecimal and BCD: 251, 141

(b) What are flip-flops? Explain the working principle of a clocked flip-flop. What is excitation table?

(c) What are NAND gates ? Why is it called a universal gate ? Draw a digital circuit to obtain a EX-OR and EX-NOR gate using NAND gates.

(d) What is Computer Network ? What are the advantages of computer networks ? Explain how Local Area Network is different from Wide Area Network.

(e) Write short notes on any two :

(i) ISDN

(ii) CSMA/CD

(iii) ATM

(f) What do you mean by network topology ? Explain the following in brief :

(i) Star topology

(ii) Bus topology

(iii) Ring topology.

4. Attempt any **four** parts of the following : **5 x 4 = 20**

(a) What is World Wide Web ? How is World Wide Web related with the term website?

(b) What is data Encryption ? Differentiate between public key and private key encryption.

(c) Write short notes on any two :

(i) Web browser

(ii) HTML

(iii) FTP

(d) What is E-commerce ? Explain different types of E-commerce.

(e) What is firewall ? Distinguish between static and dynamic firewall.

(f) What do you mean by electronic payments ? Explain with a suitable example, how a customer pays electronically to the merchant for the product he buys through internet.

5. Attempt *any four* parts of the following : 5 × 4 = 20

(a) "Operating System is a resource manager", justify this statement by giving suitable reasons.

(b) Differentiate between internal and external commands of DOS. Give three examples for each category.

(c) Why is Windows called GUI based system ? How does recycle bin help to prevent accidental deletions ?

(d) How are the charts prepared in MS-EXCEL ? List the types of charts which may be prepared by MS-EXCEL.

(e) Discuss the general Architecture of Database Management System. Explain the role of transaction manager.

(f) Discuss the scientific, business and educational applications of IT in India.

INFORMATION TECHNOLOGY

B.Tech.

FIRST SEMESTER EXAMINATION, 2005–06

Time: 3 Hours *Total Marks : 100*

Note: *Attempt* **all** *questions*

1. Attempt any **four** parts of the following : **4 × 5 = 20**
   - (*a*) What do you understand by Information Technology ? What are its applications? Explain in brief.
   - (*b*) What is the drawback of using LZ78 algorithm ? Encode the message "MAHAN*MAHABHARATH" using this algorithm. Show all the steps.
   - (*c*) What do you understand by 'Self Information'? For a given message "DADBADCADBAADAC" calculate the following :
     - (*i*) Self information associated with characters A and B in the message
     - (*ii*) Average self information of message
     - (*iii*) Entropy of message.
   - (*d*) Differentiate between the following :
     - (*i*) Static coding and dynamic coding
     - (*ii*) Digital computer and hybrid computer
     - (*iii*) JPEG and GIF
     - (*iv*) Data and information
   - (*e*) What is computer animation? Explain its basic concepts.
   - (*f*) (*i*) What is difference between compression and encryption?

     (*ii*) What do you understand by Internet?
2. Attempt any **four** parts of the following : **4 × 5 = 20**
   - (*a*) Compare the features of various generations of computer.
   - (*b*) Explain the hierarchy of memories used in computer system. Compare the characteristics of all the memories shown in the hierarchy.
   - (*c*) Differentiate between a program and an algorithm. Draw a flowchart to show whether a given number is positive or negative.
   - (*d*) What is a digitizer ? Is it an input device or an output device ? Justify your answer.
   - (*e*) Answer the following questions :
     - (*i*) What do you understand by software development life cycle ?

(*ii*) List various stages of waterfall model.

(*iii*) What are the main objectives of feasibility study phase in software development ?

(*iv*) What is SRS ?

(*v*) Differentiate between debugging and testing.

(*f*) What do you mean by quality assurance ? Write a short note on ISO 9000.

3. Attempt any **four** parts of the following : **4 × 5 = 20**

(*a*) Convert (011010111101001100)2 in decimal, octal and hexadecimal number system.

(*b*) Draw a full adder using two half adders. Also give the truth table for full adder.

(*c*) What do you mean by modulation ? Differentiate between Amplitude modulation and Frequency Modulation.

(*d*) Draw and explain the following network topologies:

(*i*) Star topology

(*ii*) Bus topology

(*iii*) Ring topology

(*e*) Differentiate between various types of transmission mode ?

(*f*) What do you mean by client server architecture ? Discuss the pros and cons of it ?

4. Attempt any **four** parts of the following : **4 × 5 = 20**

(*a*) What is e-commerce? Justify that Electronic Data Interchange (EDI) is a part of E-commerce.

(*b*) What are fire walls? Differentiate between the static and dynamic firewalls.

(*c*) What is a credit card? Discuss the problems faced with credit cards.

(*d*) Explain the purpose of the following HTML tags:

(*i*) BODY

(*ii*) LIST

(*iii*) HEADINGS

(*iv*) HREF

(*v*) IMG

(*e*) Differentiate between any two of the following :

(*i*) Applet and servlet in Java

(*ii*) Public key cryptography and private key cryptography

(*iii*) FTP and Telnet.

(*f*) What technologies are used for server side programming ? Discuss any one ?

5. **Attempt any four parts of the following :** **4 × 5 = 20**

(*a*) **Name three models of database management system and explain any one in detail.**

(*b*) **How will you perform following in Windows environment ?**

(*i*) **Open a file**

(*ii*) **Copy a file or folder from one disk to another**

(*iii*) **Change background of desktop**

(*iv*) **Create a shortcut**

(*v*) **Rename a file**

(*c*) **Write down five advantages of using MS Excel for accounting purpose.**

(*d*) **What is SQL? Write syntax of SELECT command and illustrate it with an example.**

(*e*) **Write a short note on weather forecasting.**

(*f*) **Write a short note on NICNET.**

INFORMATION TECHNOLOGY

B.Tech.

FIRST SEMESTER EXAMINATION, 2006–07

Time: 3 Hours *Total Marks : 100*

Note: *Attempt* **all** *questions*

1. Attempt any **two** parts of the following : **10 x 2 = 20**

(*a*) (*i*) Differentiate between data and information giving suitable examples. Explain the various data formats.

(*ii*) Discuss entropy of information. What is its significance ?

(*b*) For the following data :

Symbol	*Frequency*
A	.80
B	.15
C	.05

Calculate the difference between average number of bits required for one, symbol in the Huffman's and Extended Huffman coding techniques. Also discuss which coding technique is better and why ?

(*c*) (*i*) What *is* LZW compression technique ? What are the advantages of LZW compression over LZ78 compression technique ? For the test string "DIDIDDIDI$ DIDIA$DIDI", show all the steps of LZW compression including dictionary formation.

(*ii*) Write short notes on :

(1) JPEG (2) MPEG

2. Attempt any **two** parts of the following : **10 × 2 = 20**

(*a*) (*i*) Draw the block diagram of a digital computer. Explain its each block in detail giving suitable examples.

(*ii*) What do you understand by Fourth Generation Languages ?

(*b*) Explain in detail different Testing Techniques used for testing a software.

(*c*) Write short notes on any three of the following :

(*i*) SDLC

(*ii*) CMM standard for IT industry

(*iii*) Static and Dynamic RAM

(*iv*) Data Flow Diagram

3. Attempt any **four** parts of the following : **5 × 4 = 20**

(*a*) Convert the following decimal number to equivalent binary and hexadecimal number, system :

(*i*) 24.25 (*ii*) 133.15 (*iii*) 56

(*b*) What are Flip Flops ? What are the problems in SR flip-flops ? Explain by using the characteristic table of SR flip-flop.

(*c*) What do you mean by digital modulation ? Explain briefly the various digital modulation techniques.

(*d*) What do you understand by token based protocols ? Explain the working of any such protocol.

(*e*) Give an overview of ISO OSI layers. Also discuss the basic functioning of each layer.

(*f*) Write short notes on *any two* :

(*i*) CSMA/CD

(*ii*) Network Topology

(*iii*) Client-Server Architecture.

4. Attempt any **four** parts of the following : **5 x 4 = 20**

(*a*) What is TCP/IP ? Why TCP/IP is so important for internet users ?

(*b*) Explain Local Area Networking. How it is different from MAN ? Give example to support your answer.

(*c*) What is data encryption ? Differentiate between public key and private key encryption.

(*d*) How Business to Business E-Commerce is different from Business to Consumer E-Commerce ? Explain by giving suitable example.

(*e*) What are the factors that influence the selection of an ISP (Internet Service Provider)?

(*f*) Write short notes on *any two* :

(*i*) Search Engines

(*ii*) WWW

(*iii*) Electronic Payment System

5. Attempt any **four** parts *of* the following : **5 x 4 = 20**

(*a*) Differentiate between internal and external commands of DOS. Give three examples of each category.

(*b*) List the basic working of each of the following :

(*i*) MS - Word

(*ii*) MS - Excel

(*iii*) MS - Power Point.

(*c*) Discuss the different levels of Data Abstraction.

(*d*) Briefly explain the different components of Data Base Management System.

(e) Explain the salient features of NICNET? List other specialized and dedicated network existing in the country.

(*f*) Discuss the application of Information technology in various areas.

INFORMATION TECHNOLOGY

B.Tech.

SECOND SEMESTER EXAMINATION, 2006–07

Time: 3 Hours *Total Marks : 100*

Note: *Attempt* **all** *questions*

1. Attempt any **four** parts of the following : 5 x 4 = 20
   (*a*) Define Entropy. Explain its significance.
   (*b*) Explain the compression process used by MPEG.
   (*c*) Let X represent the outcome of a single roll of a fair die. What is entropy of X ?
   (*d*) Explain LZW coding algorithm. What are its advantages and disadvantages?
   (*e*) Why do we need data compaction? Explain the Huffman Coding Algorithm.
   (*f*) Explain various file formats used for multimedia data.
2. Attempt any **four** parts of the following ; 5 x 4 = 20
   (*a*) Describe the software development methodology.
   (*b*) (*i*) Differentiate between sequential access and random access devices.
   (*ii*) Explain different types of ROM devices.
   (*c*) Explain the role of hard disk in a computer system. Draw the internal design of a hard disk.
   (*d*) What is cache memory? Compare various parameters of cache memory, main memory, auxiliary storage devices.
   (*e*) (*i*) Describe the major developments in different generation of computer evolution.
   (*ii*) How do fourth generation languages differ from third generation languages?
   (*f*) Explain CMM standards for IT industry,
3. Attempt any **four** parts of the following ; 5 x 4 = 20
   (*a*) Differentiate between frequency-division multiplexing and time-division multiplexing.
   (*b*) Explain the phase modulation concept Compare it with Amplitude modulation and frequency modulation.
   (*c*) Convert the following:
   (*i*) FFFF hexadecimal to Decimal format.
   (*ii*) Decimal 31.54 to Binary format.
   (*iii*) Binary 11.0001 to Decimal format.
   (*iv*) Decimal 15 to Gray code format.
   (*v*) Hexadecimal 7F2 to Octal format.

(*d*) Define BCD code. What is the disadvantage of using BCD code? How do we remove this problem? Is BCD code weighted code? If yes, show else explain.

(*e*) Explain the role of various network elements in a mobile communication network. Which cell shape is used in it and why?

(*i*) Explain the concepts of CSMA/CD.

(*ii*) What is client-Server architecture.

(*iii*) Draw star, BUS, Ring network topologies.

4. Attempt any **four** parts of the following : **5 x 4 = 20**

(*a*) What do you understand by mark up language? How they differ from conventional programming language? Discuss clearly.

(*b*) What is cryptography ? Why do we use it in Internet ? Differentiate between public key and private key cryptography techniques.

(*c*) What is a domain name? How does computer resolves IP address corresponding to a domain name?

(*d*) What is the role of firewalls in the Internet ? Explain various types of firewalls,

(*e*) Explain the various requirements of E-commerce system. What is the role of security in E-commerce? How do we implement security in E-commerce?

(*f*) Discuss Gopher, FTP, Telnet, HTTP. E-mail.

5. Attempt any **four** parts of the following : **5 x 4 = 20**

(*a*) What is an operating system? Write its major functions. List the name of some popular operating systems.

(*b*) What is word processing? Name some features of word processors. What are advantages of word processing package MS-word ?

(*c*) Define SQL. What are advantages of using it? Give the classification of SQL statements.

(*d*) Explain die concept of e-governance? What are its advantages and disadvantages? Briefly explain the possible threats to such system.

(*e*) What is database management system, Write the advantages and disadvantages of DBMS. Explain different components of DBMS.

(*f*) Explain the role of I.T. in weather forecasting. What is the impact of I.T. use in this on common people in India?

INFORMATION TECHNOLOGY

B.Tech.

FIRST SEMESTER EXAMINATION, 2007–08

Time: 3 Hours *Total Marks : 100*

Note: *Attempt* **all** *questions*

1. Attempt any **two** parts of the following : **10 × 2 = 20**

(*a*) What do you understand by information entropy? How entropy can be used in coding? Describe the concept of static and dynamic code.

(*b*) What is Data Compression? Explain extended Huffmann codes in context with the data compression techniques.

(*c*) Explain how information representation is done in digital media, text, graphics and animation system.

2. Attempt any **two** parts of the following : **10 × 2 = 20**

(*a*) Describe the history of computer generations in terms of devices, hardware, software, mean time between failures (MTBF) and high level languages.

(*b*) (*i*) Describe the working of compilers and interpreters.

(*ii*) What is the difference between flow charts and data flow diagrams (DFD)?

(*c*) Write notes on:

(*i*) Software testing and maintenance.

(*ii*) Firmware.

3. Attempt any **two** parts of the following : **10 × 2 = 20**

(*a*) Explain the differences between decimal, hexadecimal and binary number systems. Add the following binary numbers and represent the result in octal:

(i) 10110110 + 01101101 = ________

(ii) 10101010 + 10101010 = ________

(*b*) (*i*) Describe the concepts of LAN, WAN and Mobile Communication.

(*ii*) What are ISDN and ATM systems?

(*c*) (*i*) What do you understand by Amplitude and Frequency modulation?

(*ii*) What is Multiplexing and where it is used?

4. Attempt any **two** parts of the following : **10 × 2 = 20**

(*a*) Describe the following:

(*i*) Search Engines

(*ii*) ISP

(*iii*) EDI

(*iv*) Net Surfing

(*v*) E-Commerce.

(*b*) What do you understand by encryption? What are the security threats in online business transactions? Describe the safety measures required for business transactions on web.

(*c*) Explain the working of a Firewall. How it is useful in checking unauthorized access in a network?

5. Attempt any **two** parts of the following : **10 × 2 = 20**

(*a*) Describe the difference between DOS, MS WINDOWS and LINUX.

(*b*) (*i*) Creation, modification and deletion of tables in MS-WORD.

(*ii*) Graphics features in MS-EXCEL.

(*iii*) Presentation in MS Powerpoint.

(*iv*) Database handling in FoxPro.

(*c*) What do you understand by electronic governance? How does it affect the faster dissemination of information from Parliament to Block Development Offices?

INFORMATION TECHNOLOGY

B.Tech.

SECOND SEMESTER EXAMINATION, 2007–08

Time: 3 Hours *Total Marks : 100*

Note: *Attempt* **all** *questions*

1. Attempt any **four** parts: 4 × 5 = 20

   (*a*) Define the term information representation. How is it represented in digital media?

   (*b*) What do you mean by quality of information? Explain.

   (*c*) Convert the following binary numbers to decimenal numbers:

   (*i*) 101011.11 (*ii*) 111011.10

   (*d*) Differentiate between Huffman-tree and Shannon-Fano tree, which is more effective and why?

   (*e*) Define the term data compression. Why is it required?

   (*f*) Define the following:

   (*i*) JPEG (*ii*) MHEG

2. Attempt any **four** parts: 4 × 5 = 20

   (*a*) Draw a block diagram to illustrate the basic organisation of a computer system and explain and functions of various units.

   (*b*) A computer has no intelligence of its own. Discuss.

   (*c*) Machine language programs written for one computer with a different CPU. Why?

   (*d*) Differentiate between static RAM and Dynamic RAM

   (*e*) What is an interpreter? How does it differ from a complier?

   (*f*) What is a linker? Why is it required.

3. Attempt any **two** parts: 10 × 2 = 20

   (*a*) (*i*) Draw the logic circuit for the following expressions:

   $$A \cdot \overline{B} \cdot C \cdot D + A \cdot B \cdot C \cdot D + \overline{A.B.C.D}$$

   (*ii*) What are registers ? What are used for? Draw a schematic diagram of 4-bit register.

   (*b*) (*i*) Explain the terms "bandwidth" and "band" with suitable example.

   (*ii*) What do you understand by modulation and demodulation?

   (*c*) (*i*) Define the terms—(*i*) Routa and (*ii*) Gateway.

   (*ii*) Describe the OSI model of network architecture with the functions of each layer.

4. Attempt any two parts: 10 × 2 = 20

(*a*) (*i*) List out three main characteristics features of the internet that may be used to define it.

(*ii*) What do you mean by TCP/IP? Explain.

(*b*) Define the following with example:

(*i*) Hypertext Markup language.

(*ii*) Public key and Private key

(*iii*) ISP

(*iv*) Electronic payment system.

(*c*) Define E-Commerce. Give in detail the basic infrastructure for E-Commerce.

5. Attempt any two parts: 10 × 2 = 20

(*a*) (*i*) Differentiate between internal and external commands of MS-DOS, with ex amples.

(*ii*) Name any four popular O.S. and describe the main feature of any one of them.

(*b*) (*i*) What do you mean by word processing? List important features, which makes MS-Word suitable for word processing applications.

(*ii*) What are macros in the MS-Word? What does they do? Explain.

(*c*) Define the following:

(*i*) Database Management System

(*ii*) BR NET

(*iii*) IT application in education

(*iv*) FoxPro commands to create a datable.

MODEL TEST PAPER – 1

Time: 3 Hours *Total Marks : 100*

Note: *Attempt* **all** *questions*

1. Attempt any **four** of the following: **4 × 5 = 20**

(*a*) What do you understand by Information Technology? What are its applications? Explain in brief.

(*b*) Define Entropy. What does the entropy function measure? Explain with an example.

(*c*) What is drawback of using LZ78 algorithm? Encode the message "MAHA*MAHABHARATH", using this algorithm. Show all the steps.

(*d*) Discuss LZW coding. Compress the text "/WED/WE/WEE/WEB", using this algo.

(*e*) Differentiate between the following any two:

(*i*) Data Compression and Encoding.

(*ii*) Lossless and Lossy Data Compression.

(*iii*) JPEG and MPEG.

(*f*) Write all the steps of Shannon-Fano Algorithm. How the Huffman Algorithm differs from Shannon-Fano? Explain.

2. Attempt any **four** of the following: **4 × 5 = 20**

(*a*) Draw the block diagram of digital computer. Explain the function of the each block?

(*b*) What is Digitizer? Is it an input device or output device? Justify your answer.

(*c*) Discuss the Memory hierarchy used in computer system.

(*d*) Differentiate between any **two** :

(*i*) System S/w & application S/w

(*ii*) Alpha Testing & Beta Testing

(*iii*) Multi-programming & multi-tasking

(*e*) What do you mean by Software Quality Assurance? Explain the SEI-CMM levels.

(*f*) Explain the Software Development Methodology. Explain the Waterfall Model.

3. Attempt any **four** of the following: **4 × 5 = 20**

(*a*) Draw the circuit diagram, characteristics table & excitation table of J-K Flip Flop.

(*b*) What is ISO OSI reference model? Compare with TCP/IP layers.

(*c*) Define ATM. Why does ATM use small, fixed length cells?

(*d*) Convert the following:

(*i*) $(5214)_{10}$ = ()16

(*ii*) (1011.11)2 = () 10

(*iii*) (5A8)16 = () 8

(*iv*) (1011)gray = () binary

(*v*) (13) 10 = () bcd

(*e*) What do you mean by modulation? Give the types of modulation. Differentiate in between ASK and FSK.

(*f*) Write short note on any two:

(*i*) ISDN

(*ii*) CSMA/CD

(*iii*) Token Based Protocol

4. Attempt any two of the following: **2 × 10 = 20**

(*a*) (*i*) What is E-Commerce? Explain B2B and B2C e-commerce with suitable example.

(*ii*) Write down the full forms and the purpose of the following:

SMTP, WAP, DHTML, XML, URL, WML, WWW.

(*b*) (*i*) What are fire walls? Differentiate between Static and Dynamic firewalls?

(*ii*) Discuss Gopher, FTP, & TELNET.

(*c*) (*i*) Explain the purpose of the following HTML tags:

BODY, HEAD, HTML, AHREF, LIST

(*ii*) Discuss any three types of Internet connections?

5. Attempt any two of the following: **2 × 10 = 20**

(*a*) (*i*) Define operating system. Explain the different functions performed by an operating system?

(*ii*) Define the following terms with respect to DBMS:

Field, Record, File, database, Primary key?

(*b*) Write short note on the following:

(*i*) MS Word, MS Power point,

(*ii*) Textual Vs GUI Interface

(*c*) (*i*) What is NICNET or ERNET? What are the objectives of establishing of this network?

(*ii*) Write a short note on Weather forecasting?

MODEL TEST PAPER – 2

Time: 3 Hours *Total Marks : 100*

Note: *Attempt* **all** *questions*

1. Attempt any **four** of the following : 4 × 5 = 20

   (*a*) What do you mean by quality of information? Write about the various levels of Information in Business Organisation with suitable example.

   (*b*) "ILOVEMYCOLLEGEMYCOLLEGENAMEISKEIT". Construct Huffman tree and generate Huffman codes.

   (*c*) Encode and Decode the message "DI4DID$DIDI$DIDIA$DIDI", using LZW coding technique.

   (*d*) Decompress 0.41735 number using arithematic algorithm. He following data is given: Y (0.1), E(0.2), R(0.1), G(0.1), N(0.1), M(0.1), A(0.1), F(0.1), C (0.1).

   (*e*) Write short note on any **two** of the following:

   (*i*) MPEG

   (*ii*) MHEG

   (*iii*) Static and Dynamic Coding

   (*f*) What is a Microcomputer? Differentiate between Microcomputer and microprocessor?

2. Attempt any **four** of the following : 4 × 5 = 20

   (*a*) What is Digitizer? Is it an input device or output device? Justify your answer.

   (*b*) Explain the various phases of Waterfall Model in Details.

   (*c*) Explain the various types of Testing in details.

   (*d*) What are storage devices and why are they used? Explain the difference between Optical and magnetic storage devices.

   (*e*) Write a brief note on any **two** of the following :

   (*i*) CMM

   (*ii*) Impact and Non-Impact printers

   (*iii*) Difference between application and system software.

   (*f*) Answer any **three** of the following questions:

   (*i*) What is SRS?

   (*ii*) Differentiate between Debugging and Testing.

   (*iii*) Data Flow Diagram.

   (*iv*) Draw the Flowchart to find the largest of tree numbers.

3. Attempt any **four** of the following : 4 × 5 = 20

   (*a*) Mention the Truth table and Excitation table of J-K Flip-flop. Also draw the circuit diagram.

(*b*) What are Multiplexers? Explain with the help of circuit diagram.

(*c*) Convert the following:

(*i*) 38 $()_{BCD}$

(*ii*) 99 in Excess-3 Code

(*iii*) 111011 in Gray Code

(*d*) What do you mean by Digital modulation? Explain the types also.

(*e*) Explain LAN.WAN & MAN in details.

(*f*) Explain the Token Based Protocol ion details.

4. Attempt any **four** of the following : **4 × 5 = 20**

(*a*) HTML is a programming language or not. Justify. Also exaplin 4 Tags.

(*b*) Write a brief note on any **three** of the following:

(*i*) DHTML

(*ii*) WWW

(*iii*) FTP

(*iv*) Gopher

(*c*) What are the various features supported by E-mail? Explain at least 4 features.

(*d*) Explain the various types of Network Topologies in details.

(*e*) What is ISP? What are the key factors which should be kept in mind before opting for any ISP?

(*f*) Write a brief note on any **three** of the following:

(*i*) EDI

(*ii*) SEEP

(*iii*) Electronic Payment System

(*iv*) Cryptography

5. Attempt any **two** of the following : **2 × 10 = 20**

(*a*) (*i*) Operating System acts as an resource manager. Justify the statement.

(*ii*) Explain the DBMS Architecture in details with diagram.

(*b*) (*i*) What is DOS? Explain the difference between Internal and External DOS Commands with three examples of each.

(*ii*) Textual Vs GUI Interface.

(*c*) (*i*) What is NICNET or ERNET? What are the objectives of establishing of this network?

(*ii*) Write a short note on Industry Automation.

INDEX

D

E

F